GEORGE STEINER
AT
THE NEW YORKER

Also by George Steiner
available from New Directions

My Unwritten Books

GEORGE STEINER
AT
THE NEW YORKER

EDITED AND WITH AN INTRODUCTION BY ROBERT BOYERS

A NEW DIRECTIONS BOOK

Manufactured in the United States of America
New Directions Books are printed on acid-free paper.
First published as a New Directions Paperback Original (NDP1129) in 2009
Published simultaneously in Canada by Penguin Books Canada Ltd.
Designed by Rodrigo Corral and Gus Powell

Library of Congress Cataloging-in-Publication Data

Steiner, George, 1929-
George Steiner at the New Yorker / edited and with an introduction
by Robert Boyers.
    p. cm.
Essays.
Includes index.
ISBN 978-0-8112-1704-0 (pbk. : acid-free paper)
I. Boyers, Robert. II. Title.
PR6069.T417G46 2009
814'.54—dc22
                          2008047188

NEW DIRECTIONS BOOKS ARE PUBLISHED FOR JAMES LAUGHLIN
BY NEW DIRECTIONS PUBLISHING CORPORATION
80 EIGHTH AVENUE, NEW YORK, NY 10011

CONTENTS

III. THINKERS

IV. LIFE STUDIES

IN MEMORY OF MR. SHAWN

AN INTRODUCTION BY ROBERT BOYERS

BETWEEN 1967 AND 1997, George Steiner wrote for *The New Yorker* more than one hundred and thirty pieces. Most of them were reviews, or review-essays, many quite lengthy by the standards of a weekly magazine. Often in the course of his tenure at *The New Yorker* Steiner was said to be the ideal successor to Edmund Wilson, who, like Steiner, had written over several decades on a great range of issues and had made new books and old, difficult ideas and unfamiliar subjects, seem compelling not only to literary intellectuals but to what was once called "the general reader."

In the years when he wrote regularly for *The New Yorker* Steiner contributed often to other publications as well, collecting only a small proportion of his reviews in miscellaneous volumes like *Language and Silence, On Difficulty,* and *Extraterritorial.* Remarkably, Steiner also wrote several important academic books during this period, including major works like *After Babel* and *Antigones.* Though he was sometimes attacked for spreading himself too thin and taking on subjects beyond his own "field" of comparative literature, his books were more often praised in the highest terms by writers like Anthony Burgess and John Banville, and by leading scholars in several disciplines, from Bernard Knox and Terrence des Pres to Donald Davie, from Stephen Greenblatt to Edward Said and John Bayley. Said regarded him as an "exemplary" and properly passionate guide to much of the best in contemporary writing and ideas, and Susan Sontag praised his generosity and his willingness to provoke, even when "he knew that he would be attacked" for his views. "He thinks," Sontag noted in 1980, "that there are great works of art that are clearly superior to anything else in their various forms, that there is such a thing as profound seriousness. And works created out of profound seriousness have in his view a claim on our attention and our loyalty that surpasses qualitatively and quantitatively any claim made by any other form of art or entertainment." While there were those, in the American academy especially, who were all too ready to reach for "the dismissive adjective 'elitist'" to describe such a stance, Sontag was more than willing to associate herself with Steiner's commitment to "seriousness," and there were tens of thousands of *New Yorker* readers who were likewise grateful for the model of lucidity, learning, and intellectual independence exemplified by Steiner.

It is notoriously difficult to make a strong case for the enduring vitality of criticism written for a weekly or monthly magazine. We go back to the miscellaneous collections of pieces by Edmund Wilson, or Lionel Trilling, or Steiner's long-time colleague at *The New Yorker*, John Updike, and of course we find, among other things, a variety of local insights or judgments that may seem to us, and often are, ephemeral. Can it matter to us now that John Berger's novel *G* be read as "an imaginative gloss on Kierkegaard's reading of Mozart's *Don Giovanni* in *Either/Or*," as Steiner recommended back in 1973? Is it important to note, with Trilling, that certain writers—Hemingway is a prime example—become "fatuous or maudlin" only when they are writing in the first person?

But then all worthwhile insights are at bottom local, or are founded on close readings of texts, sentences, loosely or tightly formulated ideas. Trilling's view of authenticity is compelling to us because it is made to emerge from his deep absorption in particular works by Hegel, Diderot, Wilde and others. Wilson's understanding of violence in his account of Bolshevism has everything to do with his careful attention to relevant texts, speeches and incidents, many of which may not in themselves seem to us terribly consequential. When Steiner writes of Berger's novel *G*, he understands that, as a "highly literary—indeed precious—affair," the novel asks to be read with an eye to its "plainly recognizable" literary origins. To speak of Steiner's observations in such a reading as "local" is to say in fact only that he was willing to do the essential work of the critic acutely responsive to a novel he took to have some genuine value.

Of course it is no small matter that Steiner is a fabulously learned reader, that he is fluent in several languages and can speak as comfortably about Plato and Heidegger and Simone Weil as he can about Fernando Pessoa and Aleksandr Solzhenitsyn. Leading Russian scholars acknowledged, when Steiner's early book, *Tolstoy or Dostoyevski*, appeared in 1959, that his grasp of the relevant texts and contexts was impressive, and that even without a knowledge of Russian, Steiner generated enormously original insights stirring even to specialists in Slavic literature. That has been the case as well with Steiner's work in other areas often thought to be the exclusive precinct of classicists, or philosophers, or linguists. And so it is not surprising that, in his essays and reviews, Steiner has seemed an ideal guide to a great many subjects, from the Risorgimento in Italy to the literature of the Gulag, from the history of chess to the enduring importance of George Orwell or the idiom of privacy in nineteenth-century fiction.

When he confronts the work of a canonical modern figure—Brecht, for example, or Céline, or Thomas Mann—Steiner takes very little as settled or beyond dispute. He proceeds from the assumption that a case remains to be made, and that even with a fiercely original writer, context counts for a great deal, and is apt to be considerably more elusive than is often acknowledged. Brecht,

Steiner believes, requires to be placed, exactly, with respect to a variety of predecessor figures, including Lessing and Schiller, and in so placing him, Steiner reminds us that, like them, "Brecht sets out to be a teacher, a moral preceptor," in ways that become palpable to us as the plays and poems are deftly scanned. Equally illuminating is Steiner's way of positioning his man within the essential political, ethical and religious framework. Readers of *The New Yorker* could thus expect from Steiner, on a regular basis, passages astonishing for their vividness and economy, and deeply instructive in their mastery of an emotional and ideological terrain out of reach of virtually any other practicing critic. "Brecht's detestation of bourgeois capitalism," Steiner wrote,

> remained visceral, his intimations of its impending doom as cheerily anarchic as ever. But much in this prophetic loathing, in both its psychology and its means of articulation, harks back to the bohemian nose-thumbing of his youth and to a kind of Lutheran moralism. His acute antennae told him of the stench of bureaucracy, of the gray petit-bourgeois coercions that prevailed in Mother Russia. Even as Martin Heidegger was during this same time developing an inward, 'private National Socialism' (the expression comes from an S.S. file), so Brecht was expounding for and to himself a satiric, analytic Communism alien to Stalinist orthodoxy and also to the simplistic needs of the proletariat and the left intelligentsia in the West.

The palpable features of the passage on Brecht include, most obviously, the range and depth of learning, the pedagogic clarity, the movement through ideas without any trace of heavy breathing or insistence. This, we feel, is criticism as "the formal discourse of an amateur," as R. P. Blackmur once put it, with the word "amateur" signifying a person who is interested in many things, speaks for himself rather than for a "school" or an entrenched theoretical position, and doesn't at all mind owning up to an enthusiasm or an aversion. But there is also, in the passage on Brecht, as in hundreds of others I might have selected, an extraordinary speed and fluency, an ability to invoke an origin or an intellectual nexus briefly, but with no trace of superficiality or special pleading. When Steiner notes the "bohemian nose-thumbing" of Brecht, his gift for satire and his visceral antagonism to orthodoxy, he perfectly accounts for the peculiar nature of Brecht's Communism, regarding it as an expression of the man's recoil from "the stench of bureaucracy" and the "gray petit-bourgeois coercions." We understand at once, in Steiner's passage, why Stalinist Russia could not be for Brecht an attractive alternative to the capitalist societies he routinely disparaged. And we understand, too, why Edward Said was "struck," as he said, "with the energy and, at its best, the relentless concentration of [Steiner's] thought." Those features are everywhere present in this volume of criticism drawn from the pages of the *New Yorker*.

Of course a writer of Steiner's prickly independence and drive has been easy to caricature. His efforts to discriminate better from best continue to draw the epithet "elitist," and his continuing investment in masterpieces has prompted some critics to describe him as "a museum of European monuments." But the present volume gives the lie to these characterizations. Steiner has spent a lifetime not merely in the examination of classic texts—by Shakespeare, Homer, Sophocles, Tolstoy, Dante and others—but in the ongoing, always fraught encounter with the new and difficult. With what Said called Steiner's "Tory disregard for specialization," his infectious "fascination with verbal ingenuity" and his ability to put "himself at the inner core of a discourse, discipline, language, author, and then communicate outward to the uninitiated, without losing either the intimacy or the urgent clarity of each realm," Steiner has done anything but convey an impression of frozenness or unapproachable monumentality in the many hundreds of works he has taken on. Quite the contrary. Again and again in his work, everything he looks at is made to bristle with possibility, with some genuine prospect of turning out to be freshly thrilling, surprising, or chastening. Newness itself is felt to be a challenge fit to be taken on, and when its embodiment in a particular work seems spurious or pretentious or easy, Steiner's instinct is not simply to cast it into the outer darkness but to exhibit what it takes not to be unduly impressed by the mere semblance of newness. Steiner's resistance to particular manifestations of the new (see his response to John Barth's novel *Letters*) makes all the more commendable his enthusiastic embrace of other writers and thinkers.

After all, Steiner was the first regular reviewer in the United States to make the case for writers like Thomas Bernhard, Leonardo Scascia, and even selected American novelists, like Robert Pirsig, the author of *Zen and the Art of Motorcycle Maintenance*. The lengthy review-essays he devoted to Aleksandr Solzhenitsyn and other Russian authors were instrumental in easing, and shaping, their reception here. So too did Steiner's pieces on Lévi-Strauss, Gershom Scholem, and other thinkers introduce them to a great many readers well before their books were widely read by American intellectuals.

Nor has Steiner paid attention exclusively to masterworks. In fact, he has been remarkably open and generous even to less than first-rate works, fiercely resistant only to books without high ambition or clearly designed to curry favor with some constituency or to gratify an appetite for easy consolation. There is nothing "democratic" about Steiner's criticism, if by "democratic" we mean a willingness to be charitable towards virtually everything, but he has been willing to address what comes before him without a fixed theory of value or a hierarchy of principles. Unlike a number of contemporary reviewers who have made sudden reputations in this country in the last few years, Steiner has not read to be disappointed, and has never regarded criticism as an opportunity to strike fabulously dismissive postures.

In an introduction to a collection of essays and reviews by Lionel Trilling, Leon Wieseltier recently noted that Trilling "did not read to be ravished," that he was "exercised more by 'the moral imagination' than by the imagination," and that, even when he was examining works of art, he was "a historian of morality" pondering "documents for a moral history of his culture." Steiner, too, has often written as "a historian of morality." In early essays like "Night Words" (from the 1967 volume *Language and Silence*) he studied the "douche-bag idylls" of latter-day pornographers in order to ask about the price we pay for the freedom to read whatever we like. "The danger lies," Steiner wrote, "in the facile contempt which the erotic novelist exhibits for his readers, for his personages, and for the language. Our dreams are marketed wholesale." In other essays Steiner studied the relation between art and racism (as in the case of Louis-Ferdinand Céline), the erosion of privacy, the moral status newly accorded to madness and alienation. Indeed, one might well say that the exercise of the moral imagination has been central to Steiner's work.

And yet no one would think to say of Steiner that he "did not read to be ravished." Steiner is a virtuoso of ravishment. When he inhabits Thomas Bernhard's "landscape of anguish" he exhibits his own compulsive subordination to the novelist's radical, "excoriating purpose," to the "vibrancy of terror," "marmoreal purity," and "rushing but often polluted torrents" of Bernhard's prose. Steiner's language is thus properly geared to register the tenor of the work he examines, its peculiar intensity and seductiveness. Even where, as with Bernhard, he is put off by the repetitious insistence of the novelist's lesser works, by the accent of "unrelieved pain and loathing," the recoil, as expressed, is clearly that of a reader who has had rather too much of a good thing, in this case of a strangely intoxicating though malignant rant. Thus, the hatred that saturates much of Bernhard's prose is said to become "a monotone, a blunted saw buzzing and scraping interminably." That very image of the "blunted saw" sharply conveys Steiner's visceral absorption in the actual fabric of Bernhard's writing, his susceptibility to "ravishment" and thus to genuine, heartfelt revulsion.

Just so, in Steiner's resistance to the terse, "lapidary concision" of the Romanian-French writer E.M. Cioran we hear the disappointment of a would-be lover who knows the ardent satisfactions to be found in the aphoristic exactions of Andre Gide, Oscar Wilde, and others. Think of Racine, or Nietzsche, Steiner proposes, writers whose thought and writing we admire for their relentless concentration and precision. In French, Steiner says, there is the ideal associated with *"la litote,"* for which the word "understatement" is said to be "a lame translation." Better, Steiner suggests, if we would describe the quality of surprise and awe we feel when confronted by a Nietzschean epigram or an implacably unparaphrasable formulation by Gide or Borges, to think of "that rush of silence which pilots report at the center point of a hurricane." That improbable leap in Steiner perfectly captures his own restless reaching for language adequate to convey the exhilaration he has known as a reader. And thus it is that Steiner is, has always been, a writer sometimes inordinate, venturesome, never merely tame or cautious.

In the way he casts about for telling epithets and analogies, Steiner exhibits his attunement to voice and idiom in the work he studies, in this case his excitement at the "flash of authority" achieved by writers inexorably drawn, like Wilde and Laurence Sterne and La Rochefoucauld, to "mordant brevity." His disdain for Cioran has, then, to do with what he calls a "brutal oversimplification" in a writer whose work might otherwise seem attractively chaste, subtle, loaded with stirring paradox and surprise of the sort Steiner elsewhere considers with an almost amorous intensity. At a time when many other critics were singing the praises of Cioran and committing to memory his brusquely convulsive rages and dismissals, his declarations of universal rottenness, Steiner was almost alone in noting that Cioran's terse jeremiads were often "easy," consisting, here, of a "little pirouette of self-teasing irony," and there, of discreet dabs of "macabre chic." Quoting Cioran, placing him exactly, Steiner listens attentively to the ground-beat of Cioran's thought and concludes—not without some appropriate reluctance—that the proliferating paeans to darkness in this writer "flatter the writer [himself] with the tenebrous incense of the oracular." The very absence of doubt or contradiction in such a writer, Steiner argues, can only suggest that he wishes to inspire in his reader only "numbed assent or complaisant echo."

Of course Steiner could always be counted upon to make careful discriminations, and though for many years *The New Yorker* allowed him to write at unusual length about a great many subjects, it is by no means the case that his best work was invariably written for those pages. Nor should this be at all surprising. Read around in the volumes devoted to the criticism of Edmund Wilson and you do not find that the pieces he wrote for the *New Republic* and other journals were notably inferior to his *New Yorker* reviews. Though the result of such a comparison would be very different if we were examining the works of lesser reviewers—whose pieces never seem much more than a job of work, however deftly managed—with critics like Wilson and Steiner the range of reference, the sense of pedagogic mission, the sheer force of critical intelligence conspire to make us feel, in virtually all of their criticism, that a good deal is at stake, even when the assignment at hand is occasional. Certainly no other weekly favored Steiner with the space to publish an enormous essay like "The Cleric of Treason"—an unforgettably rigorous and vivid reflection on the British art-historian turned spy, Anthony Blunt, which many readers take to be Steiner's greatest *New Yorker* essay—but then Steiner published comparably tonic reflections in many other magazines.

Frequently Steiner has referred to himself as a "courier," that is, as one who brings the news and, at his best, exemplifies the virtues of what one *New Yorker* colleague called "learning without pedantry," not to mention "sober charm." If his writing could often seem—as C.P. Snow put it—"slap in the teeth of the prevailing wind," it had also the explanatory care of the writer whose primary mission is to educate and stir. Steiner as critic was always the teacher, and the pieces collected in this volume show him to be unambivalent about that sense of mission.

"It's the greatest privilege you can have," Steiner said in a particularly sobering and mischievous interview, "to help carry the mail for a great artist [or to help to promote discussion about compelling ideas], and that's what a good teacher is. [The great artists and thinkers] give us the letters and they say: 'Now, little man, get on with it,' and if you are a good little man you know which mail boxes to carry them to, so they don't get lost, wasted or misread, and it's a very exciting job, believe me." Alert always to "Wittgenstein's distinction between all the trivia you can talk about, and all the essentials you can't," Steiner has labored not ever to obscure that distinction. He is at once among the most earnest and the least complacent of critics, stirred to anger only when confronted by those who carelessly or casually throw dirt on the things that matter.

Elias Canetti described the true writer as "the thrall of his time," one who "sticks his damp nose into everything," who is "insatiable," "unintimidated by any single task." Canetti also demanded that the writer "stand against" the very "law" of his time and make his opposition "loud" and insistent. Of course there is a danger for the critic or writer adopting a programmatically oppositional stance. Is not the demand for one an encouragement to iconoclasm or posturing? But Steiner is compulsively engaged with the art and thought of his time and gives to everything he regards the gift of his whole person, with his unremitting curiosity, his passions, misgivings, and sympathies. No one who reads him with the requisite generosity and appreciation will think of him as a traditionalist savant who has buried himself in masterpieces and armored himself in unimpeachable truths the better to resist the terrors of the new. His hostility to aspects of contemporary culture, and to particular works or ideas, is more than matched by his avidity for the genuinely new and challenging. Typically he has selected for strenuous criticism only the most audacious and well-armed opponents, including, at the height of their influence, such figures as Noam Chomsky and Jacques Derrida. Those who have heard that he is overbearing and relentless will find, as they read through the pieces collected in this volume, brio and self-confidence, to be sure, but also immense patience and the joy of the writer who knows how to share his excitement. "I try to imagine someone saying to Shakespeare, 'Relax!'" said Canetti. Of Steiner's work, we may well say what Susan Sontag once wrote of Canetti's: "His work eloquently defends tension, exertion, moral and amoral seriousness."

THE CLERIC OF TREASON

IN THE SUMMER of 1937, the twenty-nine-year-old art critic of the London *Spectator* went over to Paris to see Picasso's newly unveiled "Guernica." Turbulent acclaim surrounded this great cry of outraged humanity. The critic's finding, which was printed on August 6th, was severely dismissive. The painting was "a private brain-storm which gives no evidence that Picasso has realised the political significance of Guernica." In his column for October 8th, the critic, Anthony Blunt, reviewed Picasso's ferocious series of etchings on the "Dream and Lie of Franco." Again he was negative. These works "cannot reach more than the limited coterie of aesthetes." Picasso was blind to the sovereign consideration that the Spanish Civil War was "only a tragic part of a great forward movement" toward the defeat of Fascism and the ultimate liberation of the common man. The future belongs to an artist like William Coldstream, declared *The Spectator's* critic on March 25, 1938. "Picasso belongs to the past."

Professor Anthony Blunt came back to the study of "Guernica" in a series of lectures he gave in 1966. This time, he conceded the stature of the work and its compositional genius. He located in it motifs from Matteo di Giovanni's "Massacre of the Innocents," from Guido Reni, from the allegorical paintings of Poussin, on whom he had become the world's foremost authority. Surprisingly, Blunt could show that the apocalyptic terror of "Guernica" was indebted to a passage in Ingres's marmoreal "Jupiter and Thetis." If there was in Picasso's most celebrated canvas almost no touch of immediate or spontaneous commitment, if all the main themes were already present in the "Minotauromachy" etching, of 1935, this was simply a matter of aesthetic economy. This etching had dramatized "the checking of evil and violence by truth and innocence" in precisely the way that "Guernica" would do, though on a smaller, more playful scale. The artist's underlying attitude concerning the Spanish Civil War was not, as the young Blunt had implied, one of indifference and a refusal to take sides. And in 1945, a few months after he had joined the French Communist Party, Picasso had declared, "No, painting is not done to decorate apartments. It is an instrument of war for attack and defense against the enemy."

The art critic for *The Spectator* would not have put it this way. His aesthetics, his sense of the relations between art and society were subtler. The enemy was Matisse, whose vision seemed "no longer to be one of the real world," and Bonnard, who had chosen formal experiment and color balance to the detriment of "human values." Art, as Blunt saw it in his chronicles from 1932 to early 1939, had one essential and demanding task: to find its way out of abstraction. The Surrealist solution was a spurious one. Reflecting on Max Ernst, in his review for June 25, 1937, Blunt asked, "Are we to be contented with dreams?" No, the answer lay with a concept that Blunt designated as "honesty." The term covers a fair range of meaning. Daumier is obviously honest in his satire on the ruling classes, but even more so in showing the workers that "their lives could be made the subject for great painting." But Ingres, purest of draftsmen and most bourgeois of portraitists, is no less honest. The concentration of his technique, the delicate but "unhesitating realism" of his perception were, indeed, "revolutionary." The contrast with Gainsborough is interesting. Here also was a dispassionate portrayer of the fortunate. But it is precisely a lack of technical brilliance that robs Gainsborough's studies of "condescension," of the honesty to be found in Ingres and in his eighteenth-century predecessors—Fragonard, Watteau, and Lancret. In Rembrandt (January 7, 1938), Blunt found "an honesty so obvious that it strikes one as a moral quality." The "honest" road out of the theoretical and pragmatic trap of abstraction could only be a return to some order of realism, but a return that made no concession to technical laxity. Matisse's realism was merely "empty" and "smart," like that in the late canvases of Manet.

But as Blunt combed exhibitions and galleries there were signs of a positive turn. They lurked, as it were, in the formalism of Juan Gris; they were evident in the works of a number of English artists, notably Coldstream and Margaret Fitton, whose *Ironing and Airing* was the one submission worth noting in the appalling Royal Academy show in the spring of 1937. And there was, above all, the New Realism of the Mexican masters Rivera and Orozco. It was toward them that Blunt looked with increasing excitement. Here, assuredly, was a body of work that could deal with the realities of the human condition without compromising its aesthetic responsibility, and could, at the same time, profoundly affect the emotions of the common man. The Mexican experience is central to the chapter on "Art Under Capitalism and Socialism" that Anthony Blunt, art critic and editor of publications at the Warburg Institute, in London, contributed to a volume on *The Mind in Chains,* edited by the poet C. Day Lewis and published in 1937.

Still-life as practiced by the masters of later Impressionism embodies an impulse toward flight from the serious issues of personal and social existence, according to Blunt. It "led to the various forms of esoteric and semi-abstract art which have flourished in the present century." Art is a complex phenomenon and cannot be judged according to crude psychological and social determinants. Nevertheless, Marxism "at least gives a weapon for the historical analysis of the characteristics of a style or of a particular work of art." And it does remind us most usefully that the views of the critic are themselves "facts" for which historical explanation can be given. Using the instruments of Marxist diagnosis, we arrive at a clear view of the modernist dilemma. Impressionism marked the severance of the major artist from the proletarian world. Daumier and Courbet stayed in imaginative touch with the painful realities of the social condition. Despite its flirtations with political radicalism, Surrealism is *not* a revolutionary art in social terms. Its inherent contempt for the common viewer is matched by the reflex whereby the common viewer, in turn, rejects the Surrealist work, and these attitudes stand in stark contrast to the creative interactions between painter and public in Gothic art and the early Renaissance. The purely abstract artist and his coterie-viewers have cut themselves off "from all the serious activities of life." Blunt's conclusion is categorical: "In the present state of capitalism the position of the artist is hopeless." But other models of society are emerging from the crucible of revolution. "A workers' culture" is being built in the Soviet Union. This construction does not entail an annihilation of the past. On the contrary, as Blunt characterizes Lenin's teaching, a true socialist culture "will take over all that is good in *bourgeois* culture and turn it to its own ends." Under socialism—and Blunt's dissent from Oscar Wilde's famous essay on the same topic is evident—the modern artist, like his medieval and Renaissance forebears, will be able to develop his personality far more richly than he can under the escapist and trivializing rule of anarchic capitalism. "He will take a clearly defined place in the organisation of society as an intellectual worker, with a definite function." It may well be that we in the West do "not *like* the painting produced in the Soviet Union, but it does not follow that it is not the right kind of art for the Russians at the present time." And Mexican painting, in its revolutionary and didactic phase, is producing exactly the kind of major, immediately convincing murals and canvases that are so desperately lacking in London, Paris, and New York. Rivera and Orozco are masters who, although members of the middle class and artists first and foremost, are "helping the proletariat to produce its own culture." Reciprocally, they benefit from the kind of public scrutiny and support from which the artist under late capitalism has, more or less willfully, cut himself off. The Soviet and Mexican lessons are clear. Blunt cites with approval Lenin's dictum to Clara Zetkin: "We communists cannot stand with our hands folded and let chaos develop in any direction it may. We must guide this process according to a plan and form its results." Art is too serious a matter to be left only to artists, let alone their moneyed patrons.

Throughout 1938, these stern hopes seemed to wither. The choice before the artist grew ever more stark. He could, wrote Blunt in his *Spectator* piece for June 24th, either discipline himself to paint the world as it was, paint something else as mere frivolous distraction, or commit suicide. The Mexican example was being shamefully neglected. "In the room of every young upper-class intellectual in Cambridge who belonged to the Communist party," Blunt noted in September, "there was always to be found a reproduction of a painting by van Gogh," but nothing by Rivera, nothing by Orozco. Obviously, individual exhortation and the play of unforced sensibility were no longer enough. The column dated July 8th had brought an almost desperate gesture: "Though Hitler's method of regimenting the arts is in every way to be deplored, there is nothing intrinsically wrong in the organisation of the arts by the State." The Mexican regime had shown the way, "and let us hope that it may soon happen in Europe." The hour was late.

The war effort enlisted British artists and art historians in propaganda, in graphic reportage (Henry Moore's famous air-raid-shelter drawings), and in various arts projects. These represented the planned and militant collaboration between artist and society which Blunt had called for throughout the late nineteen-thirties. Yet it was at this point—in 1939, he became Reader in the History of Art at London University and deputy director of the highly esteemed Courtauld Institute—that Anthony Blunt's writings drew sharply inward. His first learned paper had appeared in the *Journal of the Warburg Institute* for 1937–38, but the great bulk of his published work had been journalistic. After 1938, Blunt's journalism became sparsely occasional, and it was in what was, from 1939 on, the fiercely mandarin *Journal of the Warburg and Courtauld Institutes* and in the *Burlington Magazine,* a venue for fellow-experts and connoisseurs, that he issued the unbroken series of scholarly articles that made him one of the foremost art historians of the age. These articles—on Poussin, on William Blake, on Italian painting and French architecture of the seventeenth and eighteenth centuries, on the relations between the baroque and antiquity—constitute the foundations and, very often, the preliminary form of the more than twenty-five monographs, catalogues, and books that were produced after 1939 by Sir Anthony Blunt (he was knighted in 1956), Slade Professor of Fine Art successively at Oxford and Cambridge, Fellow of the British Academy (1950), Fellow of the Society of Antiquaries (1960), and, above all else, Surveyor of the Queen's Pictures and Adviser for the Queen's Pictures and Drawings (from 1952 and 1972, respectively).

Nicolas Poussin (1594–1665) has been at the center of Blunt's scholarship and sensibility. More than thirty Poussin studies appeared between *A Poussin-Castiglione Problem,* of 1939–40, and an article on *Poussin and Aesop,* in 1966. Five major papers on the French classical master were published in 1960 alone, three more the following year. It is no exaggeration to say that Blunt is as closely identified with Poussin as another great art historian, Charles de Tolnay, has been with Michelangelo or as Erwin Panofsky was, at certain times in his career, with Dürer. It was via Poussin that Blunt organized and tested his responses not only to classical and neoclassical art and architecture but also to Cézanne's spatial compositions, Roualt's religious art, and the figure groupings and dissemination of light in Seurat. This lifelong passion culminated in a two-volume study of Poussin—incorporating the A. W. Mellon Lectures that Blunt gave in Washington and a catalogue raisonné of the artist's output—which was published by the Bollingen Foundation, in New York, in 1967.

Blunt's scholarly-critical prose is cool to a degree. It seems to repudiate explicitly the dramatized, personal lyricism that marked the writings on art of Pater and Ruskin and of their most fascinating successor, Adrian Stokes. With rare exceptions, Blunt's style avoids even those flashes of impressionism and sinuous rhetoric that ornament the art studies of Kenneth Clark. The lucid unobtrusiveness of the French classical manner, which Blunt has analyzed and treasured, has passed into his own idiom. Nevertheless, there are in his reflections on Poussin indices of his central vision. Poussin's art is ennobled by deliberate intent. It embodies "a carefully thought-out view of ethics, a consistent attitude to religion, and, toward the end of his life, a complex, almost mystical conception of the universe." Blunt sees in Poussin a master who countered Plato's dismissive finding that the representative arts are merely imitations of reality. A decisive passage on Poussin draws as near as Professor Blunt will allow himself to eloquence:

> His pursuit of a rational form of art was so passionate that it led him in his later years to a beauty beyond reason; his desire to contain emotion within its strictest limits caused him to express it in its most concentrated form; his determination to efface himself, and to seek nothing but the form perfectly appropriate to his theme, led him to create paintings which, though impersonal, are also deeply emotional and, though rational in their principles, are almost mystical in the impression that they convey.

Only disciplined governance, rigorous self-effacement, and absolute technical mastery can lead an artist, a human consciousness, to that immediacy of revelation (the mystical) which reason generates but does not wholly contain. Vehement feeling is guarded by the calm of form. It is with obvious approbation that Blunt cites Poussin's own testimony: "My nature compels me to seek and love things that are well ordered, fleeing confusion, which is as contrary and inimical to me as is day to the deepest night." This great tradition of austere nobility is essential to the French genius from Racine to Mallarmé, from the brothers Le Nain to Braque. Very few Englishmen have felt at home in its formality. Blunt, who passed long periods of his youth in France, found in the French tradition the primary climate of his feelings. He came to recognize in Poussin a late Stoic, a Senecan moralist passionate in his very rationality but fastidiously detached from public affairs. Montaigne's, observes Blunt, is the voice—and a voice quintessentially French—of this passionate dispassion. Though these qualities are preëminent in Nicolas Poussin, they can be found in other masters and media: in the French architect Philibert de l'Orme (c. 1510–70), to whom Blunt devoted a monograph in 1958; in the great painter Claude Lorrain (1600–82); in the architect and sculptor Francesco Borromini (1599–1667), of whom Blunt published an incisive, elegant study in 1979. In Borromini's aesthetics, Stoicism joins with Christian humanism to underwrite the view that God is "supreme reason." No less than Poussin in his late years, Borromini conceives of man as inevitably puny and miserable but endowed with the capacity for reflection—for translating into disciplined form certain aspects of cosmic energy and order. And this reflection suffuses a Poussin canvas, a Borromini façade, a Fouquet drawing with the light of reasoned mystery.

It is a mark of Blunt's distinction and of the fineness of his antennae that his authority extends to certain artists who at first sight seem contrary to the Gallic ideal. His papers on William Blake go back to 1938. His study *The Art of William Blake* appeared in 1959. Again, the criterion is that of concordance between vision and technique of execution. As in Poussin, though expressed in an altogether different code, there is in Blake's paintings a "complete integrity of thought and feeling." In Blake's case, the analysis was fundamentally political. Blake had set his face against materialism—against the money fever of the new industrial age—and against the cant of a sclerotic state religion. He was "a minority fighter," in severe peril of isolation, of mere eccentricity. His powers as a craftsman, the vital intelligence of his understanding of classic art and modern society enabled him to produce designs of a totally individual character yet of an unmistakable universality of meaning. "To those who are themselves trying to escape from the dominance of materialism," says Professor Blunt, Blake is of dramatic aid and comfort. And the radicalism of the protest lies in the controlled line of the composition. Such "extraordinary mixture of severity and fantasy" was to delight Blunt in his study of Borromini's façade for the Collegio di Propaganda Fide, in Rome.

To his professional colleagues, Blunt is not only an art historian and an analytic critic of great stature. He is one of the principal cataloguers of our time. The disciplines required, the significance of the product for the study and interpretation of the fine arts as a whole are not easy for the layman to grasp, let alone summarize. As the life-force of speech and writing is, finally, determined by the quality of our dictionaries and grammars, so the access to and valuation of the works of great artists depend on exact attribution and dating. Who painted this canvas? Who drew this drawing? What is the relation of this print to the original plate? When was this statue carved or cast? To what year do we assign this colonnade or that vestibule? Am I looking at individual work or at the product of an atelier working collaboratively with the master or, perhaps, according to his more or less finished maquette? The catalogue raisonné—the chronological listing and precise description of the output of an artist or of his school—is to the historian of art and culture, to the art critic, and to the connoisseur the primary instrument of ordered perception. The means required of the compiler, as of a master lexicographer or grammarian, are of the most stringent and uncommon sort. The cataloguer must, in the first place, be totally versed in the mechanics of the medium he is classifying. He must, for instance, be able to reproduce mentally but also, as it were, at his own fingertips the idiosyncrasies of the etcher's tool if he is to identify the etcher's hand. He must know the metallurgy of the relevant period if he is to judge the state of the plate. The particular texture of the ink used, the exact history of the paper and its watermarks, the aesthetic and commercial considerations that dictated the number of impressions made will be familiar to him. In attributing and dating paintings, the indexer may resort to laboratory techniques: to X-ray and infrared photography, in order to reveal successive layers of pigment; to the minute analysis of wood, canvas, and metal, in order to fix the chronology and compositional history of the object. Yet mastery of these intricate minutiae is only the preliminary step. The right ascription of a painting, of a statue, of a baptistery to this or that painter, sculptor, or architect, its right dating and placement within the man's work as a whole are, in the last analysis, the result of acute rational intuition. Memory, the retention before the mind's eye of a great range of surrounding, ancillary, comparable, or contrasting art, is indispensable. So is historical imagination, the stab of precise sympathy that enables a historical novelist, a historian, a great stage designer to image the past. Sheer erudition—that is, a voluminous intimacy with the artist's biography, with his professional habits, with the material distribution and the survival of his works as they left his atelier and began their often tortuous journey toward the modern museum, auction room, neglected attic, or private collection—is essential. But these are not the crux. What matters most are "tactile values" (Berenson's phrase)—requiring an ability to bring taste and sensory awareness to bear unswervingly on the art object both in its minutest detail and in its over-all effect. The master cataloguer has perfect pitch.

Blunt's catalogue of *The Drawings of Nicolas Poussin* began appearing in 1939. *The French Drawings in the Collection of H.M. the King at Windsor Castle* was published in 1945. Nine years later followed *The Drawings of G. B. Castiglione and Stefano della Bella in the Collection of H.M. the Queen at Windsor Castle.* Blunt's descriptive catalogue of seventeenth- and eighteenth-century Venetian drawings in Her Majesty's collection was published in 1957. Three years later came the catalogue of the Roman drawings for this same period in the Sovereign's possession. Anthony Blunt provided the catalogue for the extensive Poussin exhibition in Paris in 1960, and his definitive listing of the artist's paintings came six years later. In 1968, Blunt surveyed the James A. de Rothschild Collection at Waddesdon Manor. In 1971, he published supplements to his previous listings of French and Italian drawings. In all his monographs, moreover, such as the handsome study of *Neapolitan Baroque & Rococo Architecture* (1975) and the Borromini book, attribution, exact description, and datings play a major role. Blunt has literally put in intelligible order central rooms in the house of Western art. As I said, only the expert can fully gauge the labor, the scruple, the degree of flair and concentration involved.

"Scruple" is worth insisting on. The business of attribution, description, dating demands complete integrity on the technical level. Margins must be measured to the millimetre; successive impressions from an original plate or woodblock must be almost microscopically differentiated if the sequence is to be numbered correctly. But in this domain there are also pressures of a moral and economic kind. The outright value of a painting or drawing or engraving, the worth of a sculpture on the crazed art market depend immediately on expert attribution. The temptations are notorious. (Berenson allegedly yielded to them on occasion.) Blunt's austerity was above question. His scholarship, his teaching exemplify formidable standards of technical severity and intellectual and moral rigor. His catalogues, his art history and criticism, the decisions he arrived at in regard to the identification and valuation of pictures and drawings in public and private holding illustrate the motto adopted by Aby Warburg, founder of the institute with which Blunt was closely associated: "God lurks in the detail." At this level of learning and connoisseurship, deception and the exposure that follows would be irreparable. There was hardly a day on which Professor Sir Anthony Blunt, Knight Commander of the Royal Victorian Order and honored guest of the Queen, did not make this clear to his colleagues and to his students.

They responded unstintingly. The *Studies in Renaissance & Baroque Art Presented to Anthony Blunt on His 60th Birthday* (Phaidon, 1967) is more than a ritual gesture. Here some of the most distinguished historians of art and of architecture paid genuine tribute to a master in the field and to an exemplary teacher by publishing essays that mirrored his own high standards and catholicity of insight. But even beyond the honor done to the scholar and the expositor there is the homage to the man. What Professor Blunt's peers and associates throughout the academic world, at the National Art Collections Fund, in the National Trust (the foremost body for the preservation of Britain's historical heritage), in museums, and, one has reason to believe, in the royal entourage wished to express unreservedly was their sense of Sir Anthony's "qualities of intellect and moral integrity." The two so obviously went together.

I do not know just when Blunt was recruited into Soviet espionage. It is thought likely that he became actively interested in and sympathetic to Communism as an undergraduate at Trinity College, Cambridge, between 1926 and 1929. Elected a Fellow of the college in 1932, he appears to have acted mainly as a talent spotter and guru for the K.G.B. The evidence points to his extraordinary influence over a circle of young men that included Kim Philby, Guy Burgess, and Donald Maclean, all of whom later took flight to Moscow. Blunt saw service in France in 1939 and 1940 after an attempt, whose details remain murky, to enlist in military intelligence. In 1940, during the chaos and crisis set off by Hitler's breakthrough in the west, Anthony Blunt succeeded in his project. He was now a member of the MI5 branch of the wartime secret service. No outsider seems to know precisely what Blunt's functions were or how senior he became. Initially, he seems to have been monitoring the communications and activities of various foreign embassies and exile governments in London. By passing his findings on to his Soviet control, he would have helped the Russians to plan and carry out their murderous policies in the newly liberated countries of Eastern Europe in 1944 and 1945. Blunt himself has declared that his activities consisted only in keeping the Russians abreast of what MI5 was finding out about German intelligence networks and in passing on occasional routine information about the work and views of his colleagues. Margaret Thatcher, in her statement to the House of Commons in the third week of November, 1979—the statement that revealed Blunt's treason to the public at large—said merely this: "We do not know exactly what information he passed. We do know, however, to what information he had access." The implication was that the latter was obviously sensitive. Outwardly, Blunt's membership in MI5 ceased at the end of the war. In reality, of course, the British intelligence community, like its counterpart in every other country, is a kind of permanent club, in which "old boys" and sometime activists continue on call. In 1950, Blunt seems to have offered his assistance to the security section of the Foreign Office when it was trying to trace a major leakage of classified information from the Washington Embassy. This kind act led Blunt straight to the heart of the Burgess-Maclean file. To this day, the precise mechanism whereby Burgess and Maclean were tipped off seventy-two hours before Maclean was to be interrogated and were thus able to find refuge in the Soviet Union remains known only to a very few. Blunt almost certainly had a hand in the escape. It is not clear whether he acted as initiator and organizer of the operation or merely as a conveyer of urgent signals. What is known is that it was Anthony Blunt who phoned Burgess on the morning of May 25, 1951—a Friday—to tell him that the net would close in on Maclean on the Monday following. British security services keep the Sabbath. That night, Burgess and Maclean took the ferry from Southampton to Saint-Malo. It was Blunt, moreover, who combed Burgess's London apartment for evidence that might incriminate him and Philby. Philby's nerve held under severe interrogation. According to Mrs. Thatcher's Parliamentary statement, Blunt had admitted to helping Philby make contact with Soviet intelligence "on one occasion" between 1951 and 1956—the year in which the Queen dubbed Blunt her faithful knight. The evidence suggests, however, that Blunt served as courier between the K.G.B. and the gradually cornered agent. As Philby later put it, from his sunlit bench in a Moscow public park (he was more or less allowed to defect safely in 1963), he received "through the most ingenious of routes" a message of good cheer from his Kremlin masters and friends. "It changed the whole complexion of the case. I was no longer alone."

Nor was Blunt. Needled into action by the Burgess-Maclean farce and by the outrage of the United States intelligence and counterintelligence agencies, which had vainly sought to alert their British colleagues to the presence of "moles" at the highest levels of the secret service, interrogators from MI5 saw Blunt eleven times beginning in 1951. As far as one can gather, Blunt repudiated all suspicions with chill aloofness. Burgess's alleged revelations were the product of an alcoholic notorious for his pranks and fantasies. Some interrogators were convinced that Blunt was lying but could not make the evidence stick. With every year, moreover, Blunt's prestige in public life, his access to royalty and to the near-immunity such access brings were growing. The years from 1952 to 1964 were golden ones for the guardian and surveyor of royal art. But the climate was beginning to sour. The unearthing and trial in 1961 of George Blake, a veteran

Soviet spy, Philby's homecoming to Moscow and the spate of revelations that ensued, and the essentially trivial but unnerving scandal of the Profumo affair in the summer of 1963 brought on a general alarm and sense of betrayal. A new round of investigations began. This time, according to the official narrative, Blunt cracked, and made a deal with his hunters. He would confess his treason and cooperate with MI5 as it saw fit in exchange for absolute discretion and personal immunity. The obvious lure lay in the possibility that the K.G.B., not knowing that Blunt had been "turned," would continue to use his services, and that these would be revealed to British counterintelligence. This appetizing bargain was to be kept a complete secret. Among the very few who were told was Sir Michael Adeane, the Queen's Private Secretary. He seems to have taken the news with condign aplomb, the more notable because the Assistant Keeper of the Queen's Pictures was one Oliver Miller, a former member of the secret service. As things worked out, the K.G.B. did not take the bait, and Blunt's own cooperation with his new masters was almost nonexistent. It looked to his bitterly exasperated controls in MI5 as if he had outplayed them once again. The glitter of Sir Anthony's public honors made matters worse. Leaks and insinuations, very likely planted by the angry intelligence network, began circulating in Fleet Street, in the senior common rooms of Oxford and Cambridge colleges, and through the synapses of establishment gossip. Two journalists, Richard Deacon and Andrew Boyle, were hot on the scent. Threats of prosecution for libel forced Deacon to withdraw the book he had written on the case. Boyle, confident of his facts, and very probably encouraged in certain powerful quarters, published his book (the American edition of which was entitled *The Fourth Man*) on November 5th of last year. The choice of date was a wry hit: to Englishmen, Guy Fawkes Day is an annual reminder of mortal conspiracy. Ten days later, the Prime Minister spoke out.

These, summarily, are the facts as they have been retailed to an avid public by Mr. Boyle and other journalists in an avalanche of exposés, by pundits and ex-secret-service figures of every description, by John le Carré acolytes (and, indeed, the Master himself) since Mrs. Thatcher's revelations in Parliament. A cursory look at the tale shows that it is so full of gaps, unanswered questions, and implausibilities as to be almost useless. Granted that recruitment in 1940 was chaotic—nevertheless, how was it possible, at the very time of the Hitler-Stalin entente, for MI5 to overlook the political sentiments expounded by Blunt in his *Spectator* art reviews and his 1937 essay? Who buried or withdrew a dossier given to MI5 as early as 1939 by the Soviet defector General Walter Krivitsky—a dossier that all but identified Blunt and his connection with Maclean (though, presumably, in a garbled and fragmentary way)? The implication of efficient protection in very high places is inescapable. Blunt's double life was charmed from the start. How was it that Blunt, who had actually shared a flat with Burgess, was allowed to slip through the net (or was he?) during the 1951 fracas? Everything about the confession and guarantee of immunity in 1964 is implausible. Why should Blunt have caved in just at this time, and of just what category of importance and seniority were his services to the K.G.B. if his interrogators thought him worth sparing public exposure and prosecution for treason? Lord Home, Prime Minister at the time, and Harold Wilson, his successor, have affirmed that they were told nothing, though both were, by virtue of their office, heads of the security services. Why should this have been? And who took the decision, politically trivial but psychologically bizarre in the extreme, either to inform or not to inform Her Majesty that her honor-laden art adviser and regular palace guest was a self-confessed K.G.B. operative? Is it not distinctly conceivable that Blunt's 1964 confession was itself a tactical fraud, and that he continued to do services either as a K.G.B. informant or, more probably, as a classic double agent, "turned" by both sides but loyal only to one? How else is one to account for the fact, first disclosed in a somewhat oblique statement by Edward Heath, Prime Minister at the time, that the Blunt file had been reopened in 1973 but that three successive attorneys general had, during the ensuing six years, found nothing that was usable as evidence on which to base a prosecution? Evidence supplied by "moles" and defectors does take a long time to filter through the intelligence channels. But can the information supplied by Anatoli Dolnytsin, a ranking K.G.B. agent who sought cover in the United States in 1962 and appears to have known the entire Philby setup and Blunt's connection, really have been ignored by British counterintelligence? Once more, the suggestion of a guardian angel or coven of angels in very lofty quarters is palpable. A senior Oxford philosopher of impeccable shrewdness, himself a member of the charmed circle of British mandarin socialites, has said to me outright that the Blunt story, as told to the world at large, is in many respects a fabrication. It was devised and revealed precisely in order to lay a smoke screen behind which other eminent characters in the drama could scuttle to safety. Crucial points are "in fact the exact opposite of what you have been led to believe." Historians to come will burrow. This or that startling tracer will turn up in as yet unpublished records, letters, personal memoirs. Blunt himself will have his say and rake in the royalties (a predestined pun, that). But it is very doubtful whether any coherent truth will ever emerge. What *is* certain is simply this: Anthony Blunt was a K.G.B. minion whose treason over thirty years or more almost certainly did grave damage to his own country and may well have sent other men—Polish and Czech exiles, fellow intelligence agents—to abject death. The rest is tawdry gossip.

Espionage and treason are, one is given to understand, as ancient as whoredom. And, obviously, they have often engaged human beings of some intelligence and audacity, and, in certain cases, of elevated social standing. Yet the enlistment in this nauseating trade of a man of great intellectual eminence, one whose manifest contributions to the life of the mind are of high grace and perception, and who, as scholar and teacher, made veracity, scrupulous integrity the touchstone of his work—this is indeed rare. I can, with reference to modern times, think of no genuine parallel. Professor Blunt's treason and duplicity do pose fundamental questions about the nature of intellectual-academic obsession, about the coexistence within a single sensibility of utmost truth and falsehood, and about certain germs of the inhuman planted, as it were, at the very roots of excellence in our society. There lies the significance and fascination of the case. I have neither the competence nor the interest to contribute anything to the spate of armchair detection and spy fantasies unleashed by the Blunt affair. But I would like to think for a moment about a man who in the morning teaches his students that a false attribution of a Watteau drawing or an inaccurate transcription of a fourteenth-century epigraph is a sin against the spirit and in the afternoon or evening transmits to the agents of Soviet intelligence classified, perhaps vital information given to him in sworn trust by his countrymen and intimate colleagues. What are the sources of such scission? How does the spirit mask itself?

The Marxist sentiments voiced in Blunt's art reviews and in his contribution to *The Mind in Chains* are banal. They constitute the widespread routine of anger of a middle-class generation caught up in the threefold context of Western economic depression, rising Fascism and Nazism, and what were believed to be the dynamic, libertarian successes of the Russian Revolution. Nothing Blunt writes exhibits any particular grasp either of the philosophical aspects of Marxist dialectical materialism or of the economic and labor theory on which this materialism is founded. It is parlor-pink talk in the approved nineteen-thirties style. Except, perhaps, in one respect. Blunt had arrived early at the conviction that great art, to which he ascribed preëminent value in human consciousness and society, could not survive the fragmented, anarchic, and always modish governance of private patronage and mass-media trivialization. If Western painting, sculpture, and architecture were to regain classic stature, they must do so under the control of an enlightened, educative, and historically purposeful state. However, as one looks closely at Blunt's reiterated call for a central authority over the arts, the basis for the argument is not notably Marxist. The ideal precedent lies much earlier. Like so many of the "radical élite," Blunt cherishes two possibly antithetical persuasions. He holds great art to be of matchless significance to man; and he would want this significance to be accessible to the community as a whole. The solution is, more or less unavoidably, Plato's: "guardians," chosen for their intellectual force and their probity, are to insure the positive, life-enhancing quality of art and are to organize the presentation of such art to their entire society. And this quality and public presentation will elevate collective sensibility to a higher plane. Blunt seems to have felt that something very like this mechanism of authority and diffusion was at work in the autocratic city-states of Renaissance Italy and, above all, in the century of Louis XIV and his immediate successor. The patronage of the Medici or of Versailles was at once centrally authoritarian and progressive. It commanded the production of pictures, statues, and buildings of enduring merit but made of this production a political-social benefit and stimulus, in which the body politic as a whole was actively involved. In this way, the individual artists were integrated into the live fabric of society. However private and singular their inspiration, the canvas, the monument, the loggia or façade that they designed and produced had come under the rationalizing and humanizing pressures of public occasion and of the need to communicate both to high patrons and to the city at large. The art dealer and the private collector, the tycoon and the journalist-critic, as they mushroom under capitalism, cannot match such coherence. On the contrary, it is the cash nexus that has fatally split the world of art into the esoteric, at one end, and kitsch, at the other. Blunt seems to locate the crisis somewhere between Ingres, still working under essentially hierarchic and public conditions, and, say, Manet. The available counterpart of the Medici or the ancien régime would be the Leninist commissariat for the fine arts, the revolutionary ministry of culture in Mexico, or, very nearly, as we have seen, the propaganda office and official chamber of art in the Third Reich. Blunt is shrewd enough to know that the price may be steep, at least during a period of historical transition. But how else are the arts, without which man would recede into animality, to be rescued from their isolation, from the prostitution of the money market? It may well be because he found no other answer to this question that Anthony Blunt slid from undergraduate and salon Marxism into the practicalities of treason.

A related, more unusual motive may also have been at work, though I cannot evidence my instinct on this. There is some suggestion that Blunt, when he began serious art studies, was drawn at least as vividly to Claude Lorrain as he was to Poussin. And Lorrain is, arguably, the more original, more haunting master. But, for reasons that involved the very different relations of these two painters to their patrons and public, Poussin's works were largely accessible to students, whereas much of Lorrain was in private and often closed collections at the time. We touch here on a problem about which I feel considerable ambivalence. The private ownership of great art, its seclusion from the general view of men and women, let alone from that of interested amateurs and scholars, is a curious business. The literal disappearance of a Turner or a van Gogh into some Middle Eastern or Latin-American bank vault to be kept as investment and collateral, the sardonic decision of a Greek shipping tycoon to put an incomparable El Greco on his yacht, where it hangs at persistent risk—these are phenomena that verge on vandalism. Ought there to be private possession of great art, with everything that such possession entails of material risk, of greed, of removal from the general currents of thought and feeling? The question is particularly urgent where the painting or statue or architectural motif in question was intended for public display in the first place—as is, of course, the case with the overwhelming majority of medieval, Renaissance, and seventeenth- and eighteenth-century works. To say that private collectors, especially in the United States, have been generous in allowing scholarly guests a look at their treasures (not always, in fact) is no answer. Should mere wealth or the speculative fever of the investor determine the location, the accessibility of universal and always irreplaceable products in the legacy of man? There are times when I feel that the answer ought to be emphatically negative—that great art is not, cannot be, private property. But I am not certain. My conjecture is that Blunt was certain, and that the young scholar-connoisseur, barred from certain paintings and drawings of genius because they were locked up in private keeping, experienced a spasm of contemptuous loathing for capitalism. In the Soviet Union, he knew, great art hangs in public galleries. No scholars, no men and women wanting to mend their souls before a Raphael or a Matisse need wait, cap in hand, at the mansion door.

The second main perspective in which to try and comprehend the Blunt phenomenon is that of homosexuality. Reams have now been written about the incidence of homosexuality in the Cambridge University circles from which the Soviet intelligence services recruited their galaxy of agents. Some of the published information is very likely responsible; much of it is more or less prurient gossip. One of the main witnesses to Blunt's homoeroticism, the late Goronwy Rees, was a brilliant but emotionally erratic and not always impeccable informant. What is not in doubt is the general fact of the strongly homosexual character of the élite in which the young Blunt flourished at Trinity and King's Colleges in Cambridge—and, most especially, of the Apostles, the celebrated semisecret society of intellectual and aesthetic souls which played so distinctive a role in English philosophical and literary life from the time of Tennyson to that of Strachey and Bertrand Russell. Neither sociology nor cultural history, neither political theory nor psychology has even begun to handle authoritatively the vast theme of the part played by homosexuality in Western culture since the late nineteenth century. The subject is so diffuse and of such methodological and emotional complexity that it would require a combination of Machiavelli, de Tocqueville, and Freud to produce the great missing book. There is hardly a branch of literature, of music, of the plastic arts, of philosophy, of drama, film, fashion, and the furnishings of daily urban life in which homosexuality has not been crucially involved, often dominantly. Judaism and homosexuality (most intensely where they overlap, as in a Proust or a Wittgenstein) can be seen to have been the two main generators of the entire fabric and savor of urban modernity in the West. In ways that C.P. Snow did not even hint at in his argument on "the two cultures," it is, by and large, the striking absence of any comparable homosexual presence in the exact and applied sciences which has helped bring on the widening gap between the general culture and the scientific. This is a vast and as yet only imperfectly understood development, of which the role of homosexuality in politics and in the world of espionage and betrayal is only a specialized, though dramatic, feature. In the case of Blunt and the apostolic youths of Cambridge and Bloomsbury, moreover, homosexuality may be too restrictive a concept.

Until very recently, the more privileged orders in English society were educated in celibate schools and in the celibate colleges of Oxford and Cambridge, which have admitted women only during these last seven or eight years. This education was underwritten by an explicit ideal of masculine friendship, of a masculine intimacy and mutual trust more lasting and radiant than the plebeian values of the outside world. Cyril Connolly's *Enemies of Promise,* Philip Toynbee's exquisite *Friends Apart* give a classic picture of this adolescent Arcadia, with its overtones of white flannel summer afternoons and heroic deaths in manly wars to come. This masculine code would comprise stages of homosexual encounter ranging all the way from the most platonic (itself an ambiguous term) of schoolboy crushes to full involvement. But even the latter was in many instances only a transitory phase before the fading of the summer light and a man's responsible entry into the colder climate of matrimony and family life. It is, therefore, not the homoeroticism that matters most but the vision of a small constellation of men, their souls attuned by shared schooling and by the shared enchanted setting of Cambridge cloisters and gardens. The strength of elective affinity in such a coterie is twofold: there are the bonds of internal affection, and there is a rejection, more or less conscious, more or less aggressive, of the vulgar usages and philistine values of "the others," of the banal multitude. The password to this whole complex of attitudes and beliefs is a very famous declaration by E.M. Forster, made first in the late thirties and repeated innumerable times since: "If I had to choose between betraying my country and betraying my friend, I hope I should have the guts to betray my country." Much overrated as a novelist—only *A Passage to India* is of absolutely the first rank—Forster was for successive Cambridge generations the tuning fork of conscience. His own homosexuality, the fastidious privacy of his ways, his place among the Apostles made of him very nearly a court of appeals in questions of ethical choice. Incidentally, one cannot but wonder how much Forster may have known of the truth concerning Burgess, Philby, Maclean, Blunt, and their praetorians. Now, there can be no doubt but that his proposition on betrayal is worth close scrutiny. I happen to feel myself strongly drawn to its implicit valuation. Nationalism is the venom of modern history. Nothing is more bestially absurd than the readiness of human beings to incinerate or slaughter one another in the name of nationhood and under the infantile spell of a flag. Citizenship is a bilateral arrangement that is, that ought always to be subject to critical examination and, if need be, abrogation. No city of man is worth a major injustice, a major falsehood. The death of Socrates outweighs the survival of Athens. Nothing dignifies French history more surely than the willingness of Frenchmen to go to the brink of communal collapse, to weaken the bonds of nationhood drastically (as they in fact did) over the Dreyfus case. Long before Forster, Dr. Johnson had defined patriotism as the last refuge of a scoundrel. It seems to me doubtful whether the human animal will manage to survive if it does not learn to do without frontiers and passports, if it cannot grasp that we are all guests of each other, as we are of this scarred and poisoned earth. One's homeland is the common patch of space—it can be a hotel room or a bench in the nearest park—that the gross surveillance and harrying of modern bureaucratic regimes, East or West, still allow one for one's work. Trees have roots; men have legs with which to leave after they have, in conscience, said no. Thus, there is in Forster's challenge an ecumenical humanism worth defending. Had Anthony Blunt renounced his gilded career, and sought barren refuge in Moscow or committed suicide rather than inform on his Cambridge brethren, one would condemn him for the traitor he is, but one would acknowledge an enactment of Forster's high paradox and see some logical culmination of a long tradition of boyish fidelity. Blunt, of course, did nothing so quixotic or elegant. He betrayed his country *and* his friends with the same cold gusto.

Nonetheless, the homosexual motif may have counted in two ways. It would have given Soviet intelligence a stranglehold of blackmail over Blunt and his circle at a time when English laws, even in respect of consenting adults, were still draconian. More significant, the homoerotic ethos may have persuaded men such as Blunt and Burgess that the official society around them, whatever prizes it might bestow on their talents, was in essence hostile and hypocritical. It was, consequently, ripe for just overthrow, and espionage was one of the necessary means to this good end. The irony is that the Stalinist Soviet Union, as André Gide reported in bitter disillusion, was far more oppressive of homosexuality than the capitalist West. Blunt, who had in the 1940 preface to his *Artistic Theory in Italy 1450–1600* thanked Guy Burgess for his aid and stimulus on "all the more basic points"—Burgess's authority in Renaissance aesthetics is not immediately obvious—could flourish both within and outside the British secret service. In Russia, they order these matters differently.

But, crucial as they are, neither Blunt's overt Marxism nor his commitment to the freemasonry of golden lads takes us to the heart of the maze, which is the radical duplicity, the seeming schizophrenia, of the scholar-teacher of impeccable integrity and the professional deceiver and betrayer. When our society troubles to think on the matter at all, it and the conventions of mutual recognition by which it orders its daily affairs take casually for granted the makeup, the status of the scholar. It is only in hoary jokes about the pure pedant's forgetfulness, corporal eccentricities, or inaptitude to the simpler, more basic needs of common existence that some ancient uneasiness and suspicion surface. The absolute scholar is in fact a rather uncanny being. He is instinct with Nietzsche's finding that to be interested in something, to be totally interested in it, is a libidinal thrust more powerful than love or hatred, more tenacious than faith or friendship—not infrequently, indeed, more compelling than personal life itself. Archimedes does not flee from his killers; he does not even turn his head to acknowledge their rush into his garden when he is immersed in the algebra of conic sections. The point of strangeness is this: the conventional repute, the material or financial worth, the sensory attraction, the utility of the object of such interest is utterly irrelevant. A man will invest his sum of living in the study of Sumerian potsherds, in the vertiginous attempt to classify the dung beetles of one corner of New Guinea, in the study of the mating patterns of wood lice, in the biography of a single writer or statesman, in the synthesis of one chemical substance, in the grammar of a dead language. Korean chamber pots of the ninth century, the question of the accent in ancient Greek—witness Browning's ironic but tensed celebration of "A Grammarian's Funeral"—can compact a man's mental and nervous powers to the pitch of ecstatic fury. Mephistopheles was wasteful when he tempted Faustus with the secrets of the universe: the one *Orchis* missing from his hothouse collection, the torn page in the Laurentian codex of Aeschylus, or the as yet undiscovered proof of Fermat's Last Theorem would have served. The scholar absolute, the mandarin, is a creature cancerous with the blank "holiness of the minute particular" (William Blake's tag). He is, when in the grip of his pursuit, monomaniacally disinterested in the possible usefulness of his findings, in the good fortune or honor that they may bring him, in whether or not any but one or two other men or women on the earth care for, can even begin to understand or evaluate, what he is after. This disinterestedness is the dignity of his mania. But it can extend to more troubling zones. The archivist, the monographer, the antiquarian, the specialist consumed by fires of esoteric fascination may be indifferent also to the distracting claims of social justice, of familial affection, of political awareness, and of run-of-the-mill humanity. The world out there is the formless, boorish impediment that keeps him from the philosopher's stone, or it may even be the enemy, mocking, frustrating the wild primacy of his addiction. To the utmost scholar, sleep is a puzzle of wasted time, and flesh a piece of torn luggage that the spirit must drag after it. The legendary teacher Alain instructed his French students, "Remember, gentlemen, that each true idea is a rejection of the human body." Hence not only the legends that cluster about Faust, the tale of the man who sacrifices wife, child, home to the breeding of the perfectly black tulip (an old story retold by Dumas), and all the terror fables about deranged cabbalists and scientists but also the sober facts concerning the obsessed, sacrificial, self-devouring lives of the abstracted ones since Thales of Miletus fell down the dark well while seeking to calculate the ecliptic conjunction of sun and moon. It is indeed a haunting and haunted business.

The more so, I think, when the spell is antiquarian. Even at the sharpest edge of autistic engagement, the scientist is oriented toward the future, with what it contains of morning light and positive chance. The numismatician laboring to identify archaic coinage, the musicologist deciphering medieval notations, the philologist at his corrupt codex, or the art historian who is endeavoring to catalogue minor baroque or rococo eighteenth-century drawings not only has entered into the labyrinth and underworld of the esoteric but has, necessarily, inverted time. For him, the pulse of most vivid presence beats from out of the past. This, again, is a social and psychological estrangement to which we pay too little heed. Today's high-school student solves equations inaccessible to Newton or to Gauss; an undergraduate biologist could instruct Darwin. Almost the exact contrary holds true for the humanities. The proposition that there is to come in the West no writer to match, let alone excel, William Shakespeare or that music will not produce again the phenomena of prodigal quality manifest in Mozart and Schubert is logically undemonstrable. But it carries a formidable weight of intuitive credibility. The humanist is a rememberer. He walks, as does one troupe of the accursed in Dante's "Inferno," with his head twisted backward. He lurches indifferent into tomorrow. The sixth-century Greek lyric fragment, the Dufay canon, the drawings by Stefano della Bella are the magnet to his steps—or, as the immemorial myth of fatal retrospection has it, they are his Eurydice. This disorientation (many of us have experienced a subtle pang of nausea and bewilderment on leaving a movie theatre in broad daylight) can generate two reflexes. The first is a hunger for involvement—an attempt, desperate at times, to hook into the warming density of "the real." The mandarin reaches out of his retrospective isolation to grab at sexual or social or political life. Except in rare cases—"As for living, we leave that to our servants," remarked a French aesthete—obsessive scholarship breeds a nostalgia for action. It is "the deed" that tempts Dr. Faustus out of the prison of "the word." It was the unhoped-for chance of applying their eerily arcane skills—the analysis of chess problems, epigraphy, number theory, the theory of grammar—that enlisted a peerage of British dons in the brilliant coding and decoding operations during the Second World War. All who look back on the days of "Ultra" and "Enigma" at Bletchley Park do so with a sense of holiday. For once, hermetic addiction and the raw needs of the time coincided.

The second reflex lies, I suspect, much nearer to the subconscious. It is one of bizarre violence. The practice of devoting one's waking hours to the collation of a manuscript, to the recension of watermarks on old drawings, the discipline of investing one's dreams in the always vulnerable elucidation of abstruse problems accessible only to a handful of prying and rival colleagues can secrete a rare venom into the spirit. *Odium philologicum* is a notorious infirmity. Scholars will lash out at one another with unbridled malignancy over what appear to the laity to be minuscule, often risible points of debate. The great Lorenzo Valla was not the only Renaissance humanist who ran for his life in the wake of bilious textual controversy. Philology, musicology, and art history, because they hinge on minute niceties of perception and judgment, are especially prone to these gusts of mutual incrimination and loathing. Because their constant focus is antiquarian and archival, they can infect their adepts with a queer, lifeless brand of detestation. In a classic essay on A.E. Housman (1938), Edmund Wilson made the acute suggestion that the macabre violence in "A Shropshire Lad" ought to be seen in conjunction with the jeering savagery of Professor Housman's learned reviews and papers on Greek and Latin philology. Both stem from the cloistered, compressed asceticism of the Cambridge scholar. Like that of T.E. Lawrence, an Oxford variant, such asceticism cuts a writer off from "the great springs of life" and can nurture a pathological need for cruelty. Today, Edmund Wilson might have felt free to press home his insight by pointing to the shared, clandestine motif of academic homosexuality. Poets such as Pope and Browning have caught the whiff of sadism in academe. So have some playwrights and novelists. Anatole France's *The Crime of Sylvestre Bonnard* handles the theme lightly; it takes on naked terror in Ionesco's playlet *The Lesson*. Fantasizing about action out there in the "real" world, spinning high dreams about the secret centrality, about the occult importance of the labors in which he has interred his existence—labors that the vast majority of his fellow-men would deem wholly marginal and socially wasteful if they knew of them at all—the pure scholar, the master of catalogues, can sup on hatred. At the ordinary level, he will exorcise his spleen in the ad-hominem nastiness of a book review, in the arsenic of a footnote. He will vent his resentments in the soft betrayals of an ambiguous recommendation or examination report and in the scorpion's round of a committee on tenure. The violence stays formal. Not, one supposes, in Professor Blunt.

Here the hair-fine exactitudes of scholarship found compensation or parodistic counterstatement—for there are sensibilities both strong and obscurely lamed which demand some kind of mocking self-subversion, which find it compelling to deride something central to their own being, as one's tongue exasperates an aching tooth—in the lies and corruptions of the mole. Here the ascetic scruple of the pedagogue who instructed generations of disciples in the merciless code of documentary truth was counterpoised by the long mastery of falsehood and of forgery. Above all, Professor Blunt was able to translate into clandestine performance, into covert mendacity and, possibly, murderousness (the men and women tagged for Soviet vengeance in Eastern Europe), those fantasies of virile action, those solicitations of violence, which bubble like marsh gas from the deeps of abstruse thought and erudition.

Blunt's remark on Borromini's suicide in 1667 sounds as near to self-disclosure as anything we have heard so far:

> To have been under a strain so violent that it drove him to this act of violence—if not of madness—and yet immediately afterwards to be able to dictate such a lucid account of the event, reveals a combination of intense emotional power and rational detachment which are among the qualities which go to make him such a great architect.

"Intense emotional power," though narcissistic, and "rational detachment," such as the scholar must cultivate in pursuit of his obsession—these seem to characterize the custodian of the Queen's art treasures no less than the K.G.B. intelligencer. The controlled duality is that of a double agent toward himself, of a betrayer of others who feeds, at some last level of irony, at once juvenile and sophisticated, on self-treason. One psychological dividend for Blunt seems to be this: he is simultaneously his own witness and his own judge; the only tribunal he recognizes as competent is that of his own duplicity.

It is Blunt's condescension, the intact carapace of his self-esteem which have struck those who have sought him out since his public exposure. Hardened souls in journalism have recoiled from the man's cold sophistries, from the edge of self-satisfaction with which he savored the smoked-trout sandwiches thoughtfully put before him by a team of interviewers in the editorial sanctum of the London *Times*. He has depicted his long years of service to the Soviet intelligence organs as marginal, almost amateurish in their insignificance. He has denied handing over information of any real importance. His implication in the Philby-Burgess-Maclean murk was only that of personal amity, of the decent thing done among kindred souls. His television performance in the third week of last November was a classic. It identified not only the tawdriness of Blunt but, even more disturbingly, that of the medium itself. Here was, as one newspaper later put it, "a man with an infinite capacity for duplicity" doing a silvery, suave little pas de deux before millions. The fine hands wove arabesques suggesting cordial complicities with inquisitors and with a great public that Blunt, fairly enough, must have read as eager and prurient. The mouth moved primly, dropping seemingly hesitant yet elegantly veneered sentences in a minor key characteristic of the Cambridge common rooms of an earlier vintage. But Professor Blunt's eyes remained throughout as flat and chill as glass. It was his younger companion, harried by the press and the vileness of it all, who jumped or fell from the window of Blunt's apartment. Blunt himself, seen in Rome in mid-September, was rumored to be working on his memoirs and apologia in sunny refuge.

This charade is of no importance. What historians will look at is the gamut of reactions the public unmasking of Blunt provoked in the English social and cultural establishment. For weeks, the letters-to-the-editor page of the *Times* hummed with an agitated chorus. Outright disgust or anathema was sparse. Mandarins and "top people" (the *Times'* own half-deprecating phrase) rallied to Blunt's support. Their apologetics took one or a combination of three principal lines. One was that the wretched creature had been sufficiently chastised by Parliamentary exposure and the baying pack of vulgar journalists. Had he not confessed and received assurance of immunity many years before? Should so *distingué* a personage suffer double jeopardy? A second mode of argument was more substantial. Blunt's conversion to Communism, pleaded some of the more representative voices in current English letters, in the arts, and in political thought, had been part of a widespread movement. To turn toward Moscow in the thirties, to flinch from the waste of decaying capitalism and the menace of Mussolini,

Franco, and Hitler, was, at the time, to do the decent, the perceptive thing. If Anthony Blunt was to be flayed, who, as Shakespeare phrased it, "should 'scape whipping"? Why should an Auden depart in the odor of sanctity and a Blunt be hounded? That most of the pro-Soviet intelligentsia had had second thoughts at the time of the Hitler-Stalin alliance and that almost none translated their sympathies into espionage and treason were points conceded but dealt with lightly. The third line of advocacy, expressed by, for example, the historian A.J.P. Taylor, was this: Blunt's exposure was based on tainted evidence, most notoriously the disclosures of an American who was a former C.I.A. agent. Little credibility could be attached to the stuff, and no man should be pilloried on such insubstantial grounds. Taylor is right when he points to the flimsiness and fabricated tenor of the affair as it was officially revealed. Nonetheless, there is no doubt as to Blunt's essential treason. The pressure of sentiment on his behalf, moreover, was not primarily judicial, or even reasoned. It stemmed from the ethos of unyielding friendship as it is proclaimed in E.M. Forster's talismanic aphorism. Roasted half to death, Tom Brown, in the infernal Arcadia of his school days, will not snitch even on the class bully. Henty's midshipmen, Kipling's subalterns, the golden youths of 1914 go to their several deaths in the aura of male fidelity. A gentleman does not tell on his friend; he does not turn on his friend when the latter has, for whatever reason, fallen on hard days. Asked what he would do if Blunt now appeared at his door, one Cambridge don answered for many: "I would offer him a drink and say, 'Bad business. Hard luck, Anthony.' I think that in Cambridge personal loyalties and friendships count for a great deal, and very rightly. And that still counts. Certainly nothing has happened that would make him less of a friend." The schoolboy idiom of the passage—"bad business," "hard luck"—and the mawkish fatuousness of the last sentence come near to exemplifying the prevailing tone.

Having been told beforehand of Mrs. Thatcher's impending

statement, Professor Blunt resigned from the less prestigious of the two clubs he belongs to in London. He continues a presumably welcome member of the other. His knighthood was withdrawn by royal decree—a very rare move, which was last made, unless I am mistaken, in respect of Sir Roger Casement when he sought to stir up trouble in Ireland during the First World War. (Casement, of course, was hanged.) Under extreme pressure, Blunt resigned his Honorary Fellowship of Trinity College before the college council had to face what would have been an anguished vote. He has neither offered nor been asked to renounce his honorary degrees, most signally at Oxford. When the British Academy met last July 3rd, amid considerable public interest, the matter of Blunt's continued membership was discussed. But the august body then moved on to other business. The letters "F.B.A." remained after Blunt's name. As it happened, I saw several Academicians the day after the meeting and asked them what their attitudes would have been had Blunt been an agent for the Nazi secret services. No clear answer emerged. Some conceded that they were, in fact, abiding by an ill-defined double standard, that pro-Nazi treason had a simple nastiness that pro-Soviet treason, particularly when embarked upon in the nineteen-thirties, did not. Even the world of the Gulag and of present danger could not wholly efface the almost aesthetic difference. Others found that they would have refused to exclude Blunt from the Academy even if he had spied for Himmler. Queried in turn, I was unable to give a plain answer. Fellowship in the British Academy honors eminent scholarship. Blunt's performance as an art historian stands luminous. Are "monuments of unaging intellect"—Yeats's proud phrase—susceptible to moral or political denial? I just don't know. I, too, have taken the vows of the cleric. And, opening the *Times Literary Supplement* a day or so later—the *T.L.S.* is the mailbox of the British intelligentsia—I read a compellingly authoritative review by Anthony Blunt of a recent work on French neoclassical architecture. Should the editor not have commissioned it? Should Blunt have had the shame, the need for shadow, not to write it? Again, I don't know. Pressures there must have been. Blunt offered his resignation to the Academy on August 18th.

Huddled in his penal cage at Pisa, Ezra Pound, whose treasons strike one as amateurish and essentially histrionic compared with Blunt's, wrote one of the great laments on man in all literature. Yet, out of lucid abjection, Canto LXXXI leaps toward morning, toward the conviction that there is in art, in high thought, a redemption for the hellish ways of our condition:

> But to have done instead of not doing
> this is not vanity
> To have, with decency, knocked
> That a Blunt should open
> To have gathered from the air a live tradition
> or from a fine old eye the unconquered flame
> This is not vanity.

Pound is referring, almost certainly, to Wilfrid Scawen Blunt, the aesthete, traveller, and lyric poet, who died in 1922, and after whom Anthony Blunt's oldest brother, himself an art connoisseur and an addict of Paris, was named. But no matter. Pound meant the name to stand for everything that is radiant and truthful in our love and study of art. For all who have treasured these lines as a touchstone of our hopes, and for all who will read them in generations to come, the damage has been done. As it stands, "Blunt" burns a derisive hole in the bright fabric of the poem. At the last, this may be Professor Anthony Blunt's strongest claim to remembrance. Damn the man.

December 8, 1980

WIEN, WIEN, NUR DU ALLEIN

THERE IS A great book to be written. It would show that the twentieth century as we have lived it in the West is, in essential ways, an Austro-Hungarian product and export. We conduct our inward lives in or in conflict with a landscape mapped by Freud and his disciples and dissenters. Our philosophy and the central place we assign to language in the study of human thought derive from Wittgenstein and the Vienna school of logical positivism. The novel after Joyce is, in the main, divided between the two poles of introspective narration and lyric experiment defined by Musil and by Broch. Our music follows two great currents: that of Bruckner, Mahler, and Bartók on the one hand; that of Schoenberg, Alban Berg, and Anton Webern on the other. Though the role of Paris was, of course, vital, it is now increasingly clear that certain sources of aesthetic modernism, from Art Deco to Action painting, can be found in the Viennese *Jugendstil* and in Austrian Expressionism. The functionalist, antiseptic ideals so prominent in today's architecture were predicted in the work of Adolf Loos. Political-social satire in London and New York, the sick joke, the conviction that the language of those who govern us is a poisonous smoke screen echo the genius of Karl Kraus. Ernst Mach had a profound influence on the development of Einstein's thinking. The logic and sociology of the natural sciences cannot be formulated without reference to Karl Popper. And where shall we place the manifold effects of Schumpeter, Hayek, von Neumann? One could prolong the roll call.

The conflagration of artistic, scientific, social, and philosophical energies in Central Europe came of fundamental instabilities. It was, as the physicists say, "implosive," a compaction of conflicting forces in a violently shrinking space. Imperial decay and ethnic emancipation, anti-Semitism and Jewish success, an archaic familial order and a pervasive sexuality—such were the antinomies between which passed great flashes and arcs of creative voltage. These, in turn, precipitated the ambience of social crisis, the nervous style, the eroticism of general sensibility which to this day characterize the Western city, the atelier of Western arts, the dishevelled conventions of Western intellectual life. Between the 1880s and 1914, between 1919 and 1938, Vienna, along with Prague and Budapest, raced through, externalized, and found hectic but poignant expression for the larger crises of European and, later, of American orders of value. In this implosion, the Jewish component—Freud, Mahler, Kafka, Schoenberg, Kraus, and so many others—was almost dominant. Thus, there is a fatal logic and finality in the fact that the person of Hitler and so much of Nazi ideology sprang from Austrian ground. (Historians have traced the key term *Judenrein,* "untainted by Jews," to the membership rules of an Austrian bicycle club at the turn of the century.) It was in Vienna that the young Hitler concocted his inspired venom. As the waltz tune has it, *Wien, Wien, nur du allein.* Vienna was the capital of the age of anxiety, the hub of Jewish genius, and the city from which the Holocaust would seep. The book I have in mind would have to be a large one.

Perhaps this thought reconciles one to the scale of Hans and Rosaleen Moldenhauer's *Anton von Webern* (Knopf). Some of Webern's finest works—three studies for cello and piano, for example—run to under a minute. Even his full-length pieces tend to extreme concision. The man himself was sparse. Yet this biography exceeds eight hundred pages. Of course, it is more than merely an account of Webern's life. The Moldenhauers, who have devoted much of their own lives to the greater glory of Webern, have produced a biography, a mildly technical commentary on much of Webern's music, and a portrayal of the culture in which he lived and composed. Webern was born in 1883 and died, absurdly and tragically, in September, 1945. These are the decades of the Viennese implosion. The patient reader—even the reader whose interests are not primarily musical—will find fascinating material leading toward an understanding of the spirit of the age. The paradox is this: Webern is a figure apart, who found fulfillment in a nearly esoteric ideal of musical purity and in the solitude of the Austrian Alps. He is, at the same time, a profoundly representative phenomenon of the psychological and social conditions of modern art. As Boulez has proclaimed, there are pieces by Webern, only a few bars long, that seem to crystallize modernity. Yet there has been no musician closer to Bach.

When it came to his craft, Anton Webern—he dropped the "von," though he remained proud of his faintly aristocratic lineage—was abrasively independent. Despite lifelong economic stress, which compelled him to earn his living as an arranger, teacher, and part-time virtuoso conductor (the finest since Mahler, said many experts), Webern would not compromise. No amount of criticism, public ridicule, or scandal—the performance of his *Six Pieces* in March, 1913, occasioned a tumult fully comparable to that unleashed two months later by Stravinsky's *Sacre du Printemps*—deflected Webern from his resolve to pack with emotional strength and formal inevitability even the smallest unit of tone, of pitch, of rhythm. There has not been a tougher musical intelligence. Yet in personal and political terms Webern's history painfully illustrates just that ache for authority, for simplistic explanations, which led to naïve pietistic grandiloquence in a Bruckner and a Mahler, and which was to be instrumental in the development and triumph of

Nazism. As in many mountaineers, so in Webern, aloneness and servitude, asceticism and rapture were inextricably meshed.

Webern's relationship to Arnold Schoenberg represents almost a parody of Freud's model of man's quest for an omnipotent father figure. "I believe that the disciples of Jesus Christ could not have felt more deeply for their Lord than we for you," Webern assured the Master. Schoenberg was the "guardian angel" without whom Webern's existence would have had no purpose. "*I can really not exist* in the thought that you could not feel friendly towards me," pleaded Webern on the occasion of a minor misunderstanding, adding, "I indeed deserve punishment!" "With terrible anxiety I have thought only of you," Webern wrote to his god at the moment of political crisis in 1933. Webern's precarious psychological and material resources were totally at Schoenberg's demanding service. The case is the more interesting because much in Webern's music, while reflecting Schoenberg's teachings and Schoenberg's adoption of a twelve-tone system, was markedly different and, as musicians and musicologists today emphasize, even signalled a break with the conservative elements in Schoenberg's work. Adlerian psychoanalysis, to which Webern had successful recourse at a stage of acute depression and creative arrest, did nothing to weaken his fixation on authority.

The political consequences were predictable. Though Webern had overcome the ready, conventional anti-Semitism in which he was brought up (and which may have given to his later worship of Schoenberg its edge of overcompensation), his chauvinism never faltered. The Hitler regime seemed to embody an awesome renascence of the German and Central European genius. Such a regime must, assuredly, side with the art of the future. One must simply "attempt to convince the Hitler regime of the rightness of the twelve-tone system." Two days before the Nazi troops stomped into Vienna, Webern informed a friend, "I am totally immersed in my work and cannot, cannot be disturbed." Webern's youngest daughter enlisted in the female counterpart of the Hitler Youth. Soon, and under the flag of the Third Reich, Webern gave her in marriage to a uniformed Storm Trooper. He had promptly furnished all requisite proof of the Webern family's Aryan purity.

His confidence in Teutonic might and victory long remained firm. In June, 1942, he reported, "Sometimes such a feeling overcomes me, such hope!" A trifling courtesy shown to Webern by a German consul in Switzerland in early 1943 evoked ecstasies of patriotic gratitude: "Never before had it happened to me that a representative of my fatherland had paid any attention to me! ... I see it as a good omen and as a reward for my loyalty." An article by Goebbels, in the autumn after the German defeat at Stalingrad, in 1943, caused Webern to ask in a letter, "Do we face something totally unexpected?" In February, 1945, Allied bombardments of his beloved Vienna reached a peak, and his son was mortally wounded in action. But almost to the twelfth hour Webern would not believe that the Germanic spirit, whose achievements dominated the history of Western music, whose lyric poetry and idealist metaphysics had given to Webern's being its talismanic center, could succumb to barbarism and ruin. The conviction he had voiced in August, 1914—"An unshakable faith in the German spirit, which indeed has created, almost exclusively, the culture of mankind, is awakened in me"—continued to animate his heart and mind. The desperate flight he made from Vienna and his sudden end represent a plunge into an unforeseen abyss.

The Moldenhauers provide the evidence with absolute scrupulousness. Their discomforts in so doing are palpable. They ask themselves and the reader whether Schoenberg's exiled, Jewish presence came to haunt Webern at his daughter's wedding. The question ought, one fears, to be different: What would have happened if the Nazis had enlisted, instead of rejecting, the talents and the prestige of Dr. Anton Webern? How would he have responded if his music had been performed in the Reich instead of being banned as decadent trash fatally tainted by its association with Schoenberg and the degenerate eroticism of Berg? Time and again, Webern sought to break out of the circle of silence which the authorities had closed around him. And he did venture a few gestures of sympathy and support for hunted Jewish friends, when even the slightest such gesture took great courage. Nevertheless, the fact is that ostracism saved Webern's moral character and subsequent reputation. In the weeks before his death, Webern was being summoned to preside over the reconstruction of the pulverized musical life of Vienna. But the problem goes far beyond myopia in an individual, in an unworldly master of high art. The almost schizophrenic duality of authoritarian and radically rebellious strains in Webern's character, of rigid constraint and utter innovation in his music, is emblematic of the self-lacerating quality of Viennese culture. Our sensibility is direct heir to this creative stress.

Moreover, if there was much blindness and sorrow in Webern's career, there was also a steady conquest. By 1920, the years of neglect were ending. The famous "Passacaglia" and the early song cycles were beginning to make their way. The first all-Webern concert took place in April, 1931. The composer's fiftieth birthday became something of an occasion: a quartet was heard on the BBC, the symphony was broadcast in Prague, the saxophone quartet was played in Winterthur. In Vienna itself, so long and vociferously hostile, there was a small festivity at the house of an American patron, and a young foursome (Polish Jews, as Webern noted) performed.

Webern never doubted either the rightness of his musical doctrines or his ultimate acceptance. At a time when his pieces were regarded as absurd cacophony or as unperformable, Webern calmly assured a pupil, "Sometime in the future even the postman will whistle my melodies!" Given the ambience of our current postal services, this may not be quite the case. But recognition has been worldwide. Six International Webern Festivals took place between 1962 and 1978. Stravinsky came to see in Webern "the just man of music," the tuning fork against which contemporary composers must test their integrity. It is to Webern's ear that so much in the music of Stockhausen, of Boulez, of Elliott Carter, of George Crumb seems to address itself.

Webern could not know of these confirmations as he lay dying, shot by a G.I. in an obscure imbroglio of trigger-happiness or mistaken identity in a village in the Austrian Alps. The episode, which remains very nearly unbearable in its aura of pure hazard and waste, was cleared up by Hans Moldenhauer's untiring research. But Webern's posthumous acclaim was precisely what he had anticipated. "I have never for a single moment lost heart." Doubters, detractors, philistines "have *always* appeared to me as 'ghosts.'" Thus, Webern would approve of the pious monumentality of this book. He would recognize its somewhat pedantic style and also its candor as typically Viennese.

June 25, 1979

DE PROFUNDIS

THE EXACTIONS ALEXANDER Solzhenitsyn makes of his clandestine readers in the Soviet Union (how many are there?) and of his vast Western public have a shrewd ferocity. He knows and despises the readiness of sympathetic response in his Western audience, the vaguely prurient appetite for distant suffering. It is not so much we who read Solzhenitsyn as it is he who reads us. As Tolstoy was during his later years, so Solzhenitsyn is a searcher-out, a harrier of men's debilities, and an embarrassment to the world.

Solzhenitsyn, a theocratic anarchist, has little esteem for reason, particularly when it stems from the "intellectual," from the man who makes his more or less mundane living by dispassion. In the presence of the inhuman, reason is often a small—indeed, a laughable—agent. It can also be subtly self-flattering, and Solzhenitsyn plays harshly on the facile "objectivity" of those who would argue with him, who would try to be "reasonable" without having been exposed to even a millimeter of the archipelago of pain. What has historical analysis to say in the presence of Solzhenitsyn's own sufferings and the cry he has sent through modern history? Each indignity visited upon a human being, each torture, is irreducibly singular and inexpiable. Every time a human being is flogged, starved, deprived of self-respect, a specific black hole

opens in the fabric of life. It is an additional obscenity to deperson-
alize inhumaneness, to blanket the irreparable fact of individual
agony with anonymous categories of statistical analysis, historical
theory, or sociological model-building. Consciously or not, anyone who offers a diagnostic explanation, however pious, or even
condemnatory, erodes, smooths toward oblivion, the irremediable
concreteness of the death by torture of this man or that woman,
of the death by hunger of this child. Solzhenitsyn is obsessed by
the holiness of the minute particular. As happens with Dante and
Tolstoy, proper names cascade from his pen. He knows that if we
are to pray for the tortured dead, we must commit to memory and
utter their names, by the million, in an incessant requiem of nomination.

But the mortal mind is so constructed that it cannot contain, in
genuine individuation, more than a thimbleful of known presences.
At least twenty million men, women, and children were done to
death in the Stalinist purges. If we possess a vivid inward perception, we can visualize, we can number, and, in some measure, we
can identify with fifty persons, perhaps a hundred. Beyond that
stretches the comfortable limbo of abstraction. So if we are to understand at all we *must* try to analyze, to classify, to put forward
those reveries of reason which are called theories.

It is a platitude older than Thucydides that in the exercise of
political power the human species can and will turn to bestiality. Massacres have punctuated the millennia with strident monotony. The routine treatment of slaves, of familial dependents,
of the crippled or the crazed in epochs and societies we now
look back to as of eminent artistic, intellectual, or civic splendor
is such as to numb the imagination. Oases of compassion were
few and far between. (Hence the Christian promise of a compen-
sating Heaven.) No one really knows whether or not grass did
grow again where Genghis Khan had passed; there was no one
left to look. Throughout large stretches of Central Europe dur-

ing the Thirty Years War, there were only wolves left to devour the wind.

But there *was* an Indian summer, a relative armistice with history, in the luckier parts of Western Europe and the United States during much of the eighteenth century, and again between the close of the Napoleonic wars and 1914. The constant of savagery lay in the hands of specialized professional armies and had been exported to the frontier or the colonies. Voltaire was not a naïve Utopian when he foresaw the disappearance of torture and mass reprisal from political life. The signs were positive. General Sherman's Hunnish tactics looked like an isolated, embarrassing atavism.

It is the Armenian massacres of 1915–16 that are at once pivotal and problematic. Were they, as some have argued, a nightmarish epilogue to a long history of "barbarian" invasion and ravage, a throwback to the world of Attila? Or were they, as others contend, the opening of the age of holocaust and genocide? And what, if any, are the psychological and technical links between the deliberate murder of one million Armenians by the Turks and the exactly contemporary hecatombs on the Western front? Whatever the diagnosis, the overwhelming fact was that political, nationalist man, equipped with unprecedented weapons, had remembered or rediscovered the logic of annihilation.

It is according to this logic that we have conducted our affairs since. The logic has entailed the insanity of mass homicide from 1914 to 1918 (almost three-quarters of a million at Verdun alone), the eradication of civilian sites and peoples, the planned poisoning of the natural environment, the wanton killing of animal species, and the Nazi murder of Jews and Gypsies. Today, this same logic entails the cold-blooded eradication of native tribes throughout Amazonia, the ubiquity in Uruguay and Argentina of a degree of torture and terror which matches anything known of Stalin's thugs and the Gestapo. Today, at this minute, it is a logic that underwrites the suicidal bloodletting in Cambodia. The Gulag has no real borders.

This is not to diminish by one jot the specificity of Solzhenitsyn's reports from Hell. But it is to ask in what ways the Soviet edifice of servitude and degradation is or is not a segment of a more general catastrophe. Solzhenitsyn himself is not clear on this issue. The first two volumes of the Gulag chronicle contained crassly peremptory asides on the distinctions to be drawn between Nazi and Stalinist practices. Solzhenitsyn made much of the (undoubted) truth that Stalin had slaughtered many millions more than had Hitler. (At full tide, as Robert Conquest has shown in his classic studies, the Soviet camps comprised some eight million inmates.) Solzhenitsyn even advanced the supposition that the Gestapo tortured to elicit the "facts," whereas the Russian secret police tortured to produce false witness. No such vulgarities mar this third volume, *The Gulag Archipelago Three* (Harper & Row), but Solzhenitsyn remains undecided as to where and how the Gulag fits into the texture of Russian history and of the Russian temper. At some points, he voices the belief that oppression from above and obeissance to brute authority by the great mass of the population characterize the Russian spirit. But at other points he hammers at the specifically Bolshevik nature of the regime of terror, a regime initiated by Lenin, brought to lunatic efficacy by Stalin, and continuing in madness today on a less apocalyptic scale. Solzhenitsyn frequently and sarcastically contrasts the relatively benign deviltries of the czarist punitive apparatus (as reported by Chekhov or Dostoevsky) with the consuming bestiality of the Soviet solution.

If Solzhenitsyn were to be asked whether the reversion of modern political man to mass torture, incarceration, and murder represents some general phenomenon, or whether each instance is an appalling singularity, he would, I imagine, say something like this: When mankind rejected the true meaning and urgency of Christ's example, when it turned to secular ideals and material hopes, it severed its history and political institutions from compassion, from the imperative of grace. A politics or a social bureaucracy divorced from theological sanction has within it, ineluctably, the mechanics of nihilism, of self-destructive wantonness. The Gulag-planet, the ubiquity of torture and homicide in our public existence, is only the most dramatic, the most shameless manifestation of a pervasive inhumanity.

It is this theological-penitential reading of man's condition which underwrites the most eccentric but also the most deeply felt of Solzhenitsyn's dogmas: his detestation of secular liberalism as it flows from the French Revolution; his distaste for the Jews, in whom he sees not merely the initial refusers of Christ but the radical libertarians whose restlessness culminates in Marxism and utopian socialism; his contempt for the "degenerate hedonism" and conspicuous consumption in Western societies; his undisguised nostalgia for the theocratic aura of Orthodox—almost of Byzantine—Russia.

This is an isolating, often maddening set of theses. It has against it an alliance, at once ludicrous and, to Solzhenitsyn, entirely natural, of the K.G.B., Mrs. Jimmy Carter (*vide* her attempt to rebut Solzhenitsyn's tirade at the Harvard commencement), and the Swiss tax authorities seeking to take their tithe of the royalties of their recent guest. Conjoined, these beliefs of Solzhenitsyn make for a "mystical" explanation of modern barbarism. It is an explanation that is, by its very nature, impossible to prove or to deny. But is there a better one?

Many have tried to find one. The late Hannah Arendt strove to locate the roots of modern totalitarianism in certain definite aspects of the evolution of the encompassing nation-state, and of the quality of economic and psychological collectivism after the Enlightenment. Others have seen in the concentration and death camps a final enactment, at once logical and parodistic, of the industrial processes of assembly lines and standardization. I have put forward the "working metaphor" whereby the erosion of God's presentness from daily life and from the legitimacy of political power generated the need to institute a surrogate damnation on earth (a Hell above ground), this surrogate being the Nazi, the Soviet, the Chilean, and the Cambodian Gulags. But none of these hypotheses are really explanatory. What we are left with is the central fact: In a way and on a scale inconceivable to educated Western man from, say, Erasmus to Woodrow Wilson, we have reverted to or contrived a politics of torment and massacre. From this fact cries out the only question that matters: Can the infernal cycle be stopped?

Solzhenitsyn, who has survived not only the Gulag but the cancer ward, is animated by a raging will. More, perhaps, than anyone since Nietzsche and Tolstoy, he is mesmerized by and master of the boundless resilience of the human spirit. His answer would be: Yes, it is possible to stop the juggernaut; it is possible to repudiate the banality of evil and to say no to those who would reduce one to a worker in the slaughterhouse. He would say—or should do so in the blaze of his own vision—that the United States could halt the genocide in Amazonia, the sadistic circus in Argentina, the degradations in Chile by withdrawing from these grotesque regimes the investments, the corporate interests, on whose largesse they operate. Solzhenitsyn can and must proclaim that the automatism of oppression can be arrested, because he has seen it arrested or, at least, ground to temporary impotence in the pits of Hell itself.

This is the testimony of the final volume of the trilogy, with its enthralling record of camp uprisings, of escapes, of defiance by individuals and groups of victims. Solzhenitsyn records the forty magnificent days and nights of the revolt of May and June, 1954, in the Kengir camp. He tells the tale—it is a classic narrative—of Georgi P. Tenno, virtuoso escaper. In poignant closing chapters, he recalls his own resurrection from the house of the dead, his own reëntry, at once agonizing and joyous, into the habitual daylight of more or less normal, licensed existence.

Yet this colossus of a man, so markedly a stranger to common humanity, does not end his epic in consolation. After nine years of clandestine writing, Solzhenitsyn closes his trilogy on the grim notice that a century has passed since the invention of barbed wire. And he, who has seen, lived, recounted the utmost of resistance, of hope against Hell, implies that it is this invention that will continue to determine the history of modern man. There is in the blackness of this great fresco no touch more desperate.

September 4, 1978

GOD'S SPIES

It has been from the start a dirty business. The first spies of whom we have record were wormed by Joshua into Jericho. They found a "safe house," as it is called in today's intelligence jargon; it was that of the harlot. The second-oldest espionage tale is that in Book X of the Iliad. It is a sordid episode of penetration and counter-penetration in the night, ending in muffled butchery. Appropriately, the narrative is regarded by scholars as a late addition, a bit of melodrama not by Homer. Yet the fascination of the genre is perennial. Among the first mature American fiction is *The Spy*. In it, James Fenimore Cooper lights on a characteristic modern motif: that of the actual or putative double agent. In the context of the American Revolution, with its shared tongue and frequent kinship between adversaries, the ambivalence of the secret agent was present almost by definition. This was again the case during the War Between the States, whose clandestine couriers and intelligence runners embodied in their own persons and murky ventures the rent of divided allegiance.

Incipient duality is the agent's demon. How could it be otherwise? The craft of spying is based on intimacy with the party being spied on. The agent must melt into the enemy city. The codebreaker insinuates his own being into the labyrinthine heart of the encoder. (John Hollander's arch and subtle long poem "Reflections on Espionage" allegorizes the mirror closeness between raveller and unraveller.) Snared in the arcane web of his own "cover," smoked, winkled out of his mask, the intelligencer is often offered the escape of a second treason. He now starts working for his captors while seeming to retain his first loyalty. He has, as the term goes, "been turned."

But further pirouettes can ensue. A double agent may in fact be just that: he may be delivering authentic goods both ways, thus becoming one of the mail drops or nerve synapses that keep even the most bitter of national foes in necessary contact. Often, the two masters, or "controls," know that they are being reciprocally but usefully betrayed. The agent is allowed the naked immunity of no man's land. At other times, only one of the paymasters will know that his man has "turned." (During the Second World War, such knowledge allowed the Allied "spooks" to filter false data into the main arteries of the German counter-intelligence network.) But there are numerous cases in which neither party to mutual deception can ever be certain where the agent's truth or falsehood finally lies. A seeming double—was the young Stalin working equally for the czarist Okhrana and the Bolsheviks; was he selling out more of the one than the other; had he turned back to his first recruiters after betraying them to the second?—burrows irretrievably into the maze of his own occult purposes. Does the spy himself, Joseph Conrad opines in *The Secret Agent,* recollect where his loyalties lie?

To this question, which can be made symbolic of the uncertainties of human identity, of those capacities for self-deception and selective forgetting which make men teeter or stumble when they descend the spiral staircase of the inward self, twentieth-century espionage and its fiction give a new answer. Even the treble agent, who sells both his employers to a third bidder, even the most venal and chameleonlike of peepers (spying, "private eyeing," is the art of the voyeur), does have an ultimate adherence. He is, in the nauseous hour before dawn when he waits for the torturer's decorous rap on the door, loyal not to the nation-states or governments that have bought and sold him; he is loyal to his profession, to the cobweb, incessantly torn, incessantly repaired, that knits in a common intimacy of mistrust all agents, all miniature-camera men in unlit filing closets, all calligraphers in invisible ink, whatever the flag under which they ply their trade. No spy ever wants to come in from the cold. His only home is the tundra of his shared craft. His only brotherhood is that of professional esteem as between hunter and hunted.

In British sentiment, this bleak paradox has taken on an obsessive edge. Kim Philby's penetration, on behalf of Soviet intelligence, to very near the top of the British secret service and the related treason of Guy Burgess and Donald Maclean, whose escape to Moscow Philby crafted, grow more haunting as time passes. Part of the reason is the ruthless effrontery of the coup together with the inefficacy of official response. (Was it worse than that—was there collusion or coverup in even higher places?) In its bumbling ugliness and high cost—United States intelligence has never again found it easy to coordinate fully with its "first cousins"—the Philby disaster has come to represent certain central infirmities of imagination and technique in British public affairs.

But there are deeper grounds for malaise. In their social background and schooling, in their idiom and guise of life, Philby and his minions embodied the genteel caste on whose absolute fidelity, on whose unargued devotion to public service, Britain has based its trust in government through and by an amateur elite. Judas had belonged to the right clubs. Worse than that: he had been on the house committee. The shock of disclosure went to the heart. It induced E. M. Forster to put forward one of the most unsettling of all modern propositions: that a true gentleman and humanist is one who would rather betray his country than his friend (the inference being that the friend also is a "gentleman," that the betrayal of a cad poses no comparable crux). The Philby drama gives a special density—though, in the most recent case, a sentimental overblownness—to the spy novels of John le Carré. It is the topic of Alan Bennett's current play *The Old Country*, in which Sir Alec Guinness gives a virtuoso performance as *Philby* in his Moscow repose. And it is, inevitably, the background of Graham Greene's twentieth novel, *The Human Factor* (Simon & Schuster), which, one understands, started out, a good many years ago, as a reflection on Philby.

Graham Greene has long been a master of the politics of sadness. In this, he is heir to Conrad, from whom the new novel takes its desolate epigraph: "I only know that he who forms a tie is lost. The germ of corruption has entered into his soul." Maurice Castle (the name points toward both Forster and Kafka) has formed a tie. He loves Sarah, his black wife, and Sam, his black stepson. Their escape from South Africa, from race laws that would have made life together and marriage impossible, was a dangerous contrivance. It could not have been managed without the help of Carson, done obscurely to death in a South African jail, and his anti-apartheid associates, Communists among them. This debt binds Castle closer to Sarah. He honors it by dishonoring his own trust and office. He is a double.

Castle occupies a mildly senior niche in a dusty dead end of British intelligence. He keeps a sad eye on former African colonies. He detests South African policies and passes to his Soviet contacts whatever information might help to inhibit the spread of apartheid and the further suppression of liberal and left-wing resistance within South Africa itself. When Sarah speaks of "our people," he experiences a momentary at-homeness more immediate, more vital to his graying heart than that of his native Englishness or official function. A leak is detected in Castle's department. Counter-intelligence suspects a "mole"—the word used to designate a traitor in one's secret midst, a burrower from within who is working under the mandate of a foreign espionage organization. The logic of suspicion, casual at first, then mendaciously coherent, points to Davis, Castle's drifty, gently careless second. Colonel Daintry wants solid proof before proceeding, but Dr. Percival, who looks after health problems in "the firm" (the intelligence team), is less sentimental. Davis dies of poison.

Meanwhile, Castle has been ordered to collaborate closely with the very man in the South African secret service who once hounded him and Sarah. Uncle Remus is the code name for one of those anti-subversion, mutual-advantage schemes in which South Africa and the United States pursue their common anti-Red interests. Castle transmits one final dossier of crucial information and, knowing that the sappers are closing in on him, presses the eject button. He is spirited out of England. At the end of the novel, the phone line that had, momentarily, brought Sarah's voice goes dead. We are left to infer that it will be a very cold time indeed before Castle will see her and Sam again. In the limbo of his Moscow flat, he is reading *Robinson Crusoe*. How long was the mariner marooned in the solitude of remembrance? "Eight and twenty years, two months and nineteen days . . ." But Moscow is an island more remote.

Throughout, we are in the spare, diminished ambience that Greene has made his own. The note is one of terminality. Castle is sterile. British spies and counter-spies operate from a base of drastically diminished power or relevance. The dreams of Marxism have turned to nightmare or staled to a set of gestures and metaphors as vacant, as corrosive as are those of classic Western liberalism. (Here Greene is even more disenchanted than le Carré, who has made the "missing center" a constant element of his plots.) What élan there is resides either with the purposeful brutality of BOSS (the South African intelligence agency) or the distant pushiness of American naïveté. In Daintry, the high code of the English gentleman and public servant has withered to ineffectuality. (The one scintillating set piece in the book shows a fumbling Daintry routed at his daughter's déclassé marriage by the hectoring wife from whom he has long been separated.) In Dr. Percival, this same code has decayed to bland murderousness.

Of the faded clubs on St. James's, of the bookstores with their line in erotica, of whiskeyed suburbia, Greene makes images of a whole society wheezing its way toward some faintly nasty future—this vision being already seminal in *Brighton Rock,* in 1938. An exchange between Castle and Davis early in the tale voices the low-keyed sardonicism of the entire narrative:

> "What was the most secret information you ever possessed, Castle?"
>
> "I once knew the approximate date of an invasion."
>
> "Normandy?"
>
> "No, no. Only the Azores."

There is mastery in that "approximate."

But although this is a lean, finely governed piece of work, it is not one of Greene's major achievements. The text is replete with self-reference. The reader is asked to flesh out the shorthand of motive and characterization by recalling closely similar episodes, snatches of dialogue, motions of pathos in *Our Man in Havana* and *The Honorary Consul.* As often in Greene, the treatment of married love, pivotal to Castle's treason, is fitful. The dialogue between Sarah and Castle goes wooden; their aching intimacy is stated, not realized. It is the rapid vignettes that stand out: Bellamy ("Philby") dropping in on Castle in Moscow.

By far the most interesting motif in *The Human Factor* is Greene's suggestion that both Roman Catholicism and espionage provide an instrument of truth and of solace which neither Protestantism nor secular rationalism (its fated offspring) can match. There must be eavesdropping upon the soul; there must be occult listeners empowered to chastise and console. The agent reporting to his controller and the Catholic kneeling before his confessor are in the same perilous boat. But via that traverse, with its stripping of the spirit, with its acquiescence in penitential labors, lies solidarity. Greene enforces the parallel. Castle once saw a genuine priest, a ministering servant of God in the Soweto shanties, and knows that there are human faces to Communism, too—that some last truth in the Communist vision has survived Prague and Budapest even as Catholicism has survived the Borgias. And in the crucial scene in the book, a scene written in explicit recall of Greene's finest work, *The Power and the Glory,* Castle, who has no church, seeks to purloin the comforts of the confessional. Like Kierkegaard, Greene knows that the loneliest of men is he who has no secret—or, more exactly, who has no one to whom to betray a secret. Thus there is a bizarre communion in all treason, and a theology echoed in Lear's mysterious admonition to Cordelia: let us be "God's spies" and sing like the birds in their cage.

The notion has its sombre spell, as do those fantasies of clandestine identity with which so many of us shore up our daydreams. It is poor Davis who lets the cat out of the bag: "What a damn silly profession ours is" (wherein "profession" carries, as always in Greene, the pull of its etymological roots). But it is just this realization that Greene, le Carré, and their swarming tribe evade. There are devices rumored to be capable of detecting the heat from a tank exhaust at seventy thousand feet. Investigative journalism and the now universal ethos of gossip flood the newsstands with top-security information. Popular magazines have diagrams on how to assemble nuclear bombs. Is there anything genuinely new or decisive in the stuff spies peddle to their clients? Did Joshua need four hooded eyes to tell him that Jericho had walls and that its denizens would not welcome invasion? It may be that the whole espionage industry has become a fatuous game, a homicidal hopscotch in a house of mirrors.

"I wish all the lies were unnecessary," Castle confides to Boris, his Soviet control. "And I wish we were on the same side." Perhaps we are, and perhaps Mr. Greene is whispering to us that it is, nonetheless, the losing side. Confiteor.

May 8, 1978

FROM THE HOUSE OF THE DEAD

ALBERT SPEER WAS Hitler's architect and minister of armaments and war production. Two features distinguish him from the rest of the Nazi thugs. First, there was in Speer's feelings for Hitler a core of disinterested affection, of warmth going beyond animal fascination. On April 23, 1945, with Berlin a sea of flames and all chances of safe exit almost forfeit, Speer returned to the capital to bid a personal farewell to the Führer. The blank coldness of Hitler's response shattered him. Second, Speer kept alive within himself a modicum of sanity and moral sense, through the lunatic circus of the Reich and then during almost twenty years of incarceration in Spandau. It is these two elements—the spell exercised upon him by the person of Hitler and the resolve to emerge sane from two decades of live burial—which dominate Speer's *Spandau: The Secret Diaries* (translated from the German, for Macmillan, by Richard and Clara Winston).

At the Nuremberg war trials, Albert Speer acknowledged that it was he who had been ultimately in charge of the use of the many millions of slave laborers in the arsenal of the Reich. He had been directly involved neither in the bestial mechanics of deportation that brought these wretched human beings from the occupied territories nor in the maltreatment and bored extermination that often followed. But the overlordship of manufacture and industrial mobilization had been his, and to this extent Speer admitted—indeed, expatiated on—his guilt. The sentence of twenty years' imprisonment seemed, from the start, brutal, and was thought to reflect Soviet insistence. Almost immediately after Nuremberg, there were whisperings to the effect that the Russian authorities had no desire to see so brilliant an impresario of weaponry and materials procurement pass safely into Western hands.

Speer entered the prison of Spandau, in Berlin, on July 18, 1947; he left it at midnight sharp on September 30, 1966. Together with the time spent in the Nuremberg jail after his sentencing, this made for exactly twenty years. Speer served the second decade of his sentence in company with only two other men—Baldur von Schirach, the former Hitler Youth leader, and Rudolf Hess. Speer entered the echoing coffin of Spandau as a man of forty-two, at the summit of his powers, and after a meteoric career. He was released at sixty-one. But during his captivity he wrote: more than twenty thousand sheets of diary notes, authorized and clandestine letters, scraps of autobiography. He wrote on calendar leaves, cardboard lids, toilet paper (the traditional papyrus of the prisoner). And he succeeded in smuggling this prodigious hoard out of Spandau despite the vigilant scrutiny of American, Russian, British, and French guards. Speer smuggled out enough material for his first book, *Inside the Third Reich*, for this prison journal, and, if certain hints are right, for what may be a full-scale study of Hitler. How did he do it? Speer's account is at once curiously circumstantial and elusive. He tells us that he must protect the identity of those who helped him. The main channel was one of the prison medical aides, who had himself, ironically, been a deportee in the Reich war machine. But there must have been other avenues. It is difficult to escape the impression that the authorities, particularly the three Western powers, must have known something of Speer's voluminous commerce with the outside world and the future. Indeed, as early as

October, 1948, the wife of a leading Jewish publisher in New York approached a member of Speer's family with regard to his memoirs (the subtle indecency of the idea repelled Speer, if not the lady).

Hitler inhabits this book like a black mist. In Speer's first years of captivity, he sought to recollect and set down methodically the history of his relationship to the Führer. Many of the vignettes are memorable. We see Hitler planning to make a world art center of his native town of Linz. We watch him during the years of his somnambular ascent to power, amid the crazed multitudes aching for his whirlwind passage in an open car, or in the intimate company of his bully boys—orating, mocking, pontificating, and lapsing, brusquely, into the silent vortex of his vision. There are extraordinary snapshots of Hitler in a domestic vein at Obersalzberg, laboring at unforced sociability amid minions, aides, camp followers whose lives hung on his breath. Speer records Hitler on literature (the man had a passion for Karl May, the German version of Fenimore Cooper), on sculpture, on the meaning of history. He calls to memory the moments of generosity shown by the Führer to early associates and backers, and tells of Hitler's obsession with fire, with the tongue of flame on the hearth and the fire storm over the city.

Speer knows that Hitler is closely meshed with the root of his, Speer's, identity. November 20, 1952: "Whatever turn my life takes in the future, whenever my name is mentioned, people will think of Hitler. I shall never have an independent existence. And sometimes I see myself as a man of seventy, children long since adult and grandchildren growing up, and wherever I go people will not ask about me but about Hitler." Three years earlier, Speer ponders the predestined logic of his encounter with the Master: "I regarded Hitler above all as the preserver of the world of the nineteenth century against that disturbing metropolitan world which I feared lay in the future of all of us. Viewed in that light, I might actually have been waiting for Hitler. Moreover—and this justifies him even more—he communicated to me a strength that raised me far above the limits of my potentialities. If this is so, then I cannot say he led me away from myself: on the contrary, through him I first found a heightened identity."

In the endless tunnel of prison days, Speer tries to arrive at a clear picture of the man who built and smashed his life. If there was cruelty—though of an oddly abstract, indifferent kind—megalomania, a rasping vulgarity, self-pity, and falsehood beyond ordinary human scope, there was also the exact opposite. Speer knew Hitler as "a solicitous paterfamilias, a generous superior, amiable, self-controlled, proud, and capable of enthusiasm for beauty and greatness." The last point haunts Speer. Hitler's policies in the arts and architecture could spring from brutal myopia. But at other moments there were real flashes of insight, flights of invention and learning. The charisma of the man was a deep, cold thing, at once numbing and magnetic. And so was his naked intellectual edge in regard to political tactics, rhetorical command, and psychological penetration of the tired or corrupt shadow players who faced him at home and abroad. "He really came from another world. . . . The military men had all learned to deal with a wide variety of unusual situations. But they were totally unprepared to deal with this visionary."

There is nothing new in any of this. Other testimony has made the nightmare image routine. But Speer does touch on matters of the first importance when he seeks to diagnose Hitler's anti-Semitism. He recalls scarcely a single exchange on the question between the Führer and himself (in the nauseating miasma of Hitler's table talk we find hardly a single allusion to the world of the concentration camps). Yet on combing more closely through the great drift of his remembrance, Speer comes to the conclusion that hatred for the Jews was the absolute, unwavering pivot of Hitler's being. The entirety of Hitler's politics and war plans "was merely camouflage for this real motivating factor." Pondering Hitler's testament, with its apocalyptic vision of Jewish war guilt and of the extermination of European Jewry, Speer comes to realize that this extermination signified more to Hitler than either victory or the survival of the German nation.

Rationalist historians have disputed the point. They have striven to find a "normal" economic-strategic framework for Hitler's career. Speer is much nearer the truth. There is little sense to be made of the Hitler phenomenon—of his poisonous magic and enormity of self-destruction—if one does not focus stringently on the central motif of anti-Semitism. In some tenebrous manner, Hitler saw in the messianic coherence of the Jewish people, in their apartness, in the metaphor of their "chosenness," an unalterable mocking counterpoise to his own most intimate drives. When he proclaimed that Nazism and Judaism could not coexist, that one or both must suffer annihilation in a final conflict, he was stating a crazy truth. Learning of the Eichmann trial and of the ever-increasing evidence of the Holocaust, Speer notes that his own desire for release from prison strikes him as "almost absurd."

But the desire persisted, of course. This is the point of all prison literature: the hope against hope that more than seven thousand unchanging days will pass, that time can be given a meaning or a comforting shape across a vacuum of twenty winters. Speer's suffocation was made worse by repeated spurts of rumor. John McCloy, the United States High Commissioner for Germany, was pressing for mitigation or release; Adenauer was sympathetic; the British Foreign Office had approached the Russians. Surely the Cold War would lead to the evacuation of Spandau and to a more opportune view of Speer's crimes. Why should the Western powers let the wizard of German armament rot when they themselves were remilitarizing Germany? But each hope proved false, and Speer came to endure, and to articulate, the conviction that he would have to serve his sentence to the last, nearly inconceivable midnight.

He kept sane by means classical in the records of entombment. He took intense, daily walks in the Spandau grounds, keeping an exact count of the distance. At the close, he had covered 31,936 kilometres. But this forced march was more than abstract exercise. Speer imagined himself hiking around the globe, from Europe, via the Middle East, to China, the Bering Strait, and then down through Mexico. As he tramped, he conjured in his mind's eye what he knew of the relevant landscape, architecture, climate. "I am already deep in India," runs a typical log, "and according to the plan will be in Benares in five months." Then, there was the prison garden. From the spring of 1959 on, Speer devoted more and more time and energy to its cultivation. Each shrub, every flower bed became the object of tenacious design and care: "Spandau has become a meaning in itself. Long ago I had to organize my survival here. That is no longer necessary. The garden has taken full possession of me."

Speer read indefatigably: history, philosophy, fiction, and, eerily, books touching on events in which he had himself played so drastic a part. Once he was allowed to see engineering and architectural journals, he labored to refresh his skills and keep in some kind of touch with the world changing outside. Speer drew: plans for family houses, much appreciated by his Russian jailers, silhouettes and contours of monuments now in rubble, and occasional strange allegoric scenes, strident with solitude. Above all, he wrote, thousands and thousands of pages. His reason hung by this stout thread.

Nevertheless, there were spells of despair and near-madness: at the end of the tenth year, when Admirals Dönitz and Raeder had been released after serving their time; in June, 1961, when fear of having mislaid one of his illegal letters brought on wild panic. When breakdown seemed imminent, Speer would allow himself a "sleep-cure," a three-week indulgence in sleeping pills, securing solid nights and blurred days. But mostly he drew on his own formidable resilience. After a week in a punishment cell, sitting motionless for eleven hours in front of blank walls, Speer emerged "as fresh as I was on the first day."

The devices of the Allied authorities—acting, to be sure, in the name of outraged humanity—do not always make for pretty reading. After eleven years of imprisonment, Speer asked for canvas and oil paints. This dangerous request was refused. The prisoners were never addressed by their names—solely by the numbers they wore on their backs—for to call a man by his name is to honor him in his humanity. Family visits were kept few and brief. They were supposed to take place in the presence of Soviet, American, French, and British observers. Sixteen years passed before Speer, through a kindly oversight, was allowed an instant alone with his wife. In the event, he was too numb even to touch her hand. National stereotypes mark the different jailers and presiding officers (control of Spandau alternates on a monthly rota among the four occupying powers). The English are punctilious. The French display a certain easy panache. There is in American innocence and spontaneity a frequent edge of brutality. During each "Russian month," the prison diet plummets. But the Soviet personnel is anxiously literate. While their Western colleagues thumb through detective stories or doze over crossword puzzles, the Russians at Spandau study chemistry, physics, and mathematics, or read Dickens, Jack London, and Tolstoy. According to shifts in the Cold War temperature, inter-Allied relations within the prison tauten or relax, and the prisoners are treated in consequence. During the Cuban missile crisis, the electric tension gives the prisoners a center of gravity. It is the Russian guard who brings news of peace.

It is snapshots like this, risible and tragic, which make these claustrophobic pages bearable. Speer has a trained eye. In Nuremberg, he passes by the cells of those of his colleagues who are waiting to be hanged: "As the rules prescribe, most of them are lying on their backs, hands on the blanket, heads turned toward the inside of the coil. A ghostly sight, all of them in their immobility; it looks as though they have already been laid on their biers." In the winter of 1953, Prisoner No. 3, Hitler's sometime foreign minister Konstantin von Neurath, is allowed an armchair (the old man's health was failing). Speer recognizes it as one that he had designed for the Berlin Chancellery, in 1938: "The damask upholstery is tattered, the sheen faded, the veneer scratched, but I still like the proportions, especially the curve of the rear legs." The proud monstrosities that Speer had built for the Reich, the bright-red pillars and the marble porticoes of triumph, lie in oblivion. Two things remain: the memory of the impalpable "cathedral of ice" that Speer created by the use of a hundred and thirty searchlight beams at a Nuremberg party rally, and this chair.

As release comes nearer, Speer's mind plays ominous tricks. He stops listening to the radio. He orders his family to cease all correspondence. Sharp dreams tell him that he will never return home, that his life unlived can never be made good. Three days to go: once more he weeds the garden so that everything will be left trim. He senses, as does every long-term prisoner, that his relationship to his prison has become "semierotic," that, in some lunatic way, he no longer wants to leave the coffin he has mastered. On the last day, waiting for his and Schirach's release, Speer adds ten kilometres to his global tour. The climax is a touch of terror and human desolation beyond the reach of fiction. Great heaps of coal are being unloaded in the prison courtyard. Speer stands next to Hess, watching: "Then Hess said, 'So much coal. And from tomorrow on only for me.'" That was September 30, 1966. The crazed old hooligan, uninvolved in the worst of Nazi atrocities, because he had flown to Scotland, is in Spandau still, alone, guarded by four miniature armies and thirty-eight thousand cubic metres of walled space. The Western powers have long urged his release. The Soviet Union refuses, lest it lose the one military toehold it has in West Berlin. Our acquiescence in Russian blackmail on this point of inhumanity is past comment.

But once this is said, and once the force of Speer's record and survival has been acknowledged, another point needs to be made.

In Spandau there were books and music, family letters, and medical care. During three months out of four the food was excellent. There were hot baths, and a garden to tend. No man was flogged, none plunged in excrement or burned piecemeal to cinders. In short, twenty years in Spandau was a literal paradise compared to a single day in Belsen, Majdanek, Auschwitz, or any of a hundred of the outhouses of Hell built by the regime that Albert Speer served so brilliantly. It is the power, the pain of this book that one has to say this to oneself, if not to him (who now professes to know it). Yet even to say this is not enough. It is not merely compared with Belsen that Spandau is a rest cure: but compared with the Gulag, with the Soviet psychiatric penitentiaries, with the jails of Chile and the unspeakable death camps of Indonesia, Speer was only one of the master builders—if perhaps the most bitterly punished. The architecture of death flourishes still.

April 19, 1976

DE MORTUIS

I do not know what goes on at the Institute of Applied Research for Tropical and Subtropical Fruits, outside Paris. I prefer to imagine. There must be white-robed mandarins equipped with the panoply of competitive qualifications that in France are indispensable to every professional caste, from literati to chiropodists. Shadowy emissaries from Papua, Cipango, and the rain forests of Amazonia circulate among them offering for inspection succulent hybrids of passion fruit and guava, of cherimoya and loquats, of scented *Dipteryx odorata* and *Litchi chinensis*. Samples are skeptically nibbled, sniffed, and caressed. The seeds of a rare fly-eating apricot plant, smuggled out of the New Guinea uplands, sprout in the window box. As the Institute is housed at Maisons-Laffitte, discreet libations are, from time to time, poured from the noble vintage of a kindred name.

Like all self-respecting institutes, that of Applied Research for Tropical and Subtropical Fruits boasts an information section, a catalogue, a desk from which to send lofty but illuminating answers to the questions that pour in from the Keeper of Parrots at the Jardin Zoologique, from those, always fairly numerous in France, seeking novel, fastidious toxins whereby to poison their wives, from crossword-puzzle setters and solvers. The director of information is one

M. Philippe Ariès. He is an industrious man. Between answering queries on the nine thousand six hundred and seventy-one varieties of inedible berries in the Ceylonese undergrowth, M. Ariès writes massive tomes on life and on death, on private man and on public history. His *Centuries of Childhood,* which appeared in English in 1962, his preliminary study of *Western Attitudes Toward Death,* translated in 1974, his *The Hour of Our Death,* which has just been published in a lively translation, by Helen Weaver (Knopf), have made of Ariès one of the "herald figures" (*figures de proue*) in the immensely influential current school of French history and historiography.

Traditional history is, as English schoolboys put it, "about maps and chaps." This somewhat literalist perspective has long been challenged by such special branches as economic history, the history of ideas, the theory and analysis of international relations, and the attempt, brilliantly represented in this country by Daniel Boorstin, to make an organic whole of the records of technology, of scientific invention, of daily life in the city and on the farm, and of the archives of social institutions and family life. The French school has striven to cut radically inward. It has sought to bring into the light of methodical narrative—and, indeed, of quantifiability—the sources and flux of human consciousness, the changes of feeling, of the habits of sentiment in a given society, milieu, or epoch. No translation is entirely adequate to the native tag *"histoire des mentalités"* with its simultaneous pointers to historicity in the old sense and to the primacy of inwardness in the new. The growth of this French school is, of itself, a fascinating piece of "internal history." Positivism, in the nineteenth-century version of Auguste Comte, had taught that history was the all-embracing analytical instrument through which a society arrives at a meaningful image of its own genesis and specific character. Comte, Hippolyte Taine, Marx had forcefully urged that sociology, the statistical investigation of social mores and demographic trends, be made an integral part of the historian's methods.

Parallel to this current was that of the great tradition of French so-cial-realistic fiction, from Balzac and Flaubert to Zola and Proust, the vividly documentary, investigative focus of literary narrative on the attitudes, institutions, psychological trends of French society both rural and urban, both aristocratic and mercantile-bourgeois. These two parallel traditions seem to conjoin in the pioneering work of historians of genius such as Marc Bloch, Fernand Braudel, and Lucien Febvre. Febvre, especially, asked the key questions. He wanted to know how men and women in the sixteenth century thought and felt about love, how they experienced and coped with the emotional stress of religious conflicts, what attitudes they had toward sickness and death. He called for full-scale "histories of joy, of compassion, of private anguish." He wondered whether the new availability of eyeglasses and improvements in artificial lighting had eroded the great civilization of smells, the busy expertness of the nose, as it had prevailed in the reeking cities of the Middle Ages and the fifteenth century. Long before McLuhan, Febvre wondered about the sensory and ideological implications of the gradual shift from manuscript to print.

A galaxy of French—and, of late, English and American—historians have followed Febvre's lead. Not only do they inquire into the structure and development of, say, marital relations in town and country in the seventeenth and eighteenth centuries; they seek to determine—and this is the point—the ways in which men and women at the time understood, symbolized, and acquiesced in or sought to rebel against what they took to be (itself a prob-lematical issue) the "realities" of marriage, of sex, of childbearing and child rearing, of the inheritance and transmission of property rights. For example, such historians as Georges Duby try to bring back to life what must have been the profound modifications in the human consciousness of distance, of community, of personal reach, as the great forests of early-medieval Europe thinned, as roads became practicable once more after the decay of the Roman mandate. Other historians want to know in what precise regards, to what extent, the expectations of Hell as preached and pictured in ecclesiastical doctrine and the very gradual but steady erosion of these expectations did or did not affect the modes of warfare and the bias toward "incestuous" intermarriage of the chivalric order on the one hand and the nascent "worldliness" of the mercantile classes on the other.

Literature and the arts, the transformative history of words and of grammar, the evidence of public and domestic architecture, the evolution of cookbooks and school primers, the files of the tax collector and the phrase book of the public scrivener (with its odd survival in the Western Union selection of ready-made messages of felicitation or lament), the sermons of the parish priest and the case notes of the physician describing to himself and his community the nature of a given illness—all these are grist to the mill of the historian of "mentality." Very nearly by definition, nothing thought, felt, recorded, but also nothing overlooked by a society is irrelevant. For if perception is a historical condition, so is oversight. Did men and women before Freud not *see* certain salient features of sexual life in children, in themselves, in their dreams? Did they not *choose* to see them? Or was there as yet no accepted vocabulary for the definition and articulation of such features? We lack histories of dreams. It had long been observed that young children in medieval and Renaissance art were diminutive adults, that the artist's realization did not extend to the native qualities of childhood in a child's mien and motion. Convincing children are all but absent from Shakespeare's "universality." The child is a discovery of the eighteenth and nineteenth centuries, he is "invented" by libertarian and romantic sensibility and Rousseauist theories of education. In his *Centuries of Childhood*, Ariès sought to trace and to document the history of this gradual, surprisingly late addendum to the range of essential personal and public recognitions. He then turned to death, to the altering modes of emotional and intellectual awareness and interpretation which Western man has brought to bear on mortality as an individual experience and a collective institution.

The raw material is immense and diverse: factual and literary accounts of fatal ailment and decease; the contracts with death recorded in last wills; the chronicles of burial practices and sites; the numerous, often dramatic changes in the idiom of epitaphs and the style of commemorative monuments; philosophical, liturgical meditations on the meaning of death; fictive explorations such as Tolstoy's "The Death of Ivan Ilyich"; medical diagnoses of the causes of death; changing representations of "afterlife"; the investigations of the economics and psychology of terminal states and demise as conducted by modern sociologists and social psychologists (since the pioneering work of Geoffrey Gorer in England). There is, in fact, a substantial sense in which the history of a society's attitudes and gestures in the face of death is a central account of that society itself.

Philippe Ariès's main argument in the present tome is difficult to summarize. This is not only because, unlike many of his peers in the Gallican stable, Ariès takes a vast topic and a vast time scale (a millennium) for his canvas. It is because the main threads of his thesis are obscured by a plethora of entrancing details, and because, in a manner at once reassuringly candid and mildly exasperating, Ariès persistently qualifies, even contradicts, the general postulates he has just advanced. In a recent set of autobiographical interviews, Ariès recalls his early years among the golden youths of the extreme right-wing Action Française. The sense of impish adventure is there still. But now Ariès combines the theoretical, rigorist determinism of much of modern French anthropology and historiography with the messy, wide-awake empiricism and flexibility of the Anglo-American persuasion.

At some point in the twelfth century, Ariès contends, an archaic, essentially collective experiencing of death yielded, certainly as far as the elite went, to a personalized sense of extinction, to the concept that a specific, "biographical" individual was passing away. Throughout the medieval and early modern periods, both social and personalized agencies of mourning, of burial, of the depiction and commemoration of the dead were at work in a complex variety of models and institutionalized practices. These, in turn, depended on social class, on locale, on the prevailing confessional framework (Catholic or Protestant). They depended also on changing types of property relations. According to Ariès, romanticism brought with it an immense transformation. The social role of mourning did not cease altogether, but it was little by little overtaken by the licit expression of emphatic—even histrionic—pain. The unique, numinous identity of the dear departed was now exalted. In its ritualized negation of death ("Thou art with us now, thou shall be with us always"), in its lyric assurance of undying remembrance and evocation, romantic pathos was intended to assist the bereaved, to buttress the solitude of widow and orphan with a shared convention of transcendence. The life of the lost one continued *in memoriam*. (Witness the triumph of this theme in Shelley, in Tennyson.) Ariès argues that this romantic transformation was so pervasive as to seem to us, who come after, to represent some natural constant in human nature. But we, too, are experiencing deep alterations in the status of death. If the romantic investment in the enduring presence of the dearly beloved is operative, there is at the same time a contrary current of discretion. The dying are removed from sight. In 1967, in New York, seventy-five per cent of all deaths occurred behind the veil of the hospital room. Ostentatious grief is no longer acceptable in a society of agnostic hygiene, or, rather, it is regarded as a relic of former ways characteristic of immigrant or "Mediterranean" mores; it is Mafia burials that preserve the flamboyant desolation of the romantics. Or so it was, notably in the United States, until very lately. Drawing on a number of recent studies—in particular on Elisabeth Kübler-Ross's *On Death and Dying* (1969)—Ariès concludes his monumental survey by backtracking disarmingly. He finds more "visible," more psychologically dramatized styles and ceremonies of death coming back. These would counter the tidal drag toward clinical anonymity, toward emotional blandness in late-twentieth-century urban existence. *"Timor mortis conturbat me"* proclaimed the Psalmist and the medieval poet: "Fear of death wrings my guts." This alone has not altered.

Such an outline gives little idea of the particular densities and forces of suggestion in this book. Numerous sections—on medieval graveyards and charnel houses, on the testaments of the seventeenth-century propertied households, on baroque funerary chapels and lapidary inscriptions, on the poetry of death in the Brontës, on the clashes between traditional morticians' techniques and the rise of modern sanitation, on the millennial history of one single French rural cemetery, on the growing popularity, if this term be allowed, of cremation and the spiritual-social significance of this option—could form arresting monographs on their own. Philippe Ariès is alert to the oddities, the atavisms, the play of fantasy and of terror in human behavior. He interweaves poetry and statistics, legal briefs and folktales, metaphysics and the advertisements of funeral parlors. Where else would we find Gothic horror stories of live burial linked with contemporary debates on neurophysiology and with public unease about the amount of valuable terrain being swallowed up by the necropolis? *The Hour of Our Death* is a feast for the imagination.

In the charm and fascination of so panoptic an approach lie its obvious vulnerabilities. It is one thing to cite a poignant passage from a medieval epic or to invoke the inspired anatomy of death in a Tolstoy novella, and quite another to demonstrate that such texts are representative—that we can legitimately infer from them the attitudes of an entire society and era. It is one thing to instance the changes in the phrasing of wills and epitaphs, and quite another to arrive at a confident reading of the mental attitudes that underwrite such "encodings" or to deduce from them chronological transformations in Western sensibility. In all historical writing, the historian's own frame of perceptions plays an inevitably selective and ordering part. In "histories of consciousness," the process of refraction is a twofold one, and the light of distant evidence passes twice at least through the prism of interpretation. Certain magnitudes, moreover, seem to defy the often "literary," almost "aesthetic" reconstitutive tact and intuitions of the *historien des mentalités*. In what ways and measure have the facts of mass annihilation in global warfare and in totalitarian mass murder and the possibility of nuclear destruction as we now face it affected the Western apprehension of personal death? Ariès all but leaves this topic to one side. It may well be that he will return to it.

To "think death," the famous, challenging phrase of the philosopher Heidegger, is at once a fearfully private and a fully communal act. To marshal evidence as to the long history and current conditions of this act is to come very near the bone of our being. This book is a moment of passionate awareness and, therefore, strangely bracing.

June 22, 1981

ONE THOUSAND YEARS OF SOLITUDE

UNDER THE WHITE, leathery heat, the rock hills of Sardinia are like the spine of an antediluvian lizard. In the first sun, the air shimmers and smokes off the dead shale. By noon, it is motionless but cuts like a barb. Even the sea is silent. Inland, the light hammers at the sudden gaps of black shadow between the shuttered, tightfisted houses. The heat seeps into the shadows. Where one of the spines is sharpest perches the town of Nuoro. Still higher, up a cindery and twisting road, lies Orgosolo, known to this day for its merciless banditry and the serpentine interminability of its blood feuds. My wife and I never made it to that famed aerie. When we stepped out of the rented car in Nuoro, we choked on the heat, in the still furnace of noontime. And it was only June.

There is a bookstore in Nuoro. Most of its stock is current pulp and vaguely garish magazines. But there is at the back a wistful corner of older books, among them early editions of Grazia Deledda, whose stately, romanticized fictions of Sardinian life won the Nobel Prize in 1926. What I had come for was a rarer item. On May 18, 1979, there took place in a café in Nuoro a *dibattito,* a round-table discussion of a book: Salvatore Satta's *Il Giorno del Giudizio.* Leonardo Sole, Maria Giacobbe, and Father Giovanni Marchesi, S.J., presented their readings of different aspects of the work. From the floor, Natalion Piras expounded *una lettura altra,* "a different read-ing." These several texts were published in a brochure of twenty-nine pages for the local library, named in honor of another member of the Satta family. Surprised at my inquiry, the owner of the book-store produced, dusted off, and sold me what seemed to be about the last remaining copy.

Waiting for the heat to lose at least something of its rank, dead-ening edge, my wife and I went to see the café (called Tettamanzi in the book), and the Corso, and the cemetery, on its twisted spur of bleached rock. We stood in the Piazza S. Satta, with its assem-blage of prehistoric cairns. The breath that comes out of the fur-nace door of day is that of silence. When late afternoon releases the shadows, these move, Satta wrote, "as does a dream in that burnt land." The trip there is a blank and parching one; Nuoro is a shut place. But there is truly no way of visualizing fully except by visit-ing Nuoro one of the masterpieces of solitude in modern literature, perhaps in all literature, and of sensing its bone structure. Patrick Creagh's translation, *The Day of Judgment* (Farrar, Straus & Gir-oux), does not to my mind and ear altogether capture the genius of Satta's prose—its marmoreal ferocity, the slow fire inside the stone. Tacitus' Latin and the style of Hobbes come nearest. The availabil-ity in English of *Il Giorno del Giudizio* is nonetheless ground for celebration and thanks. A major chord is added to the register of our recognitions.

The resemblance to Tacitus and to Hobbes is no accident. Sal-vatore Satta (1902–75) spent most of his life teaching law and juris-prudence in Rome, and his sensibility was schooled in the harsh, lapidary Latinity of Roman historians and Roman law. His *Com-mentario al Codice di Procedura Civile* is a monumental work, and a standard one in Italian legal teaching. His *De Profundis,* a laconic, harrowing recollection of wartime experiences, which Satta pub-lished in 1948, is instinct with Latinity and with the high sorrow of Tacitus' image of human political folly. Satta appears to have carried inside himself for half a century the material for and the design of a book about his native Nuoro and a sclerotic, somnambular epilogue to its ancient ways. Time and again, he put the work to one side and pursued his academic career. *Il Giorno* was published only in 1979. It is posthumous not only in that it appeared after Satta's death but also in that it is in many respects a book of and for the dead. For a Sardinian, for a Nuorese, only one lodging can admit to its own wealth: the cemetery.

Il Giorno is a difficult book to describe. The stoic voice of the chronicler intervenes, and inquires of itself whether the incidents, gestures, dramatis personae of pre- and post-First World War Nuoro ought to be summoned back to spectral presence—whether the dead should not, as Christ has it in one of the most enigmatic, dismissive of his biddings, be charged with burying the dead. Satta mocks the vanity of his enterprise, its pretense of resurrection. At the same time, he acknowledges the claims upon remembrance—the gentle but insistent calling of the departed on the recollection of the living. No remembrancer save Walter Benjamin conveys more poignantly than Salvatore Satta (note the omen in his first name) the right of the defeated, the ridiculous, and the outwardly insignificant to be precisely recalled. In northern climes, the leaf-blown murmur of their coming is allowed once a year, on All Hallows' Eve. In Nuoro, that night stretches through the year. The departed are perennially in reach, begging, soliciting the alms of memory. Satta's responses are teasing: "I am writing these pages that no one will read, because I hope to be lucid enough to destroy them before I die." For whom, then, is he writing them? For the dead, the palpable density of whose audience gives to Satta an at-homeness in time and in the charred land which no individual in a traditional *communitas* can, or would seek to, attain for himself.

The composition of the text, at once episodic and internally close-woven, recalls, distantly, that of the *Spoon River Anthology;* there are moments of vivid social satire, voices in pomp or tumult, of the kind heard in *Under Milk Wood*. But neither Edgar Lee Masters nor Dylan Thomas has the philosophical intelligence, the patience of feeling which enable Satta to produce a well-nigh flawless form. Painters afford a better analogy. The effects achieved in "Il Giorno" possess the mysterious authority that inhabits the grain of things in a Chardin, the opaque luminosity that comes at us from the human bodies in La Tour.

The house and family of Don Sebastiano Sanna Carboni provide the axis of Satta's *"romanzo antropologico"* (the classification of the book offered by Italian critics, but accurate only if we take "anthropology" to include a fundamental and philosophical account of the condition of naked man). The family, or clan, is a large one: we hear of seven sons. But a loud, acrid silence obtains between Don Sebastiano and his wife, Donna Vincenza. Family dinners cause the master of the house to suffer dizzy spells. He eats alone, in the upstairs room where he pursues the tenacious, spidery arts of legal consultation and advocacy. His sons' unending studies, the immemorial Nuorese inertia that seems to lie in their bones infuriate Don Sebastiano. Do the children of millionaires in distant, phantasmagoric America not earn a youthful living selling newspapers? Donna Vincenza, goaded past martyrdom by her husband's cold anger, by the pressures upon her sere frame of housework, cloistered monotony, and carnal disappointments as numbing as old dreams, protests. People in America "have every comfort," she says. "They're not like us." Her husband's reply is one of the most savage sentences in literature—it is, literally, a death sentence: *"Tu stai al mondo soltanto perchè c'è posto."* Creagh's translation—"You're only in this world because there's room for you"—is more or less exact, but falls short. The Italian connotes an obscure, predestined niche in which insignificant, captive lives are inserted and from which there is no escape. And it is just this lack of escape that gives to such lives their utterly humiliating contingent rationale.

There is a sense in which the entirety of the work spirals out of this chilling verdict. In Nuoro, it can be said of almost all men, women, and beasts that they are on this incinerated native ground solely because there was some passing entry for them in the Doomsday Book of works and days. Maestro Fadda, with the dolorous features of an Etruscan king, is there to teach the fourth and fifth grades in the Nuoro school and to amuse the idlers at the café. Chischeddu "was one of those wrecks who for some unknown reason drift into churches, and are allowed by God or the vicar to take part in the life of the spirit as vergers or sacristans." Fileddu, the half-wit, is the licensed jester when the winds blow like banked fires out of Africa. Do any of these bespoken lives have reality? Take Pietro Catte:

> There is not the least doubt that Pietro Catte in the abstract has no reality, any more than any other man on the face of the earth. But the fact remains that he was born and that he died, as those irrefutable certificates prove. And this endows him with reality in actual fact, because birth and death are the two moments at which the infinite becomes finite; and the infinite can have no being except through the finite. Pietro Catte attempted to escape from reality by hanging himself on that tree at Biscollai, but his was a vain hope, because one cannot erase one's own birth. This is why I say that Pietro Catte, like all the hapless characters in this story, is important, and ought to be interesting to everyone: if he does not exist, then none of us exist.

The unbidden imperative of existence is borne, certainly in the world before 1914, almost timelessly. For the hill shepherds and sharecroppers, there is neither past nor future, only the coercion of custom. Insights and joys have the depthless patience of an order of things before literacy. Satta is innovative and convincing in his implicit analysis of the ways in which illiteracy and preliteracy relate to timelessness:

> Donna Vincenza was highly intelligent, even though she scarcely knew how to read and write, and for this reason she overflowed with love, without knowing it. She loved the humble furniture in her house, the embroidery on the pillowcases, which she used to work on with her mother all day. . . . She loved the *cortita* of the house, with figs and tomatoes laid out on boards to dry amid the eager buzzing of bees and wasps. And above all, she loved the garden, where she still went to pick flowers and fruit, even though her swollen legs bore her up less and less well. And she had loved Don Sebastiano, the man who had come to ask for her hand and was destined to take her to live in another house.

Even for the highly literate, such as Don Sebastiano's boys and the canons or lawyers, texts do not, as for us, entail a forward motion. Old books, obsolete pandects, wormholed commentaries retain their authority in a dusty present. The bells, which play a fascinating role in the architecture of *Il Giorno,* chime an unchangingness. The engagement between Ludovico and Celestina lasts twelve years. It ends in parting. Chastity modulates, imperceptibly, into the plenitude and comforts of bereavement.

Yet the narrative teems with actions: stately, comical, and violent. There is suicide and murder. The newly harvested grapes come into Don Sebastiano's courtyard in October—one of "waves of memories rolling in one upon the other in absurd disorder, as if the whole of existence had taken place in a single instant." The gates are flung wide "in austere expectancy" (a characteristic Satta phrase). The oxen lumber as if their great eyes were truly blind.

Crushed by the rollers in the cavernous vat, the grapes pour their heady perfume into the nocturnal house:

> But in that many-colored mass there is a hidden god, for not many hours will pass before a liquid purple fringe will appear all around the edge, and then the mass will heave up as if taking a giant breath, and will lose its innocence, and a low gurgling sound will betray the fire that is devouring it.... Everything happens at night, because both life and death are daughters of night.

The allusion is an exact one: it points to preclassical Greek and Mediterranean cosmogony. The rites of Nuorese existence are at least as antique as Homer. But when Satta tells of how an artifice of self-declared poverty builds barriers against the natural opulence and generosity of the world, the intonation, the ironies are those of the Roman satirists and of the moderns.

Another bravura chapter tells of the coming to Nuoro of electric lighting, on one freezing October evening. The whole town has gathered, suspicious, vaguely resentful, even hoping for the worst:

> And all of a sudden, as in an aurora borealis, the candles did light up, and light flooded every street, all the way from San Pictro to Sèuna, a river of light between the houses, which remained immersed in darkness. An enormous shout rose all over the town, which in some mysterious way felt that it had entered history. Then, chilled through and with eyes weary from staring, people gradually drifted back to their houses or their hovels. The light stayed on to no purpose. The north wind had risen, and the bulbs hanging in their shade in the Corso began to sway sadly, light and shadow, shadow and light, making the nighttime nervous. This had not happened with the oil lamps.

An even more penetrating passage follows. The now unwanted but regretted oil lamps of Nuoro are sold to Oliena, a village across the valley. When the evening falls, the Nuorese turn out to see Oliena light up "one lamp after another, so that one could count them," Satta writes. "And who knows whether the children didn't run after the lamplighter there as well, picking up the spent matchsticks." Only in Joyce's "The Dead" is the tread of spent time as poignant.

The temptation to quote—from con-brio chapters on ecclesiastical imbroglios and reclusive, unforgiving deaths, from one on political oratory and elections in Nuoro, from analyses of the transformations brought on by those who returned from the fronts and cities of 1914–18—is difficult to resist. But the text should be savored as a whole, and no first reading comes near to plumbing its laughter or its desolation. More often than not, these two are inseparable. Dying, Father Porcu has strength for one last prayer in God's house. He can scarcely master the flagstoned slope of the Corso. Stares of curiosity follow his spectral sortie. Then his voice resounds in the stillness: "Lord, you see how old I am and ill. Take me to you. I can no longer say Mass to you, as I can't stay on my feet. Lord, take me to you. And for the good of the Church, take Canon Floris as well. Then all will be at peace." The counterpoint of the original is unrecapturable: *"Prendetevi anche l'arciprete. Così tutto sarà pace."*

The best introduction to this masterpiece is Salvatore Satta's own:

> As in one of those absurd processions in Dante's *Paradiso,* but without either choruses or candelabra, the men of my people file by in an endless parade. They all appeal to me, they all want to place the burden of their lives in my hands, the story, which is no story, of their having been. Words of supplication

or anger whisper with the wind through the thyme bushes. An iron wreath dangles from a broken cross. And maybe while I think of their lives, because I am writing their lives, they think of me as some ridiculous god, who has summoned them together for the day of judgment, to free them forever from their memory.

The reader will not find such liberation easy, nor will he wish for it.

October 19, 1987

KILLING TIME

IF THE NOVEL published by Secker & Warburg in London on June 8, 1949, and by Harcourt, Brace in New York on June 13th (it was a Book-of-the-Month Club choice for July) had been entitled *The Last Man in Europe,* a title still under active consideration by author and publisher as late as February, 1949, this coming year would be different. It would be different so far as journalism, publishing, political commentary, editorial and partisan pronouncements, academic colloquia, and the general enterprise of letters go. More subtly but incisively, it might be quite different in political mood and social sensibility, in the ways in which literate men and women picture and find shorthand expression for the image they have of themselves, of their communities, and of their chances of survival on a planet ideologically divided and armed to the teeth.

As everyone knows, however, George Orwell and Fred Warburg, his close friend and publisher, chose another title. (Both possible titles are mooted in a letter from Orwell to Warburg dated October 22, 1948.) Having completed the manuscript in November of that year, Orwell simply reversed the last two digits. Because of this more or less adventitious device—had Orwell finished writing in 1949 we would presumably be waiting for 1994—next year will be not so much 1984 as "1984."

The attribution of the year to the book promises to be on a megalithic, soul-wearying scale. The novel—"It isn't a book I would gamble on for a big sale," wrote Orwell to his publisher in December, 1948—has now appeared in some sixty languages, and total sales are thought to be in eight figures. In Britain, radio and television treatments began last August. A seventy-minute film, entitled *The Crystal Spirit,* will portray Orwell's isolated, literally moribund existence on the Isle of Jura, in the Inner Hebrides, where much of *Nineteen Eighty-Four* was first written. Two further television programs are to show the relations between the life of the novelist and his works. Debate is reportedly raging over the question of scheduling. The dates under most active discussion are January 21st, the anniversary of Orwell's death, in 1950; June 25th, the anniversary of his birth, in 1903; and April 4th, the fictive date on which the antihero of the novel, Winston Smith, makes the first entry in his clandestine diary. A seventeen-volume, deluxe complete works is to be issued by Secker & Warburg. The original, four-volume edition of Orwell's *Collected Essays, Journalism and Letters,* issued in 1968, is to be augmented by four further volumes, running to more than half a million previously ungathered words. Penguin is to launch across the earth a newly designed *Nineteen Eighty-Four.* Sir Peter Hall is actively considering a stage production of Orwell's *Animal Farm,* first published in 1945, at the National Theatre. The summer school on Orwell to be held under the aegis of Orwell's "most authorized" biographer, Professor Bernard Crick (this absurd rubric is needed because Orwell himself expressly asked that there be neither memorial service nor biography), is only one, though doubtless the most prestigious, among dozens of similar academic literary seminars, lectures, roundtables, conferences to be held throughout the length and breadth of the land that Orwell renamed Airstrip One.

On June 7th of this year, the *Wall Street Journal* declared that the time had come for all good men to decide whether 1984 would be like *Nineteen Eighty-Four*. The response in America looks to be extensive. Television and radio have already announced numerous programs presenting or dramatizing Orwell and the novel. The Institute for Future Studies and Research at the University of Akron will bid its guests reflect on "After 1984, What Futures for Personal Freedom, Political Authority, and the Civic Culture?" A University of Wisconsin conference has as its theme "Premonitions and Perspectives from *1984:* Has the Orwellian World Arrived?" The Smithsonian is commemorating *Nineteen Eighty-Four* by examining whether or not the mass media can in fact exercise thought control. Scores of universities, educational institutes, adult-education programs, and high-school syllabi are following suit. Yet even these projects—and they can be matched by similar lists in just about every more or less open society across the globe—will be dwarfed if a project variously reported from Tokyo comes to be: it is nothing less than a summons to *all* living Nobel Prize winners to gather in Japan and propound their views on the truth, on the measure of fulfillment, of Orwell's nightmare of thirty-five years ago.

No other book has ever been publicized, packaged, and searchlit in quite this way. By statistical comparison, Shakespeare centennials have been discreet. But then no other book has sought to prëempt, has prëempted for itself, a calendar year in the history of man. This, of course, is the point. Like no other literary artifact, Orwell's *Nineteen Eighty-Four is* its title. *The Last Man in Europe* would have matched far more precisely the underlying politics of the book: its monitory plea for a social-democratic Europe resistant to both the totalitarian system of Stalinism and the detergent inhumanity of a technocracy and mass-media hypnosis of the kind toward which the United States seemed to Orwell to be moving. By opting for *Nineteen Eighty-Four,* George Orwell achieved an uncanny coup. He put his signature and claim on a piece of time. No other writer has ever done this. And there is, I think, only one genuine parallel in the records of consciousness. Kafka knew (we have his witness to this realization) that he had made his own a letter in the Roman alphabet. He knew that "K" would for a long time to come stand for the doomed mask that he assumed in his fictions, that it would point ineluctably to himself. The litany of the letter is spelled out by the English poet Rodney Pybus in his "In Memoriam Milena":

> K and again K and again K
> K for Kafka
> K from *The Castle*
> K from *The Trial*
> K the mnemonic of fear:
>
>
> O Franz I cannot
> escape that letter K after K—

But although it is now active in scores of languages (I understand that "Kafkaesque" has adjectival status even in Japanese), the identification of "K" with Kafka probably does not extend beyond a literate minority. On a scale vastly beyond the enormous readership of the novel itself, *Nineteen Eighty-Four* has been, will be drummed into man's time sense. Shakespeare does not own "S"; no twelve months are his monopoly. The *Nineteen Eighty-Four* preemption is one that neither literary theory nor semantics is really equipped to deal with.

In one of the innumerable pre-1984 opinion surveys that have been crowding the media, Len Murray, the eminently sane General Secretary of the British Trades Union Congress, put it this way: "Seldom can a year have been blackened before its time as effectively as George Orwell did to 1984." The uncertain syntax is an honest counterpart to the awesome complication of the theme. What is one to make of a work of literature, of a fiction, that "blackens before its time" a year in the lives of men? There have, to be sure, been other fated, baleful calendar years in the numerology of apocalypse. We know of the great panics that seized on Western European communities at the approach of the year 1000, and of the cultists now burrowing their way to Southern California in the expectation of a doomsday 2000. The year 1666 was regarded by astrologists and theologians as the year of the final coming of divine wrath, as foretold in the Book of Revelation. But such hysterical intimations do not arise from the adventitious tactic of a modern book title. Len Murray could have been more emphatic: *never* has any single man or stroke of the pen struck a year out of the calendar of hope. Should a thermonuclear catastrophe occur in this next year, should famine erupt beyond even its present empire, there will be countless men and women who will feel, in defiance of reason, that Orwell had somehow foreseen 1984, that there was in his *Nineteen Eighty-Four* some agency not only of clairvoyance but—and this is a far more unsettling notion—of self-fulfillment. And again the case of Kafka offers a possible parallel. *The Trial,* "The Metamorphosis," and, above all, "In the Penal Colony" express a hallucinatory prevision of the Nazi order and of the death camps in which Kafka's Milena and his three sisters were to perish. Does prophecy coerce? Is there in clairvoyance of so overwhelmingly exact a kind some seed of fulfillment?

The *Nineteen Eighty-Four* phenomenon poses nothing less than the question of the fundamental rights of the imagination. Debate has ranged since Plato over the permissible limits of fiction. Does the aesthetically effective representation of sexuality, of sadism, of political fanaticism, of economic obsession induce the reader, the spectator, the audience to imitative conduct? In this perspective, censorship is not an inhibition of the freedom of social man. It creates for the average human being those spheres of spontaneity, of personal experiment, of therapeutic ignorance or indifference in which the immense majority of human beings wish to conduct their everyday lives. Has the artist, has the literary or philosophic imaginer of absolutes any right to live our inward lives for us? Need we, ought we to, entrust our dreams or nightmares to his mastering grip? Orwell himself was nervously, puritanically concerned with the effects of pulp fiction and of more or less sadistic crime stories on society and the imagination at large. Hence two of his most penetrating essays: "Boys' Weeklies" of 1939 and "Raffles and Miss Blandish" of 1944. Looking at the fiction of James Hadley Chase, Orwell finds in it a streak of corrupting sadism. Its gestures and values are those of Fascism. Orwell read closely. In Chase's *He Won't Need It Now* notes Orwell, "the hero . . . is described as stamping on somebody's face, and then, having crushed the man's mouth in, grinding his heel round and round in it." In *Nineteen Eighty-Four,* this precise image was, if one can put it this way, to bear appalling fruit. Yet what of Orwell's own imaginings? The injection of ferocity, of vulgarity, of feverish tedium into society by pulp literature and the porn industry is an ugly but also a diffuse phenomenon, and one whose actual effects on behavior remain arguable. The preemption, the blackening in advance, of 1984 by *Nineteen Eighty-Four* is a far more specific and compelling feat. Has literature the moral license to take from the future tense its conjugation of hope?

There is no evidence that Orwell ever asked himself this question. Neither metaphysics nor grandiloquence was his forte. His grainy sensibility was as resistant to elevation as the pudding in an English café on a November evening. Moreover, as Orwell wrote *Nineteen Eighty-Four* his own time was end-stopped. The tuberculosis from which he had suffered on and off for a long time declared its full virulence in 1947–48. Orwell knew himself to be a dying man. (He died some six months after publication of the book.) It may be, indeed, that terminal illness is the one constant in the inward history of *Nineteen Eighty-Four*. Despite the available letters, ancillary writings, and contemporary testimony, there is much about the genesis and aims of the work which remains unclear.

In the letter to Warburg of October 22, 1948, Orwell states that he first thought of his novel in 1943. On the twenty-sixth of December, in reference to the publisher's blurb, Orwell says that what *Nineteen Eighty-Four* is "really meant to do is to discuss the implications of dividing the world up into 'Zones of influence' (I thought of it in 1944 as a result of the Teheran Conference), & in addition to indicate by parodying them the intellectual implications of totalitarianism." The slight disparity as to the date of inception—1943 in the one statement, 1944 in the other—is trivial. What matters is that we have no other witness as to either chronology. George Orwell has an enviable reputation for honesty, and there is no reason to suppose that he was seeking to deceive either himself or others. It is wholly plausible that the idea for some kind of Utopian satire on an ideologically divided world, on a planet perilously split between superpowers, came to Orwell during the later part of the war in Europe and after one or another of the summit meetings between Churchill, Roosevelt, and Stalin. Nevertheless, one should note that an early dating was very much in Orwell's interest. For *Nineteen Eighty-Four,* as he composed it and as we now know it, depends crucially and intimately on another book. And on this cardinal point Orwell's witness is—to choose one's words with care—guarded.

Orwell's review of Y. I. Zamyatin's *We* appeared in *Tribune,* a weekly of independent left-wing persuasion, on January 4, 1946. Orwell had read the Russian text in a French translation. He termed it "one of the literary curiosities of this book-burning age." Aldous Huxley's *Brave New World,* whose own influence on *Nineteen Eighty-Four* Orwell acknowledged repeatedly and with unworried ease, "must be partly derived" from Zamyatin. Despite appearances, despite Zamyatin's self-exile from the Soviet Union and the total suppression there of his book, *We* is, according to Orwell, not aimed at any particular country or regime. It satirizes, it gives warning of, "the implied aims of industrial civilization." Proof of this, says Orwell, is the fact that Zamyatin has since coming to the West "written some blistering satires on English life." True, Zamyatin had found himself incarcerated in 1922 in the same corridor of the same prison in which the czarist police had put him in 1906, but *We* should be read as "a study of the Machine, the genie that man has thoughtlessly let out of its bottle and cannot put back again." The reviewer finds distinct qualities in Zamyatin's fantasy. Its political intuitions and its insight into "Leader worship" do make the Russian novel "superior to Huxley's." But "so far as I can judge it is not a book of the first order." Writing to Warburg on the thirtieth of March, 1949, when *Nineteen Eighty-Four* was going to press, Orwell supported the eventual issue of an English-language version of *We*. But again his enthusiasm is distinctly muted. There is no indication that he has changed his mind as to its stature.

Zamyatin's *We,* published in 1924, tells of human existence in "The Single State." This state, ruled by "The Benefactor," enforces total control over every aspect of mental and bodily life. Surveillance and chastisement are in the hands of the political police, or "Guardians." (Zamyatin's satiric pastiche of Plato's *Republic* is evident.) The Benefactor's subjects inhabit glass houses, naked to constant inspection and recording. Men and women are identified not by proper names but by numbers. Ration coupons give them the right to lower their blinds and enjoy "the sex hour." The story of *We* is that of an attempted rebellion by D-503, who is, as Zamyatin was himself, an able engineer, but is at the same time "a poor conventional creature" (Orwell's description of him in his review). D-503 falls in love and is led into conspiracy. Caught by the all-seeing police, he betrays his beloved, I-330, and his confederates. He watches I-330 being tortured by means of compressed air under a glass bell. She does not break and must be eliminated. D-503, on the contrary, is given X-ray treatments so as to cure him of a tumor called "the imagination." He will live to recognize The Benefactor's omnipotent care.

I have expressly cited those elements in Zamyatin's fiction which Orwell picked out in his book review. "The Single State" becomes the "Oceania" of "Nineteen Eighty-Four"; The Benefactor is translated into "Big Brother"; Guardians are the equivalent of Orwell's "Thought Police"; Winston Smith does retain a name, but he is officially known and summoned as "6079 Smith W." The issue of authentic as against programmed sexuality, of an act of love between man and woman as the ultimate source of libertarian insurrection, is the crux in both narratives. The psychic and physical tortures under the glass bell are closely mirrored in Room 101 in *Nineteen Eighty-Four*. The effect of Zamyatin's glass dwellings is precisely that achieved by Orwell's telescreens. Like D-503, Winston Smith will be cured of the cancer of autonomous imagining, of the malignant growth of private remembrance. So far as the plot goes, the difference is that Zamyatin's heroine dies unconquered, whereas Orwell's Julia joins her sometime beloved in betrayal and self-betrayal.

With one exception—and it is, as we will see, the touch of genius in *Nineteen Eighty-Four*—every major theme and most of the actual narrative situations in Orwell's text derive from Zamyatin. Without *We, Nineteen Eighty-Four*, in the guise in which we have it, would simply not exist. We know nothing of what may or may not have been the germ of Orwell's project in either 1943 or 1944. We do know that the actual plotting and realization of *Nineteen Eighty-Four* stemmed from a reading of Zamyatin in the winter of 1945–46. It was in August of 1946 that Orwell began his own version of the hell to come. And one must conclude that it was the absolutely central dependence of *Nineteen Eighty-Four* on its largely forgotten predecessor that made Orwell's references to Zamyatin so uneasy, so casual in their findings.

Other sources of suggestion are readily invoked. They include H. G. Wells's *The Sleeper Awakes,* Jack London's *The Iron Heel* (a book that clearly marked much of Orwell's vision), and, of course, *Brave New World.* More significant than any of these, however, seem to have been the writings of James Burnham. Orwell's "Second Thoughts on James Burnham" appeared in the periodical *Polemic* for May, 1946. Burnham's concept of "managerialism," going back to 1940, and his view of an apocalyptic levelling of human societies under technocracy strike Orwell as profoundly suggestive. He finds Burnham's portrayal of Stalin in *Lenin's Heir,* of 1945, suspect; Burnham's fascination with the great war leader and potentate has produced "an act of homage, and even of self-abasement." But certain motifs in Burnham's description will in fact surface with Big Brother. "So long as the common man can get a hearing," concludes Orwell, all is not lost, and Burnham's prophecies may yet be proved erroneous. Again, we note a theme to be developed in *Nineteen Eighty-Four.* On March 29, 1947, when work on his novel was in full progress, Orwell published in *The New Leader,* in New York, a lengthy review of Burnham's *The Struggle for the World.* Burnham's strident view that a Soviet onslaught on the West is imminent seems to Orwell excessive. Its implicit picture of the globe as irremediably divided between American capitalism and Soviet Marxism is an oversimplification. There *is,* according to Orwell, a third way—that of "democratic Socialism." And it is the historical duty of Europe, after two homicidal and, basically, internal wars, to show that "democratic Socialism" can be made to work. A "Socialist United States of Europe" may be very difficult to bring about, argues Orwell, but it is certainly not inconceivable. It may, in fact, hold the fragile, elusive key to human survival. Palpably, Orwell's debate with Burnham points to the "Eurocentric" pivot in *Nineteen Eighty-Four.* It throws into sharp relief the full meaning of the novel's discarded title *The Last Man in Europe.* Winston Smith's doomed attempt to preserve his individuality, to know and remember the historical past represents a quintessentially European refusal both of Stalinist totalitarianism and of the antihistorical mass culture of American capitalism. With Julia's and Winston Smith's defeat and abjection, "the last man in Europe" has been made extinct.

Orwell's article on "The Prevention of Literature" appeared in *Polemic* in January, 1946. Here, again, we can observe Orwell's views, and elements soon to be used in *Nineteen Eighty-Four,* ripening, as it were, with Zamyatin's suggestion. " 'Daring to stand alone' is ideologically criminal as well as practically dangerous." No totalitarian order can allow the anarchic play of individual feeling or literary invention:

> A totalitarian society which succeeded in perpetuating itself would probably set up a schizophrenic system of thought, in which the laws of common sense held good in everyday life and in certain exact sciences, but could be disregarded by the politician, the historian, and the sociologist. Already there are countless people who would think it scandalous to falsify a scientific text-book, but would see nothing wrong in falsifying an historical fact. It is at the point where literature and politics cross that totalitarianism exerts its greatest pressure on the intellectual.

In this notion of systematic schizophrenia, state-enforced and controlled, we see the origins of "Doublethink." As he worked on his novel, Orwell came to see in the mere act of writing one of the last possibilities of humane resistance. He published his reflections on "Writers and Leviathan" in the summer, 1948, issue of *Politics & Letters.* Orwell's pragmatic socialism persuaded him that group loyalties are necessary: "And yet they are poisonous to literature, so long as literature is the product of individuals." It is when Winston Smith, feeble creature that he is, starts keeping a clandestine diary, starts putting his own words on the page, that Big Brother is threatened. True writing, observed Orwell, "will always be the product of the saner self that stands aside, records the things that are done and admits their necessity, but refuses to be deceived as to their true nature."

The theme of the relations between language and politics, between the condition of human speech and writing, on the one hand, and that of the body politic, on the other, had moved to the very center of Orwell's concerns. He stated it incisively in the famous essay on "Politics and the English Language," of 1946. War propaganda, on both sides, had sickened Orwell. He sensed what would be the erosion of style brought on by the packaged mendacities of the mass media. Politics itself, wrote Orwell, "is a mass of lies, evasions, folly, hatred, and schizophrenia." And just because "all issues are political issues" this mass threatens to invade and extinguish the responsible vitalities of all human discourse. The decadence of English might still be curable. Never use a long word where a short one will do; use active modes rather than passives wherever you can; no jargon where everyday English can serve; "break any of these rules sooner than say anything outright barbarous." The close of the essay has the eloquence of impatience:

> Political language . . . is designed to make lies sound truthful and murder respectable, and to give an appearance of solidity to pure wind. One cannot change this all in a moment, but one can at least change one's own habits, and from time to time one can even, if one jeers loudly enough, send some worn-out and useless phrase—some *jackboot, Achilles' heel, hotbed, melting pot, acid test, veritable inferno,* or other lump of verbal refuse—into the dustbin where it belongs.

One notes in passing that this closing phrase echoes a celebrated

"Trotskyism." Trotsky and his rhetoric had loomed large in *Animal Farm;* they would do so again in the affairs of Airstrip One.

The perception of organic reciprocities between language and society is as old as Plato. It had been reëxamined and deepened in the political theory and theory of history of Joseph de Maistre, the great voice of reaction and cultural pessimism of the late eighteenth and early nineteenth centuries. The writings of Bernard Shaw are frequently an avowed exercise in purging private and public speech of cant and illusion. Orwell adds to this polemic tradition a special interest in the corruption of language in children's books, in the popular arts, in mass entertainment and "bad" literature (cf. the 1942 essay on Kipling, with its analysis of the spellbinding coarseness of Kipling's idiom). But between such critiques and the move Orwell makes in *Nineteen Eighty-Four* there is still a gap.

Orwell's attitude toward Jonathan Swift was ambiguous. "In a political and moral sense I am against him, so far as I understand him. Yet curiously enough he is one of the writers I admire with least reserve, and *Gulliver's Travels,* in particular, is a book which it seems impossible for me to grow tired of." It is, says Orwell, one of the six books he would preserve if all others were destined for destruction. The portrait of Swift latent in "Politics vs. Literature" (*Polemic* for September–October, 1946) comes close to being a self-portrait: "Swift did not possess ordinary wisdom, but he did possess a terrible intensity of vision, capable of picking out a single hidden truth and then magnifying it and distorting it." In Part III of *Gulliver's Travels* Orwell finds an "extraordinarily clear prevision of the spy-haunted 'police-State.'" Informers, accusers, delators, prosecutors, perjurious witnesses throng the Kingdom of Tribnia. Indictment and counter-indictment are the mechanism of pubic affairs. Swift, remarks Orwell, anticipates the macabre automatism of the Moscow Purge Trials. Filtered through Zamyatin's *We,* these several elements will be put to use in *Nineteen Eighty-Four.* But it is, I think, in another touch in Part III that Orwell came on the crucial hint. In the "Grand Academy of Lagado," fiercely satirized by Swift, there are officious savants busy inventing new, systematically simplified forms of language. They are, of course, creating "Newspeak."

Orwell's seizure, development, systematization of Swift's hint affords *Nineteen Eighty-Four* its claim to greatness. It is here that Orwell breaks away from and goes beyond the blueprint furnished by Zamyatin. "Doublethink," "Big Brother," "proles," "Ministry of Love," "Newspeak" itself have passed into the language. "Unperson" has become grimly indispensable in current accounts of the bureaucracies of terror, be they those of the Soviet Union or of Argentina, of Libya or of Indonesia. At a deeper level, and even without regard to the ghostly fun that Orwell is having with certain elements of Hegel's dialectic as these appear in Marxist logic, the famous reversals in Newspeak—"War is Peace," "Freedom is Slavery," "Ignorance is Strength"—touch the nerve centers of our politics. The Appendix on "The Principles of Newspeak" has an unsparing authority lacking in much of the fiction itself. It was as if Orwell's entire career as reporter, political analyst, literary and linguistic critic, novelist of ideas had been a prelude to this chill statement:

> A person growing up with Newspeak as his sole language would no more know that *equal* had once been the secondary meaning of "politically equal," or that *free* had once meant "intellectually free," than, for instance, a person who had never heard of chess would be aware of the secondary meanings attaching to *queen* and *rook*. There would be many crimes and errors which it would be beyond his power to commit, simply because they were nameless and therefore unimaginable. And it was to be foreseen that with the passage of time the distin-

guishing characteristics of Newspeak would become more and more pronounced—its words growing fewer and fewer, their meanings more and more rigid, and the chance of putting them to improper uses always diminishing.

This axiom of economy may be the only inaccuracy in Orwell's prevision, based as it was on Swift. The Newspeak we in fact practice is one of verbal inflation: assassination within intelligence services is reportedly labelled "separation with extreme prejudice;" recent developments in El Salvador or the Philippines are described as "hopeful perceptions of human-rights principles." But the method is the same. Clarity of representation, heresy of thought are to be made impossible by the elimination or obfuscation of the language in which they could be conceived and communicated. One of Orwell's dicta throws an almost intolerable light on much of American primary and secondary education. Complex, polysyllabic words, words difficult to pronounce, are in Newspeak held to be *ipso facto* bad words. Misheard, ambiguously registered, such words are not only élitist—they yield breathing space to nonconformity.

There is a sadistic, self-lacerating virtuosity in the uses to which *Nineteen Eighty-Four* puts this whole invention. Again, one of Orwell's judgments on Swift is illuminating: "In the queerest way, pleasure and disgust are linked together." The samples of the translation from Oldspeak into Newspeak, the stylistic detergence and stenography of lies practiced by Winston Smith as he erases or falsifies all texts out of the past which might in any way cast doubt on today's party line, are convincing. Though "good-thinkful," "crime-think," "joycamp," and "thinkpol" have not as yet found entry into Anglo-American English, they work effortlessly in the book. And we have only to open our daily papers or watch television to know just exactly how useful a term is "duck-speak": "It is one of those interesting words that have two contradictory meanings. Applied to an opponent, it is abuse; applied to someone you agree with, it is praise." Example: in Poland, martial law is a naked tyranny over basic human rights; in Turkey, it is a necessary preparation for the coming, one day, of democratic institutions. No less haunting and ingenious are Orwell's counter-examples, the explorations he proposes of Newspeak via negative inference. Chaucer, Shakespeare, Milton, and Byron cannot be expressed in the vocabulary of Big Brother. They will, of course, be translated; such translation will change them not only into something different but "into something contradictory of what they used to be." In the Newspeak of licensed intercourse and procreation, the very phrase "I love you" will be an archaic, untranslatable "sexcrime." (A number of present-day manuals on the joys of sex or its social psychology are not far from Orwell's fantastication.) Even "I dream" will become, by virtue of its aura of private and clandestine freedom, an untranslatable and soon to be eradicated piece of Oldspeak. Had the author of *Nineteen Eighty-Four*, one wonders, come across the boast of Reichsorganisationsleiter Robert Ley, bellowed shortly after the Nazi assumption of power in 1933: "Today the only individual in Germany who still has a private life is one who sleeps"?

The Newspeak theme exfoliates brilliantly. With a wink at the Britannica, Orwell tells us that the version in use in 1984 embodied the Ninth and Tenth Editions of the Newspeak Dictionary. But it is "with the final, perfected version, as embodied in the Eleventh Edition," that the Appendix is concerned. There are still prodigious masses of history, information, belles-lettres to be purged and translated. But by the year 2050 the great task will be accomplished. And at that blessed point language, as we once knew it, will not be needed: "In fact there will *be* no thought, as we understand it now. Orthodoxy means not thinking—not needing to think. Orthodoxy is unconsciousness." Or illiteracy; or a twenty-four-hour-a-day television system. Or the designation of a thermonuclear test by the title Operation Sunshine.

Little else in *Nineteen Eighty-Four* is of comparable strength.

The matter of women and of sex elicited in Orwell's writings a queasy sentimentality. Julia is no exception. The bluebells bloom thick underfoot; the thrush begins "to pour forth a torrent of song;" Julia flings aside her clothes "with that same magnificent gesture by which a whole civilization seemed to be annihilated"; her body gleams white in the sun. Sex is referred to as "it"—not in Newspeak but in Orwell ("You like doing this? I don't mean simply me; I mean the thing in itself?" "I adore it"). Much the same sentimentality, at once genuine and self-ironizing, colors Winston Smith's mutinous descent into the "old London," into the forbidden world of the antique shop. There is the Victorian paperweight with "a strange, pink, convoluted object that recalled a rose or a sea anemone" at its dusty heart. "Oranges and lemons, say the bells of St. Clement's, You owe me three farthings, say the bells of St. Martin's." Here are "girls in full bloom, with crudely lipsticked mouths," and youths chasing them. The mixture of fascination and repulsion experienced by Winston Smith, whose sensibility we are meant to recognize as humdrum and worn out, is at many points, and uncomfortably, Orwell's own.

Already, prior to *Nineteen Eighty-Four*, accounts of torture in totalitarian police cells, of the methodical infliction of pain and humiliation on the human body, were numerous. After Auschwitz and the Gulag came the systematic bestialities of the wars in Algeria and in Vietnam. One's stomach has supped its fill of graphic horror and grown hardened. Nevertheless, the third part of Orwell's "Utopia" (his own exact designation) continues to be very nearly unbearable. Overall, this is as it should be. We are meant to imagine in our marrow, as it were, the hideous physical pain visited on Winston Smith. We are meant to retch at what is being told us:

> The elbow! He had slumped to his knees, almost paralyzed, clasping the stricken elbow with his other hand. Everything had exploded into yellow light. Inconceivable, inconceivable

that one blow could cause such pain! The light cleared and he could see the other two looking down at him. The guard was laughing at his contortions. One question at any rate was answered. Never, for any reason on earth, could you wish for an increase of pain. Of pain you could wish only one thing: that it should stop. Nothing in the world was so bad as physical pain. In the face of pain there are no heroes, no heroes, he thought over and over as he writhed on the floor, clutching uselessly at his disabled left arm.

This has stark authority. It bears witness to Orwell's unforgiving sense of the claims of the human body, of the perfectly legitimate ways in which these claims can, at times, overrule even the loftiest of ideals and obligations. Like Jonathan Swift, Orwell was rooted in the truthful stench and tearing of the flesh.

But it is not this articulation of agony that makes the close of *Nineteen Eighty-Four* so hard to take. We are, I think, up against something more complicated to define: a certain macabre prurience, a strain of sadistic kitsch of precisely the kind Orwell had tracked down in his studies of pulp fiction. We have Orwell's own words for it—he may, to be sure, have been deferring to his correspondent—that he found embarrassing the notorious proceedings in Room 101. The torture of the caged rats that are to be released so as to tear out Winston Smith's eyes and then devour his tongue was not Orwell's invention. One can read about it in those louche tomes on "Chastisement" or "The History of Torture and Mutilation" still to be found in the interior of secondhand bookshops off Charing Cross Road. But its application in *Nineteen Eighty-Four* has a kind of onanistic spell. There is "sickness" here, but in more than one sense. The letter to Warburg of October 22, 1948, contains an evident clue. The book, says Orwell, "is a good idea but the execution would have been better if I had not written it under the influence of T.B." That influence strikes one as pervasive.

The tortures, the abjections, the self-betrayals enforced on 6079 Smith W. are, pretty obviously, a translation of those undergone by George Orwell in successive and utterly useless bouts of hospitalization. "It was hopeless: every part of him, even his head, was held immovably.... There was a violent convulsion of nausea inside him, and he almost lost consciousness. Everything had gone black. For an instant he was insane, a screaming animal." It is Orwell speaking, out of the pain of his wasted lungs, out of the pit of wasted therapy. How anodyne are, by comparison, the elegant, metaphysically observed encroachments of tuberculosis in Thomas Mann's *Magic Mountain*.

Finally, the difficulty with *Nineteen Eighty-Four* is its focus. During much of the composition of the novel, Orwell seems to have viewed it as a monitory satire on technocratic managerialism, on mechanization run mad. In this light, *Nineteen Eighty-Four* would have been a blacker version of Karel Čapek's *R.U.R.*—to which we owe the word "robot"—or of Charlie Chaplin's *Modern Times*. But the book is nothing of the sort. It is a thinly veiled allegory on Stalinism, in which the actual events and ideological implications of the Stalin-Trotsky conflict are central. *Nineteen Eighty-Four* is at many levels an expansion, a literal "humanization," of the schematic fable set out in *Animal Farm*. Orwell's own statement, made in answer to an inquiry from Francis A. Henson, of the United Automobile Workers, shortly after *Nineteen Eighty-Four* appeared in America, is well known:

> My recent novel is NOT intended as an attack on Socialism ... but as a show-up of the perversions to which a centralized economy is liable and which have already been partly realized in Communism and Fascism. I do not believe that the kind of society I describe necessarily *will* arrive, but I believe (allowing of course for the fact that the book is a satire) that something resembling it *could* arrive. I believe also that totali-

tarian ideas have taken root in the minds of intellectuals every-where, and I have tried to draw these ideas out to their logical consequences. The scene of the book is laid in Britain in order to emphasize that the English-speaking races are not innately better than anyone else and that totalitarianism, *if not fought against,* could triumph anywhere.

In fact, however, the specificities of the Stalin-Trotsky theme cut across the generalities of the satire. And here Orwell's attitude is highly ambivalent. "Goldstein" (Trotsky) is portrayed both with admiration and with distaste. The long extract given from Gold-stein's forbidden writings is an adroit parody of Trotsky's own prose. When Winston Smith and Julia are trapped into joining the secret Brotherhood of Trotskyite dissenters, Orwell makes plain that this organization is as homicidal, as oppressive, as dogmatic as is the regime of Big Brother. Jewishness made Orwell uncomfort-able. This reflex is patent in *Nineteen Eighty-Four.* It pierces in the bizarre motif of the woman who "might have been a jewess" being machine-gunned in the war film seen by Smith; it is made graphic in the person of Goldstein. Above all, it emerges in a little-noticed but crucial moment in the masterly Appendix: "What was required in a Party member was an outlook similar to that of the ancient He-brew who knew, without knowing much else, that all nations other than his own worshipped 'false gods.' He did not need to know that these gods were called Baal, Osiris, Moloch, Ashtaroth, and the like: probably the less he knew about them the better for his or-thodoxy. He knew Jehovah and the commandments of Jehovah; he knew, therefore, that all gods with other names or other attributes were false gods." Fair comment. But arresting in an advocate, in a descendant of Bunyan and of Milton.

At other key points, there are comparable ambiguities or con-fusions. "In the end the Party would announce that two and two made five, and you would have to believe it." Under torture, this is exactly what Winston Smith *will* believe. But there is more at work here than a fairly crass image of irrational abjection. The very right to proclaim that two and two make five, in the face of all precedent, of all orthodoxy, of all dictates of officious common sense, is that with which Dostoyevsky's "Underground Man" identifies human freedom. So long, teaches Dostoyevsky, as the human imagination can refuse assent to universal Euclidean axioms it will remain at liberty. Orwell knew this celebrated passage, of course. How, then, are we meant to read his use and reversal of it? What values, parodistic, nihilistic, or simply muddled, are we to attach to the injunction that those sane and brave enough to resist Big Brothers must be ready to "throw sulphuric acid in a child's face"? Winston Smith invents one "Comrade Ogilvy" for purposes of Party hagiography:

> It struck him as curious that you could create dead men but not living ones. Comrade Ogilvy, who had never existed in the present, now existed in the past, and when once the act of forgery was forgotten, he would exist just as authentically, and upon the same evidence, as Charlemagne or Julius Caesar.

Are we to conclude from this ingenious conceit that our own past history is unverifiable fabrication?

While working on this article, I have reread both Malraux's *Man's Fate* and Koestler's *Darkness at Noon*. In regard to impact, to diffuse influence, *Nineteen Eighty-Four* is certainly the third in the set. It stands a good deal lower, however, in intrinsic stature. Malraux's remains a major novel, convincing in its sense of the uncertain density and intricacies of human behavior. Koestler's focus is sharp, as Orwell's is not. The sheer philosophic-political intelligence, the knowledge from inside, manifest in *Darkness at Noon* is of a different class from that in *Nineteen Eighty-Four*. Such comparisons induce the interesting possibility that Orwell's book belongs to a very particular, restricted category: that of texts of tremendous force or ingenuity which should be read fairly early in life, and read thoroughly *once*. Such texts incise themselves on our minds and remembrance like a deep etching. When we come back to them, the impression of déjà vu, of imperative contrivance is, as in the case of certain famous news photographs, hard to take. Personally, I would include *Candide* and *The Red Badge of Courage* under this same rubric of the "one-time-unforgettable."

Will *Nineteen Eighty-Four* fade from immediacy and mass awareness after 1984? This is, I think, a very difficult question. "The actual outlook," reported Orwell in the *Partisan Review* for July–August, 1947, "is very dark, and any serious thought should start out from that fact." Nothing in our affairs today, domestically or internationally, refutes this proposition. For hundreds of millions of men and women on the earth, the all too famous climax of Orwell's vision, "If you want a picture of the future, imagine a boot stamping on a human face—forever," is not so much a prophecy as it is a banal picture of the present. If nuclear disaster comes to pass or our political systems collapse under the weight of armaments and greed, there may well be those—many, perhaps—who will recall Orwell's novel as an act of inspired annunciation. But it could also be that its weaknesses as an argument, as a work of art will tell. The memorations that will throng this coming year point to a work of relevance "in excess" but also to a book peculiarly flawed. Very probably, it could not be otherwise. For, as Thoreau asks, can a man kill time without doing injury to eternity?

December 12, 1983

BLACK DANUBE

THE CUTTING EDGE of satire is local. The effectiveness of the satirist depends on the precision, on the circumstantial density, of his target. Like the caricaturist, he works close to his object and aims at obtaining immediate, startled recognition. There is a sense in which satire aims not only at destruction but at self-destruction. Ideally, it would consume its topic and thus remove the cause of its own anger. The fire dies in the cold ash. Karl Kraus, of Vienna, the master satirist in our age, entitled his journal *Die Fackel (The Torch),* but he is not the only one to resort to the fire motif; flame and satire have long been kindred.

Consequently, little satire, verbal or pictorial, has proved durable. In Aristophanes, there is a kind of slapstick of the mind, a marvellously physical clowning of ideas, that insures a measure of universality, but much in even the best of his comedies reaches laughter only across thorn hedges of footnotes and learned explanation. The generality of Juvenal's themes—the war between the sexes, religious hypocrisy, the ostentatious crassness of the *nouveau* riche, the bustling corruption of urban politics—is such as to elevate his rage into a perennial sadness over man. It is striking, however, how much better Juvenal wears in quotation than as a whole. In acuity of argument, in the exactitude of the fit between the satiric scenario and its political-religious counterpart, *A Tale of a Tub* remains Swift's masterpiece. Now only scholars read this ferocious invention, just because it presumes a specialized, closely referential knowledge of the politics of church and party, of bishopric and cabinet, in early-eighteenth-century England. If *Gulliver's Travels* survives as a classic, it is largely in spite of the special satiric purposes, again political, partisan—indeed, scurrilous—that underlie the tales. Here, almost uniquely, the venom, which called for precise identifications and recognitions, has evaporated into the fantasy.

The problem faced by anyone in 1986 seeking access to Karl Kraus in any tongue other than a very special Viennese/anti-Viennese German is that of localism, of what Henry James would have called "the spirit of place." It is a problem of the formidable density, of the inwovenness of ephemeral allusion, in-group reference, and encoded assumptions of familiarity in even the widest-ranging and most apocalyptic of Kraus's writings. Vienna at the turn of the century, in the interwar period, and on the eve of catastrophe is not merely the unwavering setting, the magnetic pole of Kraus's sense of reality; it is the daily constant of his minutely observant moral reportage. That there was within Kraus a jealously guarded arcadia—a shy, tensed love of certain Bohemian and Alpine retreats—is certain. But the genius of his work, the ever-abundant fuel of his lyric hatreds, was a single seminal city—anatomized, dissected, chronicled in its political, social, artistic, journalistic life, in a day-to-day scrutiny, from the eighteen-nineties to 1936, the year of his death. Kraus's Vienna is the total milieu to his sensibility, as is Dublin to that of James Joyce.

Staring at Vienna, Kraus became possessed by clairvoyance. He perceived in its febrile cultural brilliance the symptoms of neurosis, of the fatal tensions between "civilization and its discontents." (The famous phrase of Freud, a rival seer, whom he scorned, could be Kraus's own.) He registered in the idiom of Viennese journalism, salon talk, and parliamentary rhetoric a sickness invading the life centers of the German language. Long before George Orwell, and far more comprehensively, Karl Kraus related the decay in the lucidity, in the truth values, in the personal sinew of private and public discourse to the larger decay of Central European and Western political societies. Kraus's haunted satires on the mendacities, on the class-determined operations of the law, and of criminal justice in particular, enact a lashing repudiation of the entire bourgeois order. Earlier, perhaps, than any other social critic, Kraus spotted and analyzed the subversion of aesthetic ideas in literature and in the fine arts by the almighty power of merchandising, of the mass media, of prepackaging. His anatomies of kitsch remain unsurpassed. And, in ways that defy rational explanation—here he is peer to Kafka—Kraus sensed in the twilight of the old European regime and in the insane horrors of the First World War the coming of an even blacker night. Satirizing naïve faith in scientific progress, Kraus could in 1909 set down the then wholly fantastic (now unendurable) proposition that progress of a scientific-technological kind "makes purses out of human skin."

But, however wide their implications, the occasions for prophecy in Kraus, the springboards for rage, remain strictly local and temporal. His savage language parodies and critiques take off from some article, often trivial, in the daily press, from some piece of ephemeral literary reviewing, from a blurb or advertisement. The diatribes against the brute myopias of the law and of the late imperial or interwar bureaucracy are triggered by some obscure prosecution in the suburbs or the inner city. Kraus's highly ambiguous polemics on the matter of homosexuality—he deplored its unfeeling prosecution while fearing its clandestine influence in politics and letters—presume intimate awareness of certain scandals, libel cases, suicides under stress of blackmail both in Hohenzollern Germany and in the Viennese beau monde. Who today remembers, let alone reads, the journalists, drama critics, publicists, or academic pedants whom Kraus chose for his relentless castigations? Who recalls the forensic experts, the criminologists whose blinkered complacencies Kraus held up to ridicule? Even Kraus's magnum opus—the titanic collage-drama on the First World War, entitled *The Last Days of Mankind* and patterned, superbly, after the Walpurgisnacht allegories in the second part of Goethe's *Faust*—often requires a sure knowledge not only of Viennese dialect and slang but of the minutiae of administrative and social mores in the collapsing fabric of the Austro-Hungarian Empire.

A second obstacle impedes current access to Kraus. The collected writings are vast; the two volumes of intimate letters to Baroness Sidonie Nádherný, who was the great passion of his life, are deeply revealing. But the hammering genius of the man seems to have been most manifest in his personal appearances as a reader-declaimer of his own texts, of his translations of Shakespeare and other playwrights, and of poetry. Kraus presented some seven hundred one-man readings between 1910 and 1936. We have numerous and uniformly breathless eye- and ear-witness accounts of these performances (most recently in the memoirs of Canetti). A pure force of thought, an intellectual-histrionic charisma of the most singular virtuosity seems to have emanated from Kraus's declamations and readings. Between 1916 and 1936, he adapted for solo rendition in German thirteen plays of Shakespeare. Those (still among us) who were in the audience tell of a multiplicity of voices, of a dramatic tension and pace unmatched in the actual theatre. Kraus's arts of direct presentation included music: with an accompanist on the piano, he mimed, sang, spoke singingly the operettas of Offenbach, whom, together with the nineteenth-century Viennese dramatist Johann Nestroy and the contemporary cabaret playwright Frank Wedekind, he put in the very forefront of literature and social satire. It was Kraus at his lectern, in his *Theatre of Poetry and Thought*, who exercised the utmost spell. Like other great prophets and watchmen in the night, he possessed a relation to language more physical, more immediate, than any that can be fixed in writing. One or two amateurish photographs have survived from these dramas of the word. We have no recordings.

It is these distances, from the man and from his all-informing milieu, which render rather quixotic Professor Harry Zohn's endeavors to gain a larger, English-speaking readership for Kraus. *Half-Truths & One-and-a-Half Truths* (Carcanet) seeks to set before English readers "a mosaic of Karl Kraus's views, attitudes, and ideas as he disclosed them in aphoristic form." Now, it is perfectly true that Kraus could produce lapidary maxims and barbed aphorisms. But these lack, especially out of context, the persuasive intensity, the tidal pressure, of his rhetoric. Like Kraus's poems, the aphorisms often suffer from a willed mannerism, from the self-consciousness of the sage.

There are charged, suggestive moments: "Satires which the censor understands are rightly prohibited"; "One shouldn't learn more than what one absolutely needs against life"; "I no longer have collaborators. I used to be envious of them. They repel those readers whom I want to lose myself"; "Psychoanalysis is that mental illness for which it regards itself as therapy" (a stroke as famous as it is irrefutable); "I don't like to meddle in my private affairs"; or the finding, so consonant with the maxims of La Rochefoucauld, "Ingratitude is often disproportionate to the benefaction received." Too often, however, the dicta extracted and grouped by Professor Zohn are eminently forgettable. What is more banal than the proposition that "it is regarded as normal to consecrate virginity in general and to lust for its destruction in particular"? Do we need the chastiser of sentimentality to tell us that "love and art do not embrace what is beautiful but what is made beautiful by this embrace"? How hollow is the self-dramatization in Kraus's vaunt "I and life: the case was settled chivalrously. The opponents parted without having made up." How forced is the declaration "Many share my views with me. But I don't share them with them." And could there be any generality easier to refute than the affirmation that "a poem is good until one knows by whom it is"—this from an ardent, if clumsy, translator of Shakespeare's sonnets? Without its context, what is the reader to make of what is not in fact a Kraus aphorism but a variation on that most universal of quotations: "Lord, forgive them, for they know what they do!"?

It may well be that the most celebrated of Kraus's brevities is also the most controversial: "Concerning Hitler, I can think of nothing to say," or "nothing occurs to me" *("Mir fällt zu Hitler nichts ein")*. The prophet stood speechless before the nightmare realization of his own worst apprehensions. Set down in the late spring or early summer of 1933, this abstention from discourse, this valediction to eloquence, tells of a terrible weariness. The hundreds of public performances, the thirty-seven volumes of the *Fackel,* Kraus's tormented exit from and marginal reëntry into Judaism (the point remains obscure) had been useless. A philistine hell was about to engulf European civilization and, more especially, the German language, which Kraus had loved and fought for. "Language is the only chimera whose illusory power is endless, the inexhaustibility which keeps life from being impoverished," he had written. "Let men learn to serve language." Now Kraus's chosen instrument, the sole divining rod of truth available to thinking man, would become the raucous megaphone of the inhuman. In front of Hitler, an anti-master of the word more ruthless than he was—an actor, mountebank, declaimer more mesmerizing—Kraus fell silent. At some very deep level of half-consciousness, he may have sensed in Hitler the monstrously distorted but also parodistic image of his own talents. He now found himself between crystal ball and mirror and was struck dumb.

In actuality, the marsh gas of Nazism had bubbled out of Austria. It was on the streets of Vienna, prior to 1914, that Adolf Hitler supped his fill of the racial theories, hysterical resentments, and anti-Semitism that were to make up his demonology. When Nazism came home to Vienna, in the spring of 1938, the welcome accorded it exceeded in fervor even that which it had received in Germany. Phantom forms of National Socialism, a scarcely diminished pulse of anti-Semitism, and a singular brew of obscurantism, partly ecclesiastical, partly rural, continue to characterize the climate of consciousness in the Austria of Kurt Waldheim. It is this witches' cauldron which provokes the implacable indictments and satires of Thomas Bernhard.

Unlike Kraus, Bernhard is principally a writer of fiction—of novels, short stories, and radio plays. Prolific and uneven, he is at his best the foremost craftsman of German prose after Kafka and Musil. *Amras* (not yet translated into English); *The Lime Works*, translated by Sophie Wilkins (and recently reissued by the University of Chicago Press, which has also brought out two other Bernhard novels); the still untranslated *Frost* created a landscape of anguish as circumstantial, as closely imagined, as any in modern literature. The black woods, the rushing but often polluted torrents, the sodden, malignant hamlets of Carinthia—the secretive region of Austria in which Bernhard leads his wholly private life—were transmuted into the locale of a small-time inferno. Here human ignorance, archaic detestations, sexual brutality, and social pretense flourish like adders. Uncannily, Bernhard went on to extend this nocturnal, coldly hysterical vision into the high reaches of modern culture. His novel on Wittgenstein, *Correction* (available in a Vintage paperback), is one of the towering achievements of postwar literature. His *Der Untergeher* (untranslated), a fiction centered on the mystique and genius of Glenn Gould, searches out the manic powers of music and the enigma of a talent for supreme execution. Musicology, erotic obsession, and the keynote of self-contempt distinctive of Bernhard give compelling strength to the novel *Concrete* (another of the University of Chicago volumes).

Between these peaks lie too many fictions and scripts imitative of themselves, automatically black. Yet even where Thomas Bernhard is less than himself the style is unmistakable. Heir to the marmoreal purity of Kleist's narrative prose and to the vibrancy of terror and surrealism in Kafka, Bernhard has made of the short sentence, of an impersonal, seemingly officious syntax, and of the stripping of individual words to their radical bones an instrument wholly fitted to its excoriating purpose. The early novels of Beckett will give the English reader some approximation of Bernhard's technique. But even in the most desolate of Beckett there is laughter.

Born in 1931, Bernhard spent his childhood and adolescence in pre-Nazi and Nazi Austria. The ugliness, the strident mendacity of that experience have marked his entire vision. From 1975 to 1982, Bernhard published five studies in autobiography. They span the period from his birth to his twentieth year. Now assembled into a continuous sequence, these memoirs make up *Gathering Evidence* (Knopf). They recount the early years of an illegitimate child taken in, brought up by eccentric grandparents. They chronicle Bernhard's hideous school years under a sadistically repressive system, run first by Catholic priests, then by Nazis, then again by priests, the evident point being that there is little to choose between the two. The section called "The Cellar" narrates in paralyzing detail the young Bernhard's experiences in Salzburg when the city was being bombarded by the Allied Air Forces. The immediate postwar years were an oasis for Bernhard, who became an apprentice and a shop assistant to a Viennese grocer and witness to the temporary discomfiture of the Nazis, now so suddenly and surprisingly converted to democracy. Running errands for his dying grandfather, the old anticlerical and anarchic tiger whom Bernhard loved as he had loved no one else near him, the eighteen-year-old falls ill. He is consigned to a hospital ward for the senile and the moribund. (Such wards will become perennial in his later novels and in the inspired book—part fact, part invention—*Wittgenstein's Nephew*) In the ward, Bernhard contracts tuberculosis. On the threshold of adult life, he finds himself under sentence of death. It is both in constant expectation of the fulfillment of that sentence and in defiance of it that he will escape into the armed citadel of his art.

Scrupulously translated by David McLintock, who also translated *Concrete,* this portrait of the artist as a tortured child and death-haunted young man does not make for easy reading. The note is one of unrelieved pain and loathing:

> I was soon confirmed in my suspicion that our relations with Jesus Christ were in reality no different from those we had had with Adolf Hitler six months or a year earlier. When we consider the songs and choruses that are sung to the honour and glory of any so-called extraordinary personality, no matter whom—songs and choruses like those we used to sing at the boarding house during the Nazi period and later—we are bound to admit that, with slight differences in the wording, the texts are always the same and are always sung to the same music. All in all these songs and choruses are simply an expression of stupidity, baseness, and lack of character on the part of those who sing them. The voice one hears in these songs and choruses is the voice of inanity—universal, worldwide inanity. All the educational crimes perpetrated against the young in educational establishments the world over are perpetrated in the name of some extraordinary personality, whether his name is Hitler or Jesus or whatever.

Doctors are licensed torturers no less than teachers. Their contempt for the inner life of the patient, for the complex needs of the dying is exactly proportionate to their arrogance, to their lofty but hollow claims to expert knowledge. Bernhard's minute account of near-suffocation during injections of air into his chest is, intentionally, unbearable. It stands for a larger allegory of strangulation: by family circumstances, by schooling, by political servitude. He writes, "The professor turned up at the hospital immediately and explained to me that what had happened was *nothing out of the ordinary*. He kept on repeating this emphatically, in an excited manner and with a malignant expression on his face which carried a clear hint of menace. My pneumothorax was now ruined, thanks to the professor's debate over his luncheon menu, and something new had to be devised." A worse, even more brutal intervention follows.

Within this "world-wide inanity," the inanity of Austria is by far the most loathsome. Bernhard lashes out at Austria's unctuous burial of its thoroughly Nazi past; at the megalomaniacal provinciality of Viennese culture; at the morass of superstition, intolerance, avarice in which the Austrian peasant or mountain-dweller conducts his affairs. Bernhard anathematizes a country that has made a systematic practice of ignoring, humiliating, or banishing its greater spirits, be they Mozart or Schubert, Schoenberg or Webern; an academic establishment that refuses to honor Sigmund Freud, even posthumously; a literary-critical code that exiles Broch and Canetti and relegates Musil to near-starvation. There are numerous precincts of hell, traced by human stupidity, venality, and greed. Vienna and Salzburg are the worst. In the province of Salzburg alone, two thousand human beings, many of them young, attempt suicide annually. A European record, but hardly, if we are to believe Bernhard, adequate to the motives: "The inhabitants of the city are totally cold; meanness is their daily bread and squalid calculation their characteristic trait." In a very recent novel, *Old Masters*, the palm of infamy is bestowed, beyond right of appeal, on the "stupidest," "most hypocritical" of all cities, which is Vienna.

The trouble with hatred is its shortness of breath. Where hatred generates truly classic inspiration—in Dante, in Swift, in Rimbaud—it does so in spurts, over short distances. Prolonged, it becomes a monotone, a blunted saw buzzing and scraping inter-minably. The obsessive, indiscriminate misanthropy in Bernhard, the around-the-clock philippics *contra* Austria threaten to defeat their own ends. He does not concede the fascination and genuine mystery of the case. The country, the society, that he so rightly chastises for its Nazism, for its religious bigotry, for its risible self-satisfactions happens also to be the cradle and setting for much of what is most fertile, most significant in all of modernity. The culture that spawned Hitler also bred Freud, Wittgenstein, Mahler, Rilke, Kafka, Broch, Musil, the Jugendstil, and what matters most in modern music. Excise Austria-Hungary and interwar Austria from twentieth-century history and you will lack not only that which is most demonic, most destructive, in that history but also its great springs of intellectual and aesthetic energy. You will lack the very intensities, the self-lacerating violence of spirit, that produced a Kraus and a Bernhard. What was once central to Europe became central to Western civilization. There are so many obvious ways in which American urban culture today, and particularly Ameri-can Jewish urban culture, is a coruscating epilogue to fin-de-siècle Vienna and to that dynamo of genius and neurosis defined by the Vienna-Prague-Budapest triangle. To that heartland, mere hatred is a one-eyed guide.

July 21, 1986

B.B.

THE TUMULTUOUS THRONG that poured westward through the rents in the Berlin Wall last November emptied the supermarkets and the video shops. Within hours, there was neither fast food nor deodorant left. West Berlin emporiums were stripped of their ample supplies of soft- and sometimes hard-core porno video cassettes. T-shirts and jeans, a currency across the Wall in the days of the two Germanys, flew off the shelves. Wide-eyed and knowing, moving to the beat of heavy metal and rock, which, clandestine or overt, had been the odes to freedom throughout Eastern Europe, the young and not so young enacted the first TV revolution. Once *Dallas* had come their way (it could be picked up several hundred kilometres east of Checkpoint Charlie), once tapes of Western soap operas and rock jamborees could be multiplied and sold beyond the "Dallas line," the cataclysm and saturnalia were inevitable. Television sparked the great, wild surge toward a consumer economy, and television packaged (brilliantly) the actual rush. Why live by bread alone when there is peanut butter? Why endure as a Soviet satellite when the word "satellite" means cable television?

The gains have been tremendous. Regimes of hideous stupidity, of corrupt despotism, of inefficiency beyond credence have been broken. Slowly, human beings east of Berlin and the Oder-

Neisse are regaining their self-respect, their liberty of motion, their sense of a possible future. More slowly, but tangibly nonetheless, the hidden dimensions of the iceberg of past massacres, lies, sadistic charades are surfacing. The corpses cry out, the shades of the tortured and the obliterated take on uncanny substance. History is beginning to reënter the uncertain light of truth. Not since 1789 has Europe felt so alive, so inebriate with possibility. Both the Soviet Union and the United States are receding into colossal, lamed—if occasionally belligerent—provinciality. The ancient bells of Prague and Kraków can be heard across sombre but living ground. Leningrad and Odessa are again opening their windows on the Western light (the talismanic image of Russian nineteenth-century liberals). The violence and the cant in Romania are fearsome, but even there it is difficult to envisage a recession to the lunatic past. Only an irresponsible mandarin would fail to exult in this season of hope.

But there are losses. Marxism, being itself the product of an intelligentsia, notably in East Germany, felt committed to certain archaic, paternalistic ideals of high literacy, of literary-academic culture. Classical theatre and music, the publication of the classics flourished. Because it carried within its raucous facility and mass seductiveness the germ of anarchic protest, much of what is shoddiest in modernity, in the media, in down-market entertainment was kept (partly) at bay. Now the conductors and the performers are leaving the more than seventy symphony orchestras financed by the East German government. The professors are draining away. The poets, the thinkers wonder whether they can compete on the futures market of commercial choices. Oppression happens to be the mother of metaphor. In the supermarket, Goethe is a lossmaker. These losses, however, are, at an immediate level, luxury losses, and are perhaps recoverable. The minus signs on the balance sheet cut deeper but are much more difficult to define.

After the Mosaic-prophetic summons to justice, after early Christianity, Marxism constituted the third of the major blueprints of hope. When Marx, in the famous 1844 manuscripts, imagined a society in which love and solidarity, rather than money and competitive hatreds, would be exchanged among human beings, he was simply rephrasing the summons to transcendence of Jeremiah, of Amos, and of the Gospels. When he urged a kingdom of social justice, of classless fraternity on earth, he was translating into secular terms the sunburst of the messianic. We know—I suppose we always knew—that such summonings were Utopian: that human beings are more or less gifted carnivores; and that man is wolf to man. What is even grimmer, we know now—and should have known since the Utopian fantasies of Plato—that ideals of equality, of communal rationality, of self-sacrificial austerity can be enforced only at totally unacceptable costs. Human egotism, the competitive pulse, the lust for waste and display can be suffocated only by tyrannical violence. And, in turn, those who practice such violence themselves wither into corruption. Ineluctably, collectivist-socialist ideals seem to lead to one or another form of the Gulag.

Such knowledge lessens us. It makes louder the yawp of money in the marketplaces of the West and, even more stridently, on the black markets around the Brandenburg Gate and on the once comely squares of Prague. Moribund Utopias leave venom behind. The drug pusher, the salesman of kitsch, the hoodlum have moved into the East European and Russian vacuum. The Marxist dream turned to unpardonable nightmare, but the new daydreams are rabid; tribalism, regional chauvinism, nationalist loathings are blazing from Soviet Asia to Transylvania, from the skinheads of East Berlin to the muggers of Croatia and Kosovo. With them comes inevitably the hatred of Jews—the intuition that the Marxist program of internationalism, of the abolition of frontiers, was radically tainted by Judaic universalism. Trotsky was, after all, a Jew. So once again the old crazy drums of irredentist territorial claims and ethnic autonomy are pounding in the jungle of the cities.

*   *   *

There is, of course, scarcely a sentence I have written up to this
point which does not incorporate, more or less directly, a phrase,
an idea, an ambiguity out of Bertolt Brecht. I just adapted the titles
of two early masterpieces: *Drums in the Night* and *In the Jungle
of Cities*. No lyric poet, no dramatist, no pamphleteer has given
sharper voice to the hymns of money, has rendered more palpable
the stench of greed. Few minds have seen more unsparingly into
the cant and into the fluent self-deceptions that oil the wheels of
profit and make outwardly hygienic the power relations in mer-
cantilism and mass-consumption capitalism. At the same time, and
often inside the same Aesopian, oblique texts, Brecht bore witness
to the cynicism, to the ruses (he was the most cunning of survi-
vors, catlike in his sinuous maneuvers and landings) needed if one
was to endure in the homicidal labyrinth of Leninism and Stalinism. In Brecht's greatest poems (some are among the finest in our
century), in his best plays, in the innumerable songs of rebellion
and scarred hope which he inspired and sang, the ultimate key
is minor, the beat, though sometimes imperceptibly, downward.
Man Is Man (another famous title)—man's avarice, his cowardice,
his frenetic selfishness will most likely prevail. Mother Courage,
her children slain, the land made waste, harnesses herself to her
fatal cart: armaments for sale. The stage turns and turns. History is a self-inflicted treadmill. The visions of justice turn to red
apocalypse. What will remain of our cities is, as a great early lyric
proclaims, the black winds that have swept through them. Yet the
absurd, murdering dreams were worth dreaming. Knowingness is
not knowledge, however accurate it turns out to have been. Those
who were wrong, hideously wrong, like the Bolsheviks, the Com-
munards in France in 1871, the International brigades in the Spanish Civil War, the millions who died proclaiming their fidelity to
Stalin, were, in a paradoxical, profoundly tragic way, less wrong

than the clairvoyant, than the ironists and the yuppies, than the Madison Avenue hype peddlers and the jobbers "bellowing" on the floor of the bourse. (The image is from W. H. Auden, whom Brecht knew, for a time, as Comrade Auden.) It is better to have been hallucinated by justice than to have been awakened to junk food. The cruiser whose blank shot initiated the Petrograd uprising was named Aurora, or Dawn. So felt Brecht, "who came out of the Black Forest."

And seems to have come almost fully formed, like some incubus ready to wreak mischief. The Brecht intonations, the cunning gait, the corner-of-the-mouth wit, the carapace of the tightrope walker tensed for survival are there in the earliest of the *Letters, 1913–1956,* selected, edited, and annotated by John Willett and translated into straight, faithful English by Ralph Manheim (Routledge). Bertolt Brecht is only fifteen when we pick up the trail. But the credo has been arrived at: "To combine fidelity to nature with idealism—that is art." And so is the fierce insight. Brecht has a poem in mind: "In the afternoon the enemy is defeated." (We are in November, 1914.) Joy on one side, rage and despair on the other: "This is a night when mothers weep." Nothing revelatory in that, but then the Brecht stroke: "On *both* sides." Those impotent tears were to fill his works. Mothers—militant, blind, cynical, idealistic—recur over and over. Later, Brecht would turn Gorky's *The Mother* into a play very much his own. But B.B. himself did not weep. April, 1918, a month before his call-up: "These are heavenly days. . . . At night we sing songs by Goethe, Wedekind and Brecht. Everybody loves us. . . . And I love everybody. . . . I'd sooner have victors than victory. . . . You will conquer the world and listen to my teaching, and you will die old and surfeited with life like Job who was admired by 100 camels. And then, together, we shall reform hell and make something of it." This to Caspar Neher, Brecht's lifelong colleague, collaborator, designer. The entire program is set: to reform, to make something of hell, be hell the defeated Germany after 1918, the crazed hive of refugees when Hitler came to power, the tin pots of Californian exile, or the gray gangsterism of the East German régime.

The "everybody" Brecht loves comprises a bevy of Rosies, Helenes, Ruths. Bullheaded, ungainly, prone to bohemian vulgarities, systematically promiscuous, B.B. fascinated women. He used them and used them up, as Baal does in the early autobiographical play. For Brecht, a ménage à trois meant meagre fare. At times, his caravan (those hundred worshipful camels) included at least two accredited mistresses and their brood. Helene Weigel (the association dates from 1923) was to reign supreme—officially, at least. Brecht came to find indispensable her genius as an actress and her rigor as a Communist. But other involvements proliferated. With Carola Neher, with Ruth Berlau—at a terrible cost to the women involved. When Carola Neher was sucked into the Stalinist death machine, Brecht gauged, with almost inhuman caution and dispassion, the limits to which he might go in (vain) attempts to save her. Ruth Berlau collapsed into near-madness. In Mack the Knife, there is more than a touch of Brecht's cavalier sexuality and, one suspects, contempt for the subservience of women to male appetites. "The shark has teeth": creative genius has needs and licenses.

The Threepenny Opera is by no means Brecht's best work. It is unimaginable without the brazen bark and lilt of Kurt Weill's music. But it caught and stylized precisely a certain sour-sweet eleventh hour in Western history. Like no other work, it conveys the macabre vitality, the self-lacerating grin of the Weimar twilight. "The theatre is dead," Brecht trumpets throughout 1926 and 1927, but the cadaver can be jolted into feverish life. And in terms of celebrity and earning power those three pennies made Brecht indestructible from 1928 on.

Which was more than fortunate. Hitler makes a very early appearance in the letters, "shitting on Moses Iglstein" in a Munich park in March, 1923. Brecht kept a wary eye on his fellow word-spinner. But his attitudes toward Nazism are complicated, and laced with dialectical-materialist theory. National Socialism represents for Brecht and his K.P.D. comrades the logical, perfectly predictable terminal phase of capitalism. Its organized violence and bureaucratic efficacy both fulfill and travesty the industrial-assembly-line processes and the bookkeeping conventions of Western free-market institutions. Hitler's triumph—this was the appalling, suicidal error of the German Communists—would be brief. It would unleash the authentic proletarian revolution and bring with it the final collapse of the Wall Street empire. To prevent that triumph might well be to falsify the laws of history.

The carnival of street battles, monetary collapse, and erotic emancipation suited Brecht's observant, analytic sensibility. The period from 1927 to Hitler's takeover in 1933 is one of the most fertile in his career. His several strengths came together. We follow in these letters the hammering out of Brecht's didacticism, his Aristotelian-Marxist conviction that the theatre represents a matchless teaching instrument—that a play is always also a potential manual for human sociopolitical perceptions and conduct. Very much in the manner of such German predecessors as Lessing and Schiller, Brecht sets out to be a teacher, a moral preceptor. His plays are *Lehrstücke,* or "teaching pieces." At the same time, the formal experimenter comes into his own. Even today, a "song play" such as *Mahagonny* remains radically innovative. Brecht breaks with realism and the lyric, Expressionist eloquence of his first dramas. The cabaret, the boxing ring, the cinema enter into his technical and perceptual means. Brecht is among the very earliest masters of radio drama. (See *Lindbergh's Flight.*) He experiments with choral techniques and masks. Adopting the modes of collage and montage as these were being exploited by contemporary painters and filmmakers, Brecht incorporates into his poems and dramas the texts of other

B.B.

writers. His adaptations of Gay's *The Beggar's Opera*, of Marlowe's *Edward II*, of Kipling's ballads and military tales are metamorphic. From the original source they excavate elements marvellously tailored to Brecht's tone and purpose. Jazz, blues, Negro spirituals, Lutheran German, Elizabethan tragedy, the thieves' laments of Villon are interwoven in Brecht's voice.

The best of the letters are "from the workshop." Brecht wastes little motion on personal concerns. He is no letter writer in the manner of Keats or of Proust. His letters are neither drafts of incipient texts nor introspective meditations. They are blueprints for productions, organizational bulletins, rough-edged polemics against obtuse critics and sloppy executants. Brecht keeps a cold eye on contracts, royalties, foreign rights. He labors to institutionalize and sustain a Communist stage company, a workers' theatre, a Red cultural front against the mounting Nazi tide. "The trouble with intellectuals is that what starts as feelings ends in a hangover," he writes to the director Erwin Piscator. Brecht feels at home with designers, stagehands, musicians, cabaret folk. He wears his leather jacket and chews on a wet, heavy cigar. Theory is all very well. (There are cordial, respectful exchanges with the unorthodox Marxist thinker Karl Korsch.) But it is praxis that counts. A new marching song (to the tune of "Tipperary") "could be sung with a pointer in front of projected photos." The pointer must be found, the projector must work in the smoky basement or the provincial cinema. Even a crude parable, Stalinist in spirit, such as the *Massnahme* (*The Measures to Be Taken*) can have its tactical, pedagogic uses. The masses are bewildered; the hour is late.

When the hour came, in the spring of 1933, Brecht was able to flee: Prague, Vienna, Zurich, Lugano, Paris, New York. B.B. joined the maelstrom of refugees, of the overnight stateless, of the gypsy intellectuals and artists. With a difference: he was a celebrity. He si-

135

phoned out of the Reich his immediate family and members of his entourage and found moneys abroad. He chose Denmark as asylum. The "dark times" had begun. They were to prove productive. Brecht wrestled to achieve a political diagnosis consonant with both dialectical historicism and the actual situation. His inner acrobatics make for fascinating reading. To Korsch in January, 1934:

> There are compelling reasons for German fascism, which do not apply to other countries. The bourgeois democracies may look wistfully at the way in which wages can be cut in Germany and the unemployed enslaved, but they also see drawbacks. . . . Fascism is a stiff drink; you have to be chilled to the bone, and a *quick* coup must have prospects of success. Unfortunately, we still haven't the faintest idea of the significance of the World War. Its origins remain shrouded in dense fog. The "salvation of Germany" could never have been achieved in the old democratic form. Regimented as it was, the proletariat was no longer capable of either a foreign or a domestic policy. . . . That of course is a very special situation.

Friends and fellow-exiles, among them Walter Benjamin, came to stay with Brecht. *Fear and Misery of the Third Reich*, a ferocious set of stage vignettes, could be performed by refugee troupes and left-front companies outside Germany. There was Paul Hindemith, an early collaborator, to be ironically instructed: "You seem to have tried to set phone books to music." Neoclassicism and ivory-tower distaste are no longer of any use; they are regressive, but not in the ways of National Socialist reaction and atavistic barbarism. Among Brecht's callers was Ferdinand Reyher, a Hollywood writer he had known in Berlin. Why not write a film script on the censorship and inquisitorial suppression of rational truths—on, say, the persecution and recantation of Galileo?

Brecht's *Galileo* was completed in the autumn of 1938, and is the subtlest of his major inventions. Its muted, constrained force, its oddly divided focus—this is a play about the suffocation of free intellectual inquiry *and* about the sociopolitical irresponsibility of pure scientific pursuits—point to the core crisis in Brecht's outlook. Neither John Willett's often nostalgically "Party line" commentary nor the letters here provided tell the whole story. But the main lines are evident. It was during the summer and autumn of 1938 that Brecht distanced himself from official Marxism-Leninism and the realities of the Soviet system. A number of Brecht's intimates and friends were vanishing into Stalinist camps. His own more inventive works were being attacked as "formalist" or as inappropriate to the concrete requirements of Soviet and Party policies. Brecht may have come to understand the tragic myopia of Stalin's and the Comintern's strategy of fighting against socialists—in Spain, in Germany—rather than against Fascists and Nazis. The imminent Hitler-Stalin Pact did not altogether surprise B.B.'s disenchanted eye.

The result was a largely private position of some complexity. He did not condemn the U.S.S.R. outright. On the contrary. "The regime, the state apparatus, the Party, its leadership if you will, are developing the country's productive forces," he wrote. "They are also being developed by the national form in which the Soviet Union must enter into the decisive struggle. And there you have the class character of international politics. The world civil war." Brecht's detestation of bourgeois capitalism remained visceral, his intimations of its impending doom as cheerily anarchic as ever. But much in this prophetic loathing, in both its psychology and its means of articulation, harks back to the bohemian nose-thumbing of his youth and to a kind of Lutheran moralism. His acute antennae told him of the stench of bureaucracy, of the gray petit-bourgeois coercions that prevailed in Mother Russia. Even as Martin Heidegger was during this same time developing an inward, "private National Socialism" (the expression comes from an S.S. file), so Brecht was expounding for and to himself a satiric, analytic Communism alien

to Stalinist orthodoxy and also to the simplistic needs of the proletariat and the left intelligentsia in the West. For both men, these
internalized tactics were highly generative: of a major philosophy
and aesthetics in Heidegger's case, of preëminent poetic and theatrical creations in Brecht's.

When the moment came for renewed flight, Brecht acted with
phenomenal astuteness. After an interim stay in Sweden and then
in Finland, Brecht just before the Nazi assault on Russia (in which
his son Frank was to die fighting with the Wehrmacht) travelled
across the entire Soviet Union. Keeping a very low profile, this virtuoso of survival then finessed his domestic caravan across the Pacific to Santa Monica and Hollywood. B.B. is said to have replied
when Walter Benjamin—himself soon to die a hounded fugitive—
asked whether the great playwright would seek haven in Moscow,
"I am a Communist, not an idiot."

America had long been a sort of phonetic source of wonder
to Brecht. The mere words "Minnesota" and "Mississippi" rang
with ambiguous enchantment and menace. He had felt repelled
and magnetized by the "jungle" of Manhattan and by what he read
and intuited of the slaughterhouses and crazed winds of Chicago.
In Weill's tunes to Brecht's lyrics, American elements and synco-
pations were frequent. The realities of wartime California were
somewhat different. There have in recent years been books and
plays about the German, Central European, and Jewish refugee
lives around Los Angeles. They tell a sardonic tale. Such lions as
Thomas Mann held tight-lipped court. Franz Werfel flourished in
the dulcet shade of the *Song of Bernadette* (his blockbuster best-
seller). Arnold Schoenberg strove bitterly for recognition. (He was
refused a Guggenheim.) Lesser fry buzzed and begged, improvised
hectically, scrabbled for minor teaching posts, and intrigued against
each other with the nastiness of need. Brecht observed the snake
pit and trod lightly through it. Once again, stress and marginality
proved highly productive.

These are the years of *Mother Courage* (perhaps the most convincing of the full-scale dramas) and of *The Trial of Lucullus*, a radio play later set to superb, neglected music by Roger Sessions. In the midst of Hitler's victories, Brecht shaped the enigmatic *Good Person of Setzuan*, the wryest of his parables, and *Mr. Puntila*, his dramatization of the theme of master and servant; the Hitler satire *The Resistible Rise of Arturo Ui* accompanied Brecht's luggage. Who in America but Charles Laughton could truly incarnate the towering, intricate persona of Galileo?

There were, however, few takers. Despite the understanding of translators and critics like Eric Bentley, Brecht's demands, the idiosyncrasies of his stage techniques, and the extreme discipline they required from actors and producers proved intractable. Kurt Weill's *One Touch of Venus* boomed on Broadway. Brecht found himself seeking out little theatres or offering his skills as adapter, reviser, and auxiliary director to such fringe ventures as Elisabeth Bergner's version of Webster's *Duchess of Malfi*. Only *Galileo* ever reached the New York stage. Occasional movie scripts and the sale of the rights to the novel version of Brecht's "Simone Machard" kept the pot boiling, but the princely renown of Thomas Mann, together with Weill's success, got under Brecht's skin. So did the perennial, more and more strident miseries of Ruth Berlau. "You seem determined to do everything and neglect nothing to make me really bitter," he wrote to her. "Do you really want to turn our exile into an endless lovestory with ups and downs, reproaches, doubts, fits of despair, threats, etc. etc.?"

But the root trouble, to be sure, was the false situation Brecht found himself in ideologically. As a Marxist, he saw scant virtues in Roosevelt's New Deal. What pained him about F.D.R.'s death was that it elevated the detestable Churchill to the apparent leadership of the Western alliance. Shrewdly, Brecht saw through the temporary love fest between the capitalist democracies of the West and the heroic folk of Stalingrad. He knew so much more about "Uncle

Joe" than did his entranced California hosts or the fellow-travellers who came his feline way that he anticipated both the incipient Cold War and the surge of right-wing witch-hunts in the United States. Characteristically muffled, Brecht's letters, even to familiars, give only hints of what must have been his ironic, impatient solitude. When the Un-American Activities Committee and the F.B.I. came knocking—absurdly, Brecht's links with Gerhard Eisler were thought to have possible bearing on atomic espionage—B.B. was prepared. The Washington hearing took place on October 30, 1947. Brecht landed in Paris on November 1st.

The letters translated in this generous offering allow only incomplete glimpses of the tortuous history of Brecht's final years. B.B. came home to Marxist East Germany via Zurich. An Austrian passport and a Swiss bank account were the discreet safety net. His beginnings in Paradise Regained were thorny. The place gave Brecht "the creeps." His flirtations with modernism and formalism in music and theatrical techniques displeased the gray mastiffs of "socialist realism"—as did his constant emphasis on Germany's tragic past (notably the Thirty Years' War) and on the general history of the defeated and the victimized (as in *The Days of the Commune*). The official note in the G.D.R. was one of militant optimism, of coercive hope in the Stalinist dawn. Rightly, Party bureaucrats sensed in their most illustrious writer an incorrigible streak of irony, of anarchic clairvoyance. Matters came to a dramatic head during the June, 1953, uprising of the East Berlin workers. Privately, Brecht exulted in the genuine emergence of a politicized working class and felt bitterness at its brutal suppression. In an epigram that went around the world he urged the Party to remedy its situation by "electing a new people."

Nevertheless, and despite somewhat unctuous outrage in the West, Brecht stoutly refused to condemn the regime or to break with his homeland. Mistakes had been made and would be made in the future, but for Brecht history lay on the side of centralized state socialism. The spurious democracy of mass-consumption capitalism continued to be unacceptable to him. His position bore fruit. Brecht's own Berliner Ensemble harvested support and recognition. *The Caucasian Chalk Circle* was produced exactly as Brecht wished. Directors, actors, filmmakers from far and wide came on pilgrimage to the Brecht workshops. A Stalin Prize awarded by Moscow shielded Brecht from the jealous chicaneries of East German officiousness. A calm penetrates the late letters, even to Ruth Berlau. Brecht helped prepare a visit to London of the Ensemble and its overwhelming productions of the *Chalk Circle* and *Mother Courage*. These took place, triumphantly, two weeks after Brecht's death, of a heart attack, on August 14, 1956.

During the night of last June 30th, columns of armored cars, under helicopter cover, churned into what little is left of the G.D.R. carrying millions of freshly printed Deutsche marks. Beyond the smashed Wall, crowds danced and waved Disneyland T-shirts. Nothing in this circus would have surprised Bert Brecht. Nor would the fact that the few who seek out his lapidary tomb in East Berlin are scholars or occasional theatre folk from the "rotten" West.

The best of the poems, the clutch of great plays (in modern drama, only Claudel is of comparable weight) will stay. And the cry of naked pain as it screamed, in perfect silence, out of the open, torn mouth of Helene Weigel in her performance of Mother Courage seems to be getting louder.

September 10, 1990

UNEASY RIDER

TOLD BY THE blurb that we have here "one of the most unique and exciting books in the history of American letters," one bridles both at the grammar of the claim and at its routine excess. The grammar stays irreparable. But I have a hunch that the assertion itself is valid. *Zen and the Art of Motorcycle Maintenance: An Inquiry Into Values*, by Robert M. Pirsig (Morrow), is as willfully awkward as its title. It is densely put together. It lurches, with a deliberate shift of its grave ballast, between fiction and philosophic discourse, between a private memoir and the formulaic impersonality of an engineering or trade journal. As it stands, it is a very long book, but report has it, and fault lines indicate, that a much longer text lies behind it. One hears of an eight-hundred-thousand-word draft and feels perversely deprived of it by the mere sanity and worldliness of the publisher. *Zen and the Art* is awkward both to live with and to write about. It lodges in the mind as few recent novels have, deepening its grip, compelling the landscape into unexpected planes of order and menace.

The narrative thread is deceptively trite. Father and son are on a motorcycle holiday, travelling from Minneapolis toward the Dakotas, then across the mountains, turning south to Santa Rosa and the Bay. Asphalt, motels, hairpins in the knife-cold of the Rockies, fog and desert, the waters dividing, then the vineyards and the tawny flanks of the sea. Mr. Pirsig is not the first ever to burst: Kerouac has been here before him, and Humbert Humbert, a clutch of novels, films, stories, television serials of loners on the move, lapping the silent miles, toasted or drenched under the big skies, motelling from one neon oasis to the next, and gliding at sundown through the nerve-wrenching sadness of the American suburb, honky-tonk town, and used-car crater. Pirsig is good on distance, windburn, and the uncomely occurrences in one's innards after too many hours on a cycle, after too many dusty snacks. But this would not make for the force of his book.

There are other pressures. The eleven-year-old passenger is called Chris. The weight of his nascent perceptions, of his endangered identity, grows fierce. There is a level at which this is the story of the great-shouldered ferryman of the Lord, of St. Christopher, guardian, talisman of travellers, his ribs bursting, his thighs shivering as the Child's weight almost overwhelms him in midstream. And Pirsig knows, perhaps senses with the somnambular erudition of a major artist, that the Christian image is itself a reflection of something much older—the centaur, a creature "motorcyclic" if ever there was, bearing the infant Hercules. A father and his child are riding through night and wind, enigmatically pursued, in receipt of eerie solicitations that seem to tear at the boy's soul. Yes, of course: the most famous of ballads, Goethe's "Erlkönig," some of whose multitudinous musical settings seem to resound from between the crotchets and plosives of the motorcycle engine. An erl-tale of nocturnal harrying, the human psyche being drawn back into an ancient slumber or possession, precisely as Chris may be if the cleansing Pacific is not reached in time. In short, we find a prodigality of pointers and echoes. There are the Wild Ones from Marlon Brando's pack, the Angels out of Hell (all theological inferences being allowed)—those outriders of Death whom Cocteau sheathed in leather and filmed long ago. A largesse of symbols, allusions, archetypes so spendthrift, so palpable, that only a great imaginer, shaping his material out of integral need, could afford it. A more professional contriver would have excised, he would have made his mythologies oblique, he would have felt embarrassed at the obviousness of the symbols offered. Mr. Pirsig allows himself a certain broad innocence. Everything is animate at the surface, contoured, casting exact shadows, as in the snowscape of an American primitive. Because the underlying design is covert and original to a degree.

Pirsig's work is, like so much of classic American literature, Manichaean. It is formed of dualities, binary oppositions, presences, values, codes of utterance in conflict. Father against son; the architectures of the mind against those of the machine; a modernity of speed, uniformity, and consumption (of fuel, of space, of political gimmicks) against conservancy, against the patience of true thought. But these confrontations are themselves ambiguous; they keep us off balance and straining for poise as do the swerves of the motorcycle.

Phaedrus is hunting the narrator. He is, at one level, the secret sharer, the intense questioner, the compaction of pure intellect. He has sprung directly out of the Plato dialogue that carries his name, and the device of having a living being pursued by a shadow out of Plato is by itself enough to certify Pirsig's strength, his mastery over the reader. But the chase is, to be sure, internal. It is the narrator himself who is a rent being, cloven nearly to his roots by alternate modes of identity. It is not the Demon king who is threatening the child's psyche, perhaps his life, but the father. Chris's dawning awareness of this fact, via nightmares, via the strangeness he hears in the penumbra of his father's voice, and the final duel between divided man and child on the verge of the healing sea, are of a numbing force. Chris perceives that his father has, at some dread point in the past, been out of his mind, literally ecstatic, as are the daemonically inhabited. The remembrance of a glass wall, in some hospital long ago, overwhelms him. Phaedrus, the lambent but ultimately anarchic agency of untamed thought, of speculative obsession beyond the constraints of love and of social life, is about to spring:

> His gaze fails in a sudden inward flash. Then his eyes close and a strange cry comes from his mouth, a wail like the sound of something far away. He turns and stumbles on the ground, then falls, doubles up and kneels and rocks back and forth, head on the ground. A faint misty wind blows in the grass around him. A seagull alights nearby.
>
> Through the fog I hear the whine of gears of a truck. . . .

Gears, points, engine-mounting bolts, the overhead-cam chain-tensioner, chain guards, fuel injectors play a major part. This is indeed a book about the art of motorcycle maintenance, about the cerebral concentration, about the scruple and delicacy of both hand and ear required to keep an engine musical and safe across heat or cold, tarmac or red dust. It is a book about the diverse orders of relation—wasteful, obtuse, amateurish, peremptory, utilitarian, insightful—which connect modern man to his mechanical environment. A motorcycle is "a system of concepts worked out in steel." Phaedrus and Plato, his master, believe that the steel fabric is but a shadow, necessarily inferior, of the idea of an engine generated by, perfect within, the mind. There is, the narrator allows, truth in this addiction to the ideal. But it is a perilous truth. It is the actual, the material we must endure and shape to our needs. Matter, too, has its exactitudes:

> If the fit is loose by a distance of only a few thousandths of an inch the force will be delivered suddenly, like a hammer blow, and the rod, bearing, and crankshaft surface will soon be pounded flat, creating a noise which at first sounds a lot like loose tappets. That's the reason I'm checking it now. If it *is*

a loose rod and I try to make it to the mountains without an overhaul, it will soon get louder and louder until the rod tears itself free, slams into the spinning crankshaft, and destroys the engine. Sometimes broken rods will pile right down through the crankcase and dump all the oil onto the road. All you can do then is start walking.

The two disciplines of apprehension, ideal and instrumental, are bodied forth in what is probably the wittiest, most ramified episode in the tale. The traveller returns to the college in Montana from which nervous collapse and Phaedrus' insistence on the absolute value of truth, on education as moral begetting, had driven him years before. His hosts dwell in the perfect house in the perfect canyon. Theirs is the very essence of the new American pastoral, of those chic serenities we now dress, build, and diet for. Robert De-Weese, artist-in-residence, brings out instructions for the assembly of an outdoor barbecue rotisserie which have baffled him. The discussion flows deep. It touches on the limitations of language in regard to mechanical procedure, on machine assembly as a long-lost branch of sculpture whose organic finesse is betrayed by the inert facility of commercial blueprints, on the ghost (O shades of Descartes) that inhabits the machine. Pirsig's timing and crafting at this juncture are flawless.

This is not always so. The westward journey is punctuated by lengthy meditations and lay sermons that Pirsig calls "Chautauquas." They are basic to his purpose. During these addresses to the reader, Phaedrus' insinuations are registered and diagnosed. The nature of quality, in conduct as in engineering, is debated and tested against the pragmatic shoddiness of a consumer society. Much of this discursive argument, the "inquiry into values," is finely shaped. But there are pedestrian stretches, potted summaries of Kant which betray the aggressive certitudes of the self-taught man, mis-attributions (it was not Coleridge but Goethe who divided rational humanity into Platonists and Aristotelians), tatters out of a Great Books seminar to which the narrator once took bitter exception. The cracker-barrel voice grinds on, sententious and flat. But the book is inspired, original enough to impel us across gray patches. And as the mountains gentle toward the sea—with father and child locked in a ghostly grip—the narrative tact, the perfect economy of effect, defy criticism.

A detailed technical treatise on the tools, on the routines, on the metaphysics of a specialized skill; the legend of a great hunt after identity, after the salvation of mind and soul out of obsession, the hunter being hunted; a fiction repeatedly interrupted by, enmeshed with, a lengthy meditation on the ironic and tragic singularities of American man—the analogies with *Moby Dick* are patent. Robert Pirsig invites the prodigious comparison. It is at many points, including, even, the almost complete absence of women, suitable. What more can one say?

April 15, 1974

RARE BIRD

THE WORKS OF Guy Davenport, professor of English at the University of Kentucky, are not easily come by. They include three, partly overlapping, sets of translations from archaic Greek lyrics and philosophy: *Carmina Archilochi: The Fragments of Archilochos* (University of California Press, 1964), *Herakleitos and Diogenes* (Grey Fox Press, San Francisco, 1979), *Archilochos, Sappho and Alkman* (University of California Press, 1980). There are three collections of short "fictions": *Tatlin! Six Stories* (Scribners, 1974), *Da Vinci's Bicycle: Ten Stories* (Johns Hopkins University Press, 1979), and the newly published *Eclogues: Eight Stories* (North Point Press, San Francisco, 1981). Issued at the same time, and also by the North Point Press, are forty literary essays and sketches, entitled *The Geography of the Imagination*. The Cambridge (England) literary magazine *Granta* (No. 4, 1981) features Guy Davenport's "Fifty-seven Views of Fujiyama." I have found that it is almost impossible to acquire three other Davenport titles: *The Intelligence of Louis Agassiz, Flowers and Leaves*, and *Cydonia Florentia*.

Professor Davenport illustrates his own texts with cunning collages. He keeps bowls of sugar water in the rooms of his house so that hornets, bees, and ants will feel welcome. He writes tales with such titles as "Mesoroposthonippidon." He looks to Ezra Pound for what luminous fragments of sane perception there are left in our politics, in our sense of how art can order man's civic being. He also holds the Bolshevik Revolution to have been a necessary delirium. Professor Davenport's publications are, in fact, privacies. They guard his elusiveness like masks and thorn hedges. He has a small circle of ardent readers, foremost among them Hugh Kenner. Anecdotes crop up about the arch fastidiousness of his manner. To "review" Davenport seems a crass intrusion. But in terms of the bleak condition of our current fantasies this intrusion may be justified. The fact is that Guy Davenport is among the very few truly original, truly autonomous voices now audible in American letters. Name Guy Davenport and William Gass. There are not many others to set beside Borges, Raymond Queneau, and Calvino. Adult dreams are as hard to come by just now as Davenport's more arcane imprints.

A Davenport sentence or short paragraph (the fragment, the aphorism, as in the early Greek poets and pre-Socratic thinkers, is Davenport's core) is instantaneously recognizable. "In the morning, sipping coffee, Mr. Hulme could find no proportion in the arcades, the buildings, the windows, the campanile, the duomi, the typography of the newspaper, that was not perfect. The children and the old people made him sad. All ideas rise like music from the physical." (*Eclogues*.) "A delegation came of trembling splendor, Consuls of the dead they said they were. One lifted a hand. Their patrician faces and beautiful feet seemed to me to be godlike, their eyes a fidget of light." (*Da Vinci's Bicycle*.) "There had been awful rains of stars in North America throughout my childhood and youth. For whole nights a fireworks of meteorites had hissed and sighed down the sky before I wrote my poem about the *nova* which flared before the eyes of Tycho Brahe, and I wrote my first story about the ghost of a horse leaping from a cascade of flame just after the Leonids had been more torrential than men had remembered them for centuries." (*Tatlin!*) "Corelli sarabandes, good talk by the fire, the wind in a huffle after sunset making a humpenscrump of the waves and trees." (*Eclogues.*) There would be no harm in simply using the remainder of this review to make a mosaic and montage of quotes. Let me instead transcribe one of the whole mini-chapters, welded paragraphs, that make up the "Fifty-seven Views":

> All of that again, he said. I long to see all of that again, the villages of the Pyrenees, Pau, the roads. O Lord, to smell French coffee again all mixed in with the smell of the earth, brandy, hay. Some of it will have changed, not all. The French peasant goes on forever. I asked if indeed there was any chance, any likelihood, that he could go. His smile was a resigned irony. Who knows, he said, that Saint Anthony didn't take the streetcar into Alexandria? There hasn't been a desert father in centuries and centuries, and there's considerable confusion as to the rules of the game. He indicated a field to our left, beyond the wood of white oak and sweetgum where we were walking, a field of wheat stubble. That's where I asked Joan Baez to take off her shoes and stockings so that I could see a woman's feet again. She was so lovely against the spring wheat. Back in the hermitage we ate goat's cheese and salted peanuts, and sipped whiskey from jelly glasses. On his table lay letters from Nicanor Parra and Marguerite Yourcenar. He held the whiskey bottle up to the cold bright Kentucky sunlight blazing through the windows. And then out to the privy, where he kicked the door with his hobnail boot, to shoo off the black snake who was usually inside. *Out! Out! You old son of a bitch! You can come back later.*

Guy Davenport is faithful to Ezra Pound's injunction that prose ought to be at least as well crafted as verse. He is a master of subtle pace. Seemingly short sentences and fragmentary phrases open, via unexpected commas, into sequences as opulent as Japanese paper blossoms dropped in clear water. Davenport's gait has the spare, funny lyricism of the music of Erik Satie. I say this with reference to the grammar. (Note the deft, whimsical uses, sometimes reminiscent of Gertrude Stein's, of the historical present.) The vocabulary, especially in recent texts, is a different matter. It is baroque, precious, crazily inventive. I take my examples from "On Some Lines of Virgil," a long montage story in *Eclogues* and, incidentally, one of the most hilarious, tenderly risqué accounts of sexual awakening in all modern literature. The reader must be ready for such finds as "gressorial," "tump," "grig," "nuchal," "daddled." He will find Davenport to be a virtuoso of opaque yet immediately suggestive verbs: "to jaunce," "to shirre cingles," or "to snoove," which rings precisely like something out of the dream dictionary of Shakespeare's Bottom.

This coruscating idiom is, of course, a part of Professor Davenport's ecstatic bookishness. He breathes open and hidden quotations, allusions, bibliographic references, mandarin puns. Even in the simple, mainly lyric examples I cited, the need for erudition presses on the reader. Mr. Hulme is T. E. Hulme, the Imagist guru and philosopher-poet who influenced Pound in London and who himself used to note the coincidence of his name with that of the great David Hume. Tycho Brahe's observation of an exploding nova is a benchmark in the history of astronomy and cosmology which directs us to a famous Chinese precedent. Arcangelo Corelli (1653–1713) is one among masters of Baroque and pre-modern music whose limpid texture and elegance were rediscovered by Pound et al. early in our century. A sarabande is a solemn dance, contrastive with the "huffle" of the wind. We want to know something of St. Anthony, in ancient patristics, and Flaubert, we want to be able to identify not only Joan Baez but Nicanor Parra and Mme. Yourcenar, so as to savor the full intent of the passage from the "Fifty-seven Views." And these are fairly routine demands compared to those which Davenport makes on the reader in what may be his finest fable, "The Death of Picasso," or in a vignette such as "Lo Splendore Della Luce a Bologna," itself a quotation with great resonances backward.

Such bookishness, such investment in the zany, esoteric lusts of learning, puts Davenport in a definite tradition. Coleridge, supremely of this breed, spoke of "library-cormorants," of men whose nerves are set to twanging by a footnote. Burton's *The Anatomy of Melancholy* often foreshadows Davenport's mosaic of allusions. They include Nabokov—witness the mad fun of his notes and index to Pushkin's *Eugene Onegin*—and Borges, haunter of the Universal Library. And here again Pound is essential to Davenport's perspective. There are numerous ways in which his parables and prose collages are a counterpart to, a garland woven around, the omnium-gatherum of Pound's *Cantos*. Indeed, Pound and Davenport seem to represent a cultural omnivorousness, an attempt at making a complete inventory of the world's aesthetic-poetic loot, which is radically American.

Guy Davenport is equally American in a seemingly antithetical commitment to the informalities of the wild, to the innocence of untutored space. The campfire at nightfall, the sodden slog through the Maine woods and along a Vermont trail, the dive into the quarry pool in the slow heat of the Indiana or Kentucky summer—these are talismanic to Davenport. He rivals, he echoes Thoreau and Mark Twain in the knowing sensuality of his immersions in the American Arcadia. He sings the light rust on the Virginia hills, the dark pools of the Poconos. Shelter him for the wet night in an old mill up White Mountains way and Davenport hugs his luck: "Packrats in little white pants, and spiders, and lizards, no doubt, I said, and we will make friends with them all." ("Fifty-seven Views.")

It is Davenport's genius to bring together a Byzantine high literacy and a profoundly American at-homeness on the earth. This interplay gives his whole work its offbeat freshness, its irreverent piety. Consider the complex but unforced shocks of sensuous-literate recognition in that invocation of Joan Baez as it plays against the austere classicism of Marguerite Yourcenar. Look at the closing moment in the passage. Nothing could be more robustly native than the shooing away of the blacksnake. But we know, and Davenport wants us to know, of the guardian snakes in antique holy places and of a very similar moment in what may be D. H. Lawrence's loveliest, most forgiving poem. The cardinal terms in Davenport are continuity and unison, the cross-weave of time and of space, of experience and of innocence, made possible by montage and collage. The bison painted in the prehistoric caves at Lascaux unconsciously rhyme with Goya's etchings of bulls and Picasso's "Guernica." All times, things, forms intertwine in arabesques of manifold oneness. Ovid tells of men turning into animals, Darwin of animals turning into men. Science and poetry must spring from the same music of mind, from the same intimation of harmony, or they are nothing. Art is simply a way of seeing precisely, as precisely as did Agassiz:

> He belongs to the spirit of Picasso and Tchelitchew, who have meditated on change as infinite variety within a form, theme variations made at the very beginning of creation, simultaneous. The ideas of nature were for Agassiz what an image is for Picasso. Genus and species are perhaps ideal forms from which nature matures all the possibilities. Time need not enter into the discussion. Snake and bird and pterodactyl all came from the same workshop, from the same *materia* available to the craftsman; they do not need to be seen as made out of each other. An artist fascinated by a structural theme made them all. (*The Geography.*)

Plotinus, the great Neo-Platonist visionary, could have said this. Nearer home, it is Emerson's creed. Davenport's work is one of metamorphic unity. As if the wood were alive still in the paper of his books. ("Printed by Maple-Vail on acid-free paper," says the colophon of the North Point Press.)

It follows that there are really no differences, in tactics or panache, between Davenport's "fictions" and the literary essays now assembled for the first time. The same angular elegance, erudition, and fun are manifest in both. Professor Davenport threads garlands of praise and acute definition around Charles Olson, Louis Zukofsky, Marianne Moore, and Eudora Welty (this last essay being one of the finest analyses available of Miss Welty's guarded but compassionate art). The several essays on Pound are a celebration. The concise salute to Charles Ives leads to a key complaint: a pioneering study of the composer

> fell under the evil spirit that has kept Ives himself a shy ghost in American art. How long it took us to see Melville! We still have no notion of Poe's greatness. Our Whitman and our Thoreau are not Whitman and Thoreau. We have a wrong, vague, and inadequate appreciation of Stephen Foster. And the great Formalist painter Grant Wood, who in Europe would have founded a school. (*The Geography.*)

Professor Davenport is illuminating on the Wittgenstein-Gertrude Stein language games and on their enactment in William Carlos Williams: "When he quotes, early in *Paterson,* a sign saying that dogs are not allowed in a park except on leashes, he wants to catch us in the Steinian-Wittgensteinian moment of seeing that, yes, the sign has a kind of purpose, but as dogs can't read, the sign exists in a sleep of reason." The covert reference to Goya is almost Davenport's signature. If this order of criticism has a fault, it is only that of generosity.

But this largesse and lightness of touch can betray Davenport. It will not do to say that Ezra Pound was driven mad by "the simple fact that the United States issues no money at all but borrows money issued by a private bank." He adds, "The hideous and obscene taxes which we pay our government are actually interest on this perpetual loan, ineradicable and unpayable." ("The Geography.") Davenport's phrasing leads one to suppose that he either sympathizes with or agrees with (or both) Pound's lunatic economics. It is this "Sisyphean economic insanity," argues Davenport, that explains Pound's views on the international fiscal conspiracies of the Jews. "Such was the geometry of his vision." As it happens, it was a vision that led to some of the more nauseating anti-Semitic and anti-American diatribes in the literature of hysteria and propaganda. Undoubtedly, the issue is a tangled one as far as Pound's personal actions and mental dispositions go. But Davenport's sprightly elegance defuses altogether what should be, to him, as to other "classic imaginations," a key question. Ezra Pound and the German philosopher Martin Heidegger are very probably the two great masters of humanism in our time. This is to say that they have spoken out with more authority, with more lyric energy than any other twentieth-century poets or thinkers against the ecological devastation, the vulgarization of personal style, the blind greed that characterize our mass-consumption polity. It is in Pound's "Cantos" and in Heidegger's metaphysical and anthropological writings that we find the great restatement of classical and Confucian ideals of civic comeliness, of humane at-homeness on what is left to us of our begrimed planet. Yet in the lives and pronouncements of both men there are significant involvements with totalitarian, Fascist inhumanity. What are the underlying connections? What is it that makes high literacy so vulnerable to the siren calls of barbarism? Davenport prefers to pass.

This is true also of a second compelling domain. The world of Davenport's *ficciones* and reflections is one of homoeroticism. "The Death of Picasso" is among the few masterpieces of homosexual sensibility after Proust. But when it comes to perceiving articulately the pressures of this eros on the very nerve centers of modern art, thought, and social consciousness, Davenport evades. It is this evasion which reduces his vignette of Wittgenstein, in this gathering of essays, and many of the Wittgenstein allusions and presences throughout his works, to trivia.

These are not, I think, random lapses. Pound's aesthetics, Pound's repertoire of what matters in the health of art and of man's social condition lie at the core of Davenport's enterprise. His hermetic wit, the sharp disingenuousness of his questionings of human discourse and gesture look to Wittgenstein, just as directly as so much in archaic Greek lyric poetry looks to the riddles and metaphors of the pre-Socratics. Guy Davenport's unreadiness to come to grips with the tragic substance of either Pound or Wittgenstein, with the larger implications of their positions, suggests a central reticence. Davenport seems to shield both himself and his readers from the full, perhaps anarchic deployment of his own strengths. A certain preciousness, a courtly scruple interposes between Professor Davenport and his daemon.

Already, however, anyone who cares for order and for grace in the exposed life of American letters is abundantly in Davenport's debt. He is, as the dour British locution has it, "not everyone's cup of tea." But to a growing number he will, I am confident, be nectar.

November 30, 1981

DEAD LETTERS

THE RECIPE FOR John Barth's novel *Letters* (Putnam) is of scant elegance. The first step is to take any of a number of historical-literary compendiums and, after assiduous cross-reference, spangle a seven-hundred-and-seventy-two-page text with passages like the following:

> It is the birthday of John Calvin, Giorgio de Chirico, James III of Scotland, Carl Orff, Camille Pissarro, Marcel Proust, James McNeill Whistler. The Allies are landing in Sicily, Apollo-11 has sprung a leak, Vice-President Fillmore has succeeded Zachary Taylor to the U.S. presidency, the first contingent of U.S. Marines is leaving Viet Nam, Ben Franklin is proposing a Colonial Union modeled after the Iroquois League of Six Nations, the Germans have begun their bombing of Britain and ratified the Versailles Treaty, Thor Heyerdahl's *Ra* is swamping again in rough seas and may not make it to Barbados, Korean truce negotiations have begun, the stock market continues its decline, and Woodrow Wilson has presented his League of Nations proposal to the U.S. Senate.

The purpose of these synchronic lists is to suggest that past and present, memory and dream, the material and the fictive are part of a single cat's cradle. Our being, the fugitive shadows in our thoughts are one long *Wiedertraum* (Mr. Barth's word), or dream redreamed. *Everything* connects in the pulsing spiderweb of time. Bertrand Russell asked with arch economy: What evidence is there that the entire past of the universe has not been fantasized by the mind in the latest fraction of a second? Borges can bring home this possibility in a single tranquil sentence.

Second step: You assume that the reader is perfectly familiar with the entirety of your previous works—that he has their plots, allusions, dramatis personae, and stylistic devices at his fingertips. You insert in every page more or less tricksy, more or less coy references to *The Floating Opera*, *The End of the Road*, *The Sot-Weed Factor*, *Giles Goat-Boy*, *Lost in the Funhouse*, and *Chimera*. In an ecstasy of mandarin narcissism, you go further. You have the main character in "Letters" discover, read, and comment upon all these previous stops in the hall of mirrors. And then, with a high-wire leap into the safety net of the self, you introduce into your new novel one Jacob Horner, a transparently autobiographical mask from an earlier and better book. Nay (to echo Professor Barth's pastiche of Augustan epistolary idiom), you divide the said Horner into a dual form: Jacob Horner, the inmate of Remobilization Farm, pens letters to Jacob Horner, the inmate of Remobilization Farm, in autistic abandon. A character from one's own previous novel re-dreams himself. Alas, Pirandello was here first, and with mastery.

Third step: Being an unquestionably learned professor of English and American literature, and having more than a passing familiarity with European letters of the eighteenth and nineteenth centuries, you bake your huge brick ("Letters" is longer than "The Idiot," "Ulysses," or "The Magic Mountain") with carefully prepared academic straw; i.e., it becomes a palimpsest of literary-historical-stylistic sources and allusions. Underlying this tome are Samuel Richardson's "Clarissa," Goethe's "Werther," and that greatest, coldest of epistolary fictions Laclos's "Liaisons Dangere-uses." Passage after passage is carpentered of quotations, of dou-ble-acrostic allusions, of acronymic play on names, incidents, and citations out of English and American literature from Chaucer to T. S. Eliot. Defoe, Swift, and Johnson abound in what is primarily a pastiche of an eighteenth-century epistolary novel. But so do the Metaphysicals, Shakespeare, and the American humorists. When April is come, it is, of course, "the cruellest month;" when genealo-gies are detailed, interminably, they astutely echo the dark cata-logues of inheritance in Faulkner, notably in "The Bear." But the warp and woof are not only literary in the strict sense. They are wound around arcane spools of biography. It is scarcely possible to make sense of "Letters" without close knowledge of the life, loves, and opinions of Mme. de Staël and her tormented lover Benjamin Constant. Intimacy with the erotic peregrinations of Lord Byron is equally requisite. (Mme. de Staël and Byron met.) Knowing the vital role of Napoleon in the lives and imaginings of George Noel and Corinne, one proceeds to a formidably erudite set of allusions to Napoleon's putative flight to the United States in 1815, to Jérôme Bonaparte's actual American sojourn, and to Yankee witnesses or descendants of this illustrious visitation. Re-animations of histori-cal-literary figures are nothing new or illicit. But Barth is out of luck. Titans have been there before him, and on his exact ground. The Mme. de Staël-Byron world, on the lustrous banks of Lake Ge-neva, weaves its phantom spell in Nabokov's *Ada*; *Werther* is re-born, with the vitality of complete self-control, in Thomas Mann's *Lotte in Weimar*.

In themselves, such ingredients will make a more or less in-digestible classroom soufflé. Nary a page here, sirrah, unworthy of exegesis, gloss, footnotes, hermeneutics, explication, semiotic analysis, psychohistorical and seminar-cabalistic commentary. Let timbrels sound in the warrens of academe, for not only is Professor Barth's text a cento of echoes but these echoes are frequently doubly, triply teasing. Ambrose Mensch proposes to "do a verbena." Ah! Transposition of Proust's famous *faire cattleya,* signifying "to make love." Freshman stuff, that. But wait: it is not to Proust that Dr. Barth now directs us. He asks in a parenthesis, "Do you know Maupassant's tale 'La Fenêtre,' about the verbena-scented lady who invites her suitor to her country château?" Scuttle of footsteps from the classroom to the stacks, where, indeed, a complete edition of Maupassant's tales awaits us. End of chase? Not at all. "Verbena-scented" ought to ring a bell. Egad, sir, we've cottoned on. That haunting tale "An Odor of Verbena," from Faulkner's collection *The Unvanquished.* Of course. How could we have been so slow? John Barth, Alumni Centennial Professor of English and Creative Writing at Johns Hopkins University, member of the National Institute of Arts and Letters and the American Academy of Arts and Sciences (all this and more on the flap), sits smiling.

John Barth has been an exceedingly clever, if self-indulgent, writer. His ear for parody, pastiche, *rifacimento,* satiric takeoff is exceptional. His knowledge of literature and of history, of the War of 1812 and of the development of American film, of the fauna and flora of Maryland is awesome. Crass though it so often is, his verbalization of sexuality and of the erotic pulse in human flesh carries intense conviction. No doubt he will again write better books, but in this one the virtuosities of perception and verbal technique end in mountainous waste. If Professor Barth does not wish to curtail his own prolixity, was there no one with the nerve or affection required to tell the author that a book one-third as long and stripped of its blatant mechanics of self-reference would have been funny and effective? The sadness of the whole affair goes well beyond the particular case. It involves the current climate of "big time" publishing—the hunt, at once arrogant and spineless, for the "blockbuster." It engages the absence of an authoritative body of reviewing, especially of "big-name fiction." How many harried reviewers can have had the time to plow through, let alone give critical thought to, this "new comic masterpiece"? (Blurb writers *have* to say such things.) Yet it is only where criticism is stringent and unashamed that literature is honored. Narcissism is, just now, the fashionable tag attached to the American situation. Much in that ascription is obviously modish and oversimplified. But to a degree at once precise and grotesque *Letters* seems to document such a view.

Letter to the Author: Dear John Barth, In France—where (as is said by one of your favorite masters, the Sterne Laurence) they order these matters better—there is a proverb: A bad book is the death of a good forest.

December 31, 1979

TIGERS IN THE MIRROR

INEVITABLY, THE CURRENT world fame of Jorge Luis Borges will entail for some a sense of private loss. As when a view long treasured (the shadow mass of Arthur's Seat in Edinburgh seen, uniquely, from the back of No. 60 The Pleasance, or Fifty-first Street angled to a bronze and racing canyon through a trick of elevation and light in my dentist's window), a collector's item of and for the inner eye, becomes a panoptic spectacle for the tourist horde. For a long time, the splendor of Borges was clandestine, signalled to the happy few, bartered in undertones and mutual recognitions. How many knew of his first work, a summary of Greek myths, written in English in Buenos Aires, the author aged seven? Or of Opus 2, dated 1907 and distinctly premonitory—a translation into Spanish of Oscar Wilde's "The Happy Prince"? To affirm today that "Pierre Menard, Author of the Quixote" is one of the sheer wonders of human contrivance, that the several facets of Borges's shy genius are almost wholly crystallized in that spare fable, is a platitude. But how many own the *editio princeps* of *El Jardin de Senderos Que Se Bifurcan* (Buenos Aires, 1941), in which the tale appeared? Only ten years ago, it was a mark of arcane erudition to know that H. Bustos Domecq was the joint pseudonym of Borges and his close collaborator, Adolfo Bioy Casares, and that the Borges who, with Delia Ingenieros, published a learned monograph on ancient Germanic and Anglo-Saxon literatures (Mexico, 1951) was indeed the Master. Such information was close-guarded, parsimoniously dispensed, often nearly impossible to come by, as were Borges's poems, stories, essays—themselves scattered, out of print, pseudonymous. I recall an early connoisseur, in the cavernous rear of a bookstore in Lisbon, showing me—this was in the early nineteen-fifties—Borges's translation of Virginia Woolf's *Orlando*, his preface to a Buenos Aires edition of Kafka's *Metamorphosis*, his key essay on the artificial language devised by Bishop John Wilkins, published in *La Nación* in 1942, and (rarest of rare items) *Dimensions of My Hope*, a collection of short essays issued in 1926 but, by Borges's wish, never reprinted. These slim objects were displayed to me with an air of fastidious condescension. And rightly. I had arrived late at the secret place.

The turning point came in 1961. Beckett and Borges were awarded the Formentor Prize. A year later, Borges's *Labyrinths* and *Fictions* appeared in English. Honors rained. The Italian government made Borges *Commendatore*. At the suggestion of Malraux, de Gaulle conferred on his illustrious fellow-writer and master of myths the title of Commander of the Ordre des Lettres et des Arts. The sudden lion found himself lecturing in Madrid, Paris, Geneva, London, Oxford, Edinburgh, Harvard, Texas. "At a ripe old age," muses Borges, "I began to find that many people were interested in my work all over the world. It seems strange: many of my writings have been done into English, into Swedish, into French, into Italian, into German, into Portuguese, into some of the Slav languages, into Danish. And always this comes as a great surprise to me, because I remember I published a book—that must have been way back in 1932, I think—and at the end of the year I found out that no less than thirty-seven copies had been sold!" A leanness that had its compensations: "Those people are real, I mean every one of them has a face of his own, a family, he lives in his own particular street. Why, if you sell, say, two thousand copies, it is the same thing as if you had sold nothing at all, because two thousand is too vast—I mean for the imagination to grasp. . . . Perhaps seventeen would have been better or even seven." Each of these numbers has a symbolic role, and in Borges's fables so does the cabalistic diminishing series.

Today, the secret thirty-seven have produced an industry. Critical commentaries on Borges, interviews with, memoires about, special issues of quarterlies devoted to, editions of—all pullulate. Already the five-hundred-and-twenty-page exegetic, biographical, and bibliographical Borges compilation issued in Paris by L'Herne in 1964 is out of date. The air is gray with theses: on "Borges and Beowulf," on "The Influence of the Western on the Narrative Pace of the Later Borges," on "Borges's Enigmatic Concern with 'West Side Story'" ("I have seen it many times"), on "The Real Origins of the Words Tlön and Uqbar in Borges's Stories," on "Borges and the Zohar." There have been Borges weekends in Austin, seminars in Widener, a large-scale symposium at the University of Oklahoma, where Borges himself was present, watching the learned sanctification of his other self—or, as he says, *Borges y yo.* A journal of Borgesian studies is being founded. Its first issue will deal with the function of the mirror and the labyrinth in Borges's art, and with the dreamtigers that wait behind the mirror or, rather, in its silent crystal maze. With the academic circus have come the mimes. Borges's manner is being widely aped. There are magic turns that many writers, and even undergraduates gifted with a knowing ear, can simulate: the self-deprecatory deflection of Borges's tone, the occult fantastications of literary, historical reference that pepper his narrative, the alternance of direct, bone-spare statement with sinuous evasion. The key images and heraldic markers of the Borges world have passed into literary currency. "I've grown weary of labyrinths and mirrors and of tigers and of all that sort of thing. Especially when others are using them. . . . That's the advantage of imitators. They cure one of one's literary ills. Because one thinks: there are so many people doing that sort of thing now, there's no need for one to do it any more. Now let the others do it, and good riddance." But it is not pseudo-Borges that matters.

The enigma is this: that tactics of feeling so specialized, so intricately enmeshed with a sensibility that is private in the extreme, should have so wide, so natural an echo. Like Lewis Carroll, Borges has made of autistic dreams—of a private condition that is exotic and idiosyncratic to a degree—pictures, discreet but exacting summonses, that readers the world over are discovering with a sense of perfect recognition. Our streets and gardens, the arrowing of a lizard across the warm light, our libraries and circular staircases are beginning to look precisely as Borges imagined them, though the sources of his vision remain irreducibly singular, hermetic, at moments almost moon-mad. The process whereby a fantastically private model of the world leaps beyond the wall of mirrors in which it was created and reaches out to change the general landscape of awareness is unmistakable but exceedingly difficult to talk about (how much of the vast critical literature on Kafka is baffled verbiage). That Borges's entrance on the larger scene of the imagination was preceded by a local point of view of extreme rigor and linguistic métier is certain. But that will not get us very far. The fact is that even lame translations communicate much of his spell. The message—set in a cabbalistic code, written, as it were, in invisible ink, thrust, with the proud casualness of deep modesty, in the most fragile of bottles—has crossed the seven seas (there are, of course, many more in the Borges atlas, and they are multiples of seven), to reach every kind of shore. Even those who know nothing of his masters and early companions—Lugones, Macedonio Fernández, Evaristo Carriego—or to whom the Palermo district of Buenos Aires and the tradition of gaucho ballads are little more than names have found access to Borges's *Fictions*. There is a sense in which the director of the Biblioteca Nacional of Argentina is now the most original of Anglo-American writers.

This extraterritoriality may be a clue. Borges is a universalist. In part this is a question of upbringing, of the years from 1914 to 1921 spent in Switzerland, Italy, Spain. And it arises from Borges's prodigious talents as a linguist. He is at home in English, French, German, Italian, Portuguese, Anglo-Saxon, and Old Norse, as well as in a Spanish that is constantly shot through with Argentine elements. Like other writers whose sight has failed, Borges moves with a cat's assurance through the sound-world of many tongues. He tells memorably of "Beginning the Study of Anglo-Saxon Grammar":

> At fifty generations' end
> (And such abysses time affords us all)
> I returned to the further shore of a great river
> That the vikings' dragons did not reach.
> To the harsh and arduous words
> That, with a mouth now turned to dust,
> I used in my Northumbrian, Mercian days
> Before I became a Haslam or a Borges. . . .
>
> Praised be the infinite
> Mesh of effects and causes
> Which, before it shews me the mirror
> In which I shall see no-one or I shall see another,
> Grants me now this contemplation pure
> Of a language of the dawn.

"Before I became a Borges." There is in his penetration of different cultures a secret of literal metamorphosis. In "Deutsches Requiem," the narrator becomes—*is*—Otto Dietrich zur Linde, condemned Nazi war criminal. Vincent Moon's confession, *The Shape of the Sword*, is a classic in the rich literature of the Irish troubles. Elsewhere, Borges assumes the mask of Dr. Yu Tsun, former professor of English at the Hochschule in Tsingtao, or of Averroës, the great Islamic commentator on Aristotle. Each quick-change brings with it its own persuasive aura, yet all are Borges. He delights in extending this sense of the unhoused, of the mysteriously conglomerate, to his own past: "I may have Jewish ancestors, but I can't tell. My mother's name is Acevedo: Acevedo may be a name for a Portuguese Jew, but, again, it may not. . . . The word *acevedo,* of course, means a kind of tree; the word is not especially Jewish, though many Jews are called Acevedo. I can't tell." As Borges sees it, other masters may derive their strength from a similar stance of strangeness: "I don't know why, but I always feel something Italian, something Jewish about Shakespeare, and perhaps Englishmen admire him because of that, because it's so unlike them." It is not the specific doubt or fantastication that counts. It is the basic notion of the writer as a guest, as a human being whose job it is to stay vulnerable to manifold strange presences, who must keep the doors of his momentary lodging open to all winds:

> I know little—or nothing—of my own forebears;
> The Borges back in Portugal; vague folk
> That in my flesh, obscurely, still evoke
> Their customs, and their firmnesses and fears.
> As slight as if they'd never lived in the sun
> And free from any trafficking with art,
> They form an indecipherable part
> Of time, of earth, and of oblivion.

This universality and disdain of anchor is directly reflected in Borges's fabled erudition. Whether or not it is "merely put there as a kind of private joke," the fabric of bibliographical allusions, philosophic tags, literary citations, cabalistic references, mathematical and philological acrostics that crowd Borges's stories and poems is obviously crucial to the way he experiences reality. A perceptive French critic, Roger Caillois, has argued that in an age of deepening illiteracy, when even the educated have only a smattering of classical or theological knowledge, erudition is of itself a kind of fantasy, a surrealistic construct. Moving with muted omniscience from eleventh-century heretical fragments to baroque algebra and multi-tomed Victorian *œuvres* on the fauna of the Aral Sea, Borges builds an anti-world, a perfectly coherent space in which his mind can conjure at will. The fact that a good deal of the alleged source material and mosaic of allusion is a pure fabrication—a device that Borges shares with Nabokov and for which both may be indebted to Flaubert's *Bouvard et Pecuchet*—paradoxically strengthens the impression of solidity. Pierre Menard stands before us, instantaneously substantial and implausible, through the invented catalogue of his "visible works"; in turn, each arcane item in the catalogue points to the meaning of the parable. And who would doubt the veracity of the "Three Versions of Judas" once Borges has assured us that Nils Runeberg—note the rune in the name—published "Den Hemlige Frälsaren" in 1909 but did not know a book by Euclides da Cunha ("Revolt in the Backlands," exclaims the unwary reader) in which it is affirmed that for the "heresiarch of Canudos, Antonio Conselheiro, virtue 'was almost an impiety'"? Unquestionably there is humor in this polymath montage. And there is, as in Pound, a deliberate enterprise of total recall, a graphic summation of classical and Western civilization in a time in which the latter is largely forgot or vulgarized. Borges is a curator at heart, a treasurer of unconsidered trifles, an indexer of the antique truths and waste conjectures that throng the attic of history. All this arch learning has its comical and gently histrionic sides. But a very much deeper meaning as well.

Borges holds, or, rather, makes precise imaginative use of, a cabbalistic image of the world, a master metaphor of existence, which he may have become familiar with as early as 1914, in Geneva, when he read Gustav Meyrink's novel "The Golem," and when he was in close contact with the scholar Maurice Abramowicz. The metaphor goes something like this: The Universe is a great Book; each natural and mental phenomenon in it carries meaning. The world is an immense alphabet. Physical reality, the facts of history, whatever men have created, are, as it were, syllables of a constant message. We are surrounded by a limitless network of significance, whose every thread carries a pulse of being and conducts, ultimately, to what Borges, in an enigmatic tale of great power, calls the *Aleph*. The narrator sees this inexpressible pivot of the cosmos in the dusty corner of the cellar of the house of Carlos Argentino, in Garay Street, on an October afternoon. It is the space of all spaces, the cabbalistic sphere whose center is everywhere and whose circumference is nowhere; it is the wheel of Ezekiel's vision but also the quiet small bird of Sufi mysticism, which in some manner contains all birds: "I was dizzy and I wept, for mine eyes had beheld this secret and conjectural object, whose name is usurped by men, but which no man has looked upon: the inconceivable universe." From the point of view of the writer, "the universe which others call the Library" has several notable features. It embraces *all* books, not only those that have already been written but every page of every tome that will be written and, which matters more, that could conceivably be written. Regrouped, the letters of all known scripts and alphabets as they are set down in extant volumes can produce every imaginable human thought, every line of verse or prose paragraph to the limits of the universe. The Library also contains not only all languages but those languages that have perished or are yet to come. Plainly, Borges is fascinated by the notion, so prominent in the linguistic speculations of the Kabbala and of Jacob Böhme, that a secret primal speech, an *Ursprache* from before Babel, underlies the multitude of human tongues. If, as blind poets can, we pass our fingers along the living edge of words—Spanish words, Russian words, Aramaic words, the syllables of a singer in Cathay—we shall feel in them the subtle beat of a great current pulsing from a common center, the final word, made up of all letters and combinations of letters in all tongues, that is the name of God.

Thus, Borges's universalism is a deeply felt imaginative strategy, a maneuver to be in touch with the great winds that blow from the heart of things. When he cites fictitious titles, imaginary cross-references, folios and writers that have never existed, Borges is simply regrouping counters of reality into the shape of possible other worlds. When he moves, by wordplay and echo, from language to language, he is turning the kaleidoscope, throwing the light on another patch of the wall. Like Emerson, whom he cites indefatigably, Borges is confident that this vision of a totally meshed, symbolic universe is a jubilation: "From the tireless labyrinth of dreams I returned as if to my home to the harsh prison. I blessed its dampness, I blessed its tiger, I blessed the crevice of light, I blessed my old, suffering body, I blessed the darkness and the stone." To Borges, as to the transcendentalists, no living thing or sound but contains a cipher of all.

This dream-system—Borges often asks whether we ourselves, our dreams included, are not being dreamed from without—has generated some of the most witty, uncannily original short fiction in Western literature. "Pierre Menard," "The Library of Babel," "The Circular Ruins," "The Aleph," "Tlön, Uqbar, Orbis Tertius," "Averroës' Search" are laconic masterpieces. Their concise perfection, like that of a good poem, builds a world that is at once closed, the reader inescapably inside it, yet open to the widest resonance. Some of the parables, scarcely a page long, such as "Ragnarök," "Everything and Nothing," and "Borges and I" stand beside Kafka's as the only successes in that notoriously labile form. Had he produced no more than the *Ficciones*, Borges would rank among the few fresh dreamers since Poe and Baudelaire. He has, that being the mark of a truly major artist, deepened the landscape of our memories.

Nonetheless, despite its formal universality and the vertigo breadths of his allusive range, the fabric of Borges's art has severe gaps. Only once, in the story "Emma Zunz," has Borges realized a credible woman. Throughout the rest of his work, women are the blurred objects of men's fantasies or recollections. Even among men, the lines of imaginative force in a Borges fiction are stringently simplified. The fundamental equation is that of a duel. Pacific encounters are cast in the mode of a collision between the "I" of the narrator and the more or less obtrusive shadow of "the other one." When a third persona turns up, it will be almost invariably, obliquely, a presence alluded to or remembered or perceived, unsteadily, at the very edge of the retina. The space of action in which a Borges figure moves is mythical and never social. When a setting or locale or historical circumstance intrudes, it does so in free-floating hits, exactly as in a dream. Thus the weird, cool emptiness that breathes from many Borges texts as from a sudden window on the night. It is these lacunae, these intense specializations of awareness, that account, I think, for Borges's suspicions of the novel. He reverts frequently to the question. He says that a writer whom dimmed eyesight forces to compose mentally and, as it were, at one go, must stick to very short narratives. And it is true that the first important "Ficciones" follow immediately on the grave accident Borges suffered in December of 1938. He feels, as well, that the novel, like the verse epic before it, is a transitory form: "The novel is a form that may pass, doubtless will pass, but I don't think the story will. . . . It's so much older." It is the teller of tales, on the high road, the *skald,* the raconteur of the pampas, men whose blindness is often a statement of the brightness and crowding of life they have experienced, who incarnate Borges's notion of the writer. Homer is often invoked as a talisman. Granted. But it is as likely that the novel represents precisely the main dimensions lacking in Borges. The rounded presence of women, their relations to men, are of the essence of full-scale fiction. As is a matrix of society. Number theory and mathematical logic charm Borges (see his "Avatars of the Tortoise"). There is a good deal of plain engineering in a novel.

The concentrated strangeness of Borges's repertoire makes for a certain preciousness, a rococo elaboration that can be spellbinding but also airless. More than once, the pale lights and ivory forms of his invention move away from the active disarray of life. Borges has declared that he regards English literature, including American, as "by far the richest in the world." He is admirably at home in it. But his own anthology of English works is a curious one. The writers who signify most to him, who serve very nearly as alternate masks to his own person, are De Quincey, Stevenson, Chesterton, and Kipling. Undoubtedly these are masters, but of a tangential kind. Borges is perfectly right to remind us of De Quincey's organ-pealing prose, and of the sheer control and economy of recital in Stevenson and Kipling. Chesterton is a very odd choice, though again one can make out what *The Man Who Was Thursday* has contributed to Borges's love of charade and high intellectual slapstick. But not one of these writers is among the natural springs of energy in the language or in the history of feeling. And when Borges affirms—teasingly, perhaps—that Samuel Johnson "was a far more English writer than Shakespeare," one's sense of the willfully bizarre deepens. Holding himself so beautifully aloof from the bombast, the bullying, the strident ideological pretensions that characterize so much of current letters, Borges has built for himself a center that is, as in the mystical sphere of the Zohar, also a far-out place.

He himself seems conscious of the drawbacks in this eccentric position. He has said, in more than one recent interview, that he is now aiming at extreme simplicity, at composing short tales of a flat, masculine directness. Courage, the spare encounter of knife against knife, have always fascinated Borges. Some of his earliest and best work derives from the legends of rumbles in the Palermo quarter of Buenos Aires and from the heroic *razzias* of gauchos and frontier soldiers. He takes eloquent pride in his warring forebears: in his grandfather, Colonel Borges, who fought the Indians and died in a revolution; in Colonel Suarez, his great-grandfather, who led a Peruvian cavalry charge in one of the last great battles against the Spaniards; in a great-uncle who commanded the vanguard of San Martin's army:

> My feet tread the shadows of the lances that spar for the kill.
> The taunts of my death,
> the horses, the horsemen, the horses' manes,
> tighten the ring around me. . . . Now the first
> blow, the lance's hard steel ripping my chest,
> and across my throat the intimate knife.

"The Intruder," a very short story recently translated into English, illustrates Borges's present ideal. Two brothers share a young woman. One of them kills her so that their fraternity may again be whole. They now share a new bond: "the obligation to forget her." Borges himself compares this vignette to Kipling's first tales. "The Intruder" is a slight thing, but flawless and strangely moving. It is as if Borges, after his rare voyage through languages, cultures, mythologies, had come home and found the *Aleph* in the next patio.

The Book of Imaginary Beings (Dutton) is marginal Borges. Compiled in collaboration with Margarita Guerrero, this *Manual de Zoología Fantastica* was first published in 1957. An enlarged version followed ten years later. The present collection is again expanded and has been translated by Mr. Norman Thomas di Giovanni, the most active of Borges's current "other voices." The book is a bestiary of fabled creatures, mostly animal and spectral. It proceeds alphabetically, from the A Bao A Qu of Malayan witchcraft to the whalelike Zaratan reported in the ninth-century *Book of Animals* of al-Jahiz. On the way, we meet dragons and krakens, banshees and hippogriffs. A good deal of the text is quotation from previous fabulists—Herbert Giles, Arthur Waley, Gershom Scholem, and Kafka. Often an entry consists of an extract from a poem or antique fiction followed by a brief gloss. There are, to be sure, unmistakable touches. A light-hearted entry on the brownies of Scottish farm lore moves via Stevenson to "that episode of Olalla, in which the scion of an old Spanish family bites his sister's hand." Full stop. We learn that the Holy Ghost has written two books; one is the Bible, "the second, the whole world, whose creatures had locked up in them moral teachings." In the "Fauna of Mirrors," Borges articulates the crucial vision of his own heraldic system. One day, the shapes that are frozen in the looking glass shall spring forth: "In advance of the invasion we will hear from the depths of mirrors the clatter of weapons." Borges knows that the Golem bears the word *'emeth,* meaning "truth," on its forehead; eliminate the first letter and you have *'meth,* whose meaning is "death." He supports Ibsen's biting suggestion that trolls are, above all, nationalists. "They think, or do their best to think, that the foul concoction they brew is delicious and that their hovels are palaces." But the greater part of the material is familiar and low-keyed. As Borges says, in a characteristic simile, "we should like the reader to dip into these pages at random, just as one plays with the shifting patterns of a kaleidoscope."

In a wonderful poem, "In Praise of Darkness," which equivocates with amused irony on the fitness of a man nearly blind to know all books but to forget whichever he chooses, Borges numbers the roads that have led him to his secret center:

> These roads were footsteps and echoes,
> women, men, agonies, rebirths,
> days and nights,

falling asleep and dreams,
each single moment of my yesterdays,
and of the world's yesterdays,
the firm sword of the Dane and the moon of the Persians,
the deeds of the dead,
shared love, words,
Emerson, and snow, and so many things.
Now I can forget them. I reach my center,
my algebra and my key,
my mirror.
Soon I shall know who I am.

It would be foolish to offer a simple paraphrase for that final core of meaning, for the encounter of perfect identity that takes place at the heart of the mirror. But this meaning is related, vitally, to freedom. In an arch note, Borges has come out in defense of censorship. The true writer uses allusions and metaphors. Censorship compels him to sharpen, to handle more expertly, the prime instruments of his trade. There is, implies Borges, no real freedom in the loud graffiti of erotic and political emancipation that currently pass for fiction and poetry. The liberating function of art lies in its singular capacity to "dream against the world," to structure worlds that are *otherwise*. The great writer is both anarchist and architect; his dreams sap and rebuild the botched, provisional landscape of reality. In 1940, Borges called on the "certain ghost" of De Quincey to "Weave nightmare nets / as a bulwark for your island." His own work has woven nightmares, but far more often dreams of wit and elegance. All these dreams are, inalienably, Borges's. But it is we who wake from them, increased.

June 20, 1970

OF NUANCE AND SCRUPLE

AT CERTAIN TIMES in literature, a particular writer seems to embody the dignity and solitude of the entire profession. Henry James was "the Master" not only or even mainly by virtue of his gifts but because his manner of life, his style, even on trivial occasions, expressed the compulsive ministry of great art. Today there is reason to suppose that Samuel Beckett is the writer par excellence, that other playwrights and novelists find in him the concentrated shadow of their strivings and privations. Monsieur Beckett is—to the last fibre of his compact, elusive being—métier. There is no discernible waste motion, no public flourish, no concession—or none that is heralded—to the noise and imprecisions of life. Beckett's early years have an air of deliberate apprenticeship (he was at the age of twenty-one acting as secretary to Joyce). His first publications, the essay on "Dante ... Bruno ... Vico ... Joyce" of 1929, the 1931 monograph on Proust, a collection of poems issued in 1935 by the Europa Press—a name symptomatic—are exact preliminaries. Beckett charts, in regard to his own needs, the proximate attractions of Joyce and Proust; he is most influenced by what he discards. In *More Pricks Than Kicks* (London, 1934), he strikes his own special note. War came as a banal interruption. It surrounded Beckett with a silence, a routine of lunacy and sorrow as tangible as that already guessed at in his art. With *Molloy* in 1951 and *Waiting for Godot*, a year later, Beckett achieved that least interesting but most necessary of conditions—timeliness. Time had caught up; the major artist is, precisely, one who "dreams ahead."

Henry James was representative through the stately profusion of his work, through the conviction, manifest in all he wrote, that language, if pursued with enough fastidious energy, could be made to realize and convey the sum of worthwhile experience. Beckett's sparsity, his genius for saying less, is the antithesis. Beckett uses words as if each had to be extracted from a safe and smuggled into the light from a stock dangerously low. If the same word will do, use it many times over, until it is rubbed fine and anonymous. Breath is a legacy not to be squandered; monosyllables are enough for weekdays. Praised be the saints for full stops; they keep us prodigal babblers from penury. The notion that we can express to our deaf selves, let alone communicate to any other human beings, blind, deaf, insensate as they are, a complete truth, fact, sensation—a fifth, tenth, millionth of such aforesaid truth, fact, or sensation—is arrogant folly. James clearly believed the thing was feasible; so did Proust, and Joyce when, in a last, crazy fling, he spread a net of bright, sounding words over all of creation. Now the park gates are shut, top hats and rhetoric molder on empty benches. Saints above, sir, it's hard enough for a man to get up stairs, let alone *say* so:

> There were not many steps. I had counted them a thousand times, both going up and coming down, but the figure has gone from my mind. I have never known whether you should say one with your foot on the sidewalk, two with the following foot on the first step, and so on, or whether the sidewalk shouldn't count. At the top of the steps I fell foul of the same dilemma. In the other direction, I mean from top to bottom, it was the same, the word is not too strong. I did not know where to begin nor where to end, that's the truth of the matter. I arrived therefore

at three totally different figures, without ever knowing which of them was right. And when I say that the figure has gone from my mind, I mean that none of the three figures is with me any more, in my mind.

Beckett's *reductio* of language—*Echo's Bones,* the title of his early book of verse, is a perfect designation—relates to much that is distinctive of modern feeling. "It was the same, the word is not too strong" exhibits the tense playfulness of linguistic philosophy. There are passages in Beckett nearly interchangeable with the "language exercises" in Wittgenstein's *Investigations*; both stalk the vapid inflations and imprecisions of our common speech. *Act Without Words* (1957) is to drama what "Black on Black" is to painting, a display of final logic. Beckett's silences, his wry assumption that a rose may indeed be a rose but that only a fool would take so scandalous a proposition for granted or feel confident of translating it into art, are akin to monochrome canvas, Warhol statics, and silent music.

But with a difference. There is in Beckett a formidable inverse eloquence. Words, hoarded and threadbare as they are, dance for him as they do for all Irish bards. Partly this is a matter of repetition made musical; partly it springs from a cunning delicacy of to and fro, a rhythm of exchange closely modelled on slapstick. Beckett has links with Gertrude Stein and Kafka. But it is from the Marx Brothers that Vladimir and Estragon or Hamm and Clov have learned most. There are fugues of dialogue in *Waiting for Godot*—although "dialogue," with its implication of efficient contact, is painfully the wrong word—that come nearest in current literature to pure rhetoric:

> VLADIMIR: We have our reasons.
> ESTRAGON: All the dead voices.
> VLADIMIR: They make a noise like wings.
> ESTRAGON: Like leaves.

VLADIMIR: Like sand.

ESTRAGON: Like leaves.

Silence

VLADIMIR: They all speak at once.

ESTRAGON: Each one to itself.

Silence

VLADIMIR: Rather they whisper.

ESTRAGON: They rustle.

VLADIMIR: They murmur.

ESTRAGON: They rustle.

Silence

VLADIMIR: What do they say?

ESTRAGON: They talk about their lives.

VLADIMIR: To have lived is not enough for them.

ESTRAGON: They have to talk about it.

VLADIMIR: To be dead is not enough for them.

ESTRAGON: It is not sufficient.

Silence

VLADIMIR: They make a noise like feathers.

ESTRAGON: Like leaves.

VLADIMIR: Like ashes.

ESTRAGON: Like leaves.

Long silence

A topic for future dissertations: Uses of silence in Webern and Beckett. In *Textes pour Rien* (1955), we learn that we simply cannot go on speaking of souls and bodies, of births, lives, and deaths; we must carry on without any of that as best we can. "All that is the death of words, all that is superfluity of words, they do not know how to say anything else, but will say it no more." I look, says Beckett, "for the voice of my silence." The silences that punctuate his discourse, whose differing lengths and intensities seem as carefully modulated as they are in music, are not empty. They have in them, almost audible, the echo of things unspoken. And of words said in another language.

Samuel Beckett is master of two languages. This is a new and deeply suggestive phenomenon. Until very recently, a writer has been, almost by definition, a being rooted in his native idiom, a sensibility housed more closely, more inevitably than ordinary men and women in the shell of one language. To be a good writer signified a special intimacy with those rhythms of speech that lie deeper than formal syntax; it meant having an ear for those multitudinous connotations and buried echoes of an idiom no dictionary can convey. A poet or novelist whom political exile or private disaster had cut off from his native speech was a creature maimed.

Oscar Wilde was one of the first modern "dualists" (the qualification is necessary because bilingualism in Latin and one's own vulgate was, of course, a general condition of high culture in medieval and Renaissance Europe). Wilde wrote beautifully in French, but eccentrically, to display the rootless elegance and irony toward fixed counters that marked his work and career as a whole. Kafka experienced the simultaneous pressures and poetic temptations of three languages—Czech, German, and Yiddish. A number of his tales and parables can be read as symbolic confessions by a man not fully domiciled in the language in which he chose, or found himself compelled, to write. Kafka notes in his diary for 24th October, 1911:

> Yesterday it occurred to me that I did not always love my mother as she deserved and as I could, only because the German language prevented it. The Jewish mother is no "Mutter," to call her "Mutter" makes her a little comic. . . . For the Jew, "Mutter" is specifically German. . . . The Jewish woman who is called "Mutter" therefore becomes not only comic but strange.

But the writer as linguistic polymath, as actively at home in several languages, is something very new. That the three probable figures of genius in contemporary fiction—Nabokov, Borges, and Beckett—should each have a virtuoso fluency in several languages, that Nabokov and Beckett should have produced major works in two or more utterly different tongues, is a fact of enormous interest. Its implications so far as the new internationalism of culture goes have hardly been grasped. Their performance and, to a lesser degree, that of Ezra Pound—with its deliberate sandwiching of languages and alphabets—suggest that the modernist movement can be seen as a strategy of permanent exile. The artist and the writer are incessant tourists window-shopping over the entire compass of available forms. The conditions of linguistic stability, of local, national self-consciousness in which literature flourished between the Renaissance and, say, the nineteen-fifties are now under extreme stress. Faulkner and Dylan Thomas might one day be seen as among the last major "homeowners" of literature. Joyce's employment at Berlitz and Nabokov's residence in a hotel may come to stand as signs for the age. Increasingly, every act of communication between human beings seems an act of translation.

In order to grasp Beckett's parallel, mutually informing virtuosity, two aids are necessary: the critical bibliography gathered by Raymond Federman and John Fletcher (*Samuel Beckett: His Works and His Critics* to be published later this year by the University of California Press) and the trilingual edition of Beckett's plays issued by Suhrkamp Verlag in Frankfurt in 1963–64. Roughly until 1945, Beckett wrote in English; after that, he composed mainly in French. But the situation is complicated by the fact that *Watt* (1953) has so far appeared only in English and by the constant possibility that work published in French was first written in English, and vice versa. *Waiting for Godot, Endgame, Molloy, Malone Dies, The Unnamable*, and the recent *Têtes Mortes* first appeared in French. Most of these texts, but not all, have been translated by Beckett into English (were some of them conceived in English?), usually with alterations and excisions. Beckett's bibliography is as labyrinthine as Nabokov's or as some of the multilingual *œuvres* Borges lists in his "Fictions." The same book or fragment may lead several lives; pieces go underground and reappear much later, subtly transmuted. To study Beckett's genius seriously one must lay side by side the French and English versions of *Waiting for Godot* or *Malone Dies*, in which the French version most probably has preceded the English, then do the same with *All That Fall* or *Happy Days*, in which Beckett reverses himself and recasts his English text into French. After which, quite in the vein of a Borges fable, one ought to rotate the eight texts around a common center to follow the permutations of Beckett's wit and sensibility within the matrix of two great tongues. Only in this way can one make out to what degree Beckett's idiom—the laconic, arch, delicately paced inflections of his style—is a *pas de deux* of French and English, with a strong dose of Irish tomfoolery and arcane sadness added.

Such is Beckett's dual control that he translates his own jokes by altering them, by finding in his alternative language an exact counterpart to the undertones, idiomatic associations, or social context of the original. No outside translator would have chosen the equivalences found by Beckett for the famous crescendo of mutual flyting in Act II of *Waiting for Godot*: *"Andouille! Tordu! Crétin! Curé! Dégueulasse! Micheton! Ordure! Archi...tecte!"* is not translated, in any ordinary sense, by "Moron! Vermin! Abortion! Morpion! Sewerrat! Curate! Cretin! Crritic!" "Morpion" is a subtle borrowing from the French, signifying both a kind of flea and a game analogous to Vladimir's and Estragon's alignment of insults, but a borrowing *not* from the French text initially provided by Beckett himself! The accelerando of outrage conveyed by the *cr*-sounds in the English version springs from the French not by translation but by intimate re-creation; Beckett seems capable of reliving in either French or English the poetic, associative processes that produced his initial text. Thus, to compare Lucky's crazed monologue in its French and English casts is to be given a memorable lesson in the singular genius of both languages as well as in their European interaction. A wealth of sly precision lies behind the "translation" of Seine-et-Oise, Seine-et-Marne into Feckham Peckham Fulham Clapham. The death of Voltaire becomes, appropriately yet with a distinct shift of stress, that of Dr. Johnson. Not even Connemara stays put; it suffers a sea change into *"Normandie on ne sait pourquoi."*

Stories and Texts for Nothing, recently published by Grove Press, is a case in point. This collection of three short fables and thirteen monologues is a cat's cradle. The stories seem to have been written in French in 1945 and are related to both "Molloy" and "Malone Dies." The monologues and stories appeared in Paris in 1955, but at least one had already been published in a magazine. The English edition of this book, under the title of *No's Knife, Collected Shorter Prose*, includes four items not included by Grove Press, among them "Ping," a weird miniature interestingly dissected in the February issue of *Encounter*. The Grove edition is, as has been noted elsewhere, no a compliment to Beckett's austere pedantry in matters of dating and bibliography. The few indications given are erroneous or incomplete. This is a fascinating but minor work. Slight if only because Beckett allows a number of influences or foreign bodies to obtrude. Jonathan Swift, always a ghostly precedent, looms large in the dirt and hallucinations of "The End." There is more Kafka, or, rather, more undisguised Kafka, than Beckett usually allows one to detect: "That's where the court sits this evening, in the depths of that vaulty night, that's where I'm clerk and scribe, not understanding what I hear, not knowing what I write." Joyce is very much with us, Irish ballad, end of winter's day, horsecab and all, in "The Expelled." We read in "The Calmative" that "there was never any city but the one" and are meant to grasp a twofold unity, Dublin-Paris, the venue of the great artificer and now of Beckett himself.

But although these are fragments, four-finger exercises, the essential motifs come through. The spirit shuffles like a ragpicker in quest of words that have not been chewed to the marrow, that have kept something of their secret life despite the mendacity of the age. The dandy as ascetic, the fastidious beggar—these are Beckett's natural personae. The keynote is one of genuine yet faintly insolent amazement: "It's enough to make you wonder sometimes if you are on the right planet. Even the words desert you, it's as bad as that." The apocalypse is a death of speech (which echoes the rhetorical but no less final desolation of *King Lear*):

> All the peoples of the earth would not suffice, at the end of the billions you'd need a god, unwitnessed witness of witnesses, what a blessing it's all down the drain, nothing ever as much as begun, nothing ever but nothing and never, nothing ever but lifeless words.

Yet sometimes in this kingdom of ashcans and rain "words were coming back to me, and the way to make them sound."

When that pentecostal dispensation lights, Beckett literally sings, in a low, penetrating voice, awesomely cunning in its cadence. Beckett's style makes other contemporary prose seem flatulent:

> I know what I mean, or one-armed better still, no arms, no hands, better by far, as old as the world and no less hideous, amputated on all sides, erect on my trusty stumps, bursting with ... old prayers, old lessons, soul, mind, and carcass finishing neck and neck, not to mention the gobchucks, too painful to mention, sobs made mucus, hawked up from the heart, now I have a heart, now I'm complete. ... Evenings, evenings, what evenings they were then, made of what, and when was that, I don't know, made of friendly shadows, friendly skies, of time cloyed, resting from devouring, until its midnight meets, I don't

know, any more than then, when I used to say, from within, or from without, from the coming night or from under the ground.

The laconic wit of "soul, mind, and carcass finishing neck and neck" would by itself signal the hand of a major poet. But the entirety of this eleventh monologue or murmuring meditation is high poetry, and seeks out Shakespeare with distant, teasing echo ("where I am, between two parting dreams, knowing none, known of none").

Beckett's landscape is a bleak monochrome. The matter of his singsong is ordure, solitude, and the ghostly self-sufficiency that comes after a long fast. Nevertheless, he is one of our indispensable recorders, and knows it, too: "Peekaboo here I come again, just when most needed, like the square root of minus one, having terminated my humanities." A dense, brilliantly apt phrase. The square root of minus one is imaginary, spectral, but mathematics cannot do without it. "Terminated" is a deliberate gallicism: it signifies that Beckett has mastered humane learning (these texts bristle with arcane allusions), that he has made an academic inventory of civilization before closing the lid and paring himself to the bone. But "terminated" also means finis, *Endgame, Krapp's Last Tape*. This is terminal art, making most criticism or commentary a superfluous vulgarity.

The vision that emerges from the sum of Beckett's writings is narrow and repetitive. It is also grimly hilarious. It may not be much, but, being so honest, it might well prove the best, most durable we have. Beckett's thinness, his refusal to see in language and literary form adequate realizations of human feeling or society, make him antithetical to Henry James. But he is as representative of our present diminished reach as James was representative of a lost spaciousness. Thus there applies to both the salutation spoken by W. H. Auden in Mount Auburn cemetery: "Master of nuance and scruple."

April 27, 1968

UNDER EASTERN EYES

THERE IS A contradiction about the genius of Russian literature. From Pushkin to Pasternak, the masters of Russian poetry and fiction belong to the world as a whole. Even in lame translations, their lyrics, novels, and short stories are indispensable. We cannot readily suppose the repertoire of our feelings and common humanity without them. Historically brief and constrained as it is in genre, Russian literature shares this compelling universality with that of ancient Greece. Yet the non-Russian reader of Pushkin, of Gogol, of Dostoevsky, or of Mandelstam is always an outsider. He is, in some fundamental sense, eavesdropping on an internal discourse that, however obvious its communicative strength and universal pertinence, even the acutest of Western scholars and critics do not get right. The meaning remains obstinately national and resistant to export. Of course, this is in part a matter of language or, more accurately, of the bewildering gamut of languages ranging all the way from the regional and demotic to the highly literary and even Europeanized in which Russian writers perform. The obstacles that a Pushkin, a Gogol, an Akhmatova set in the way of full translation are bristling. But this can be said of classics in many other tongues, and there is, after all, a level—indeed, an immensely broad and transforming level—on which the great Russian texts do get through. (Imagine our landscape without *Fathers and Sons* or *War and Peace* or *The Brothers Karamazov* or *The Three Sisters*.) If one still feels that one is often getting it wrong, that the Western focus seriously distorts what the Russian writer is saying, the reason cannot only be one of linguistic distance.

It is a routine observation—the Russians are the first to offer it—that all of Russian literature (with the obvious exception of liturgical texts) is essentially political. It is produced and published, so far as it can be, in the teeth of ubiquitous censorship. One can scarcely count a year in which Russian poets, novelists, or dramatists have worked in anything approaching normal, let alone positive, conditions of intellectual freedom. A Russian masterpiece exists in spite of the régime. It enacts a subversion, an ironic circumlocution, a direct challenge to or ambiguous compromise with the prevailing apparatus of oppression, be it czarist and Orthodox ecclesiastical or Leninist-Stalinist. As the Russian phrase has it, the great writer is "the alternative state." His books are the principal, at many points the only, act of political opposition. In an intricate cat-and-mouse game that has remained virtually unchanged since the eighteenth century, the Kremlin allows the creation, and even the diffusion, of literary works whose fundamentally rebellious character it clearly realizes. With the passage of generations, such works—Pushkin's, Turgenev's, Chekhov's—become national classics: they are safety valves releasing into the domain of the imaginary some of those enormous pressures for reform, for responsible political change, which reality will not allow. The hounding of individual writers, their incarceration, their banishment, is part of the bargain.

This much the outsider can make out. He looks at the harrowing of Pushkin, at Gogol's despair, at Dostoevsky's term in Siberia, at Tolstoy's volcanic struggle against censorship, or at the long catalogue of the murdered and missing which makes up the record of twentieth-century Russian literary achievement, and he will grasp the underlying mechanism. The Russian writer matters enormously. He matters far more than his counterpart in the bored and tolerant West. Often the whole of Russian consciousness seems to turn on his poem. In exchange, he threads his way through a cunning hell. But this grim dialectic is not the whole truth, or rather it conceals inside itself another truth instinctively apparent to the Russian artist and his public but almost impossible to gauge rightly from outside.

Russian history has been one of nearly inconceivable suffering and humiliation. But both the torment and the abjection nourish the roots of a messianic vision, of a sense of uniqueness or radiant doom. This sense can translate into the idiom of the Orthodox Slavophile, with his conviction that the Russian land is holy in an absolutely concrete way, that it alone will bear the footsteps of Christ's return. Or it can be metamorphosed into the messianic secularism of the Communist claim to a perfect society, to the millenary dawn of absolute human justice and equality. A sense of election through and for pain is common to the most varied shades of Russian sensibility. And it means that there is to the triangular relationship of the Russian writer, his readers, and the omnipresent state that enfolds them a decisive complicity. I had my first inkling of this when visiting the Soviet Union some time after Stalin's death. Those whom one met spoke of their survival with a numbed wonder that no visitor could really share. But at the very same moment there was in their reflections on Stalin a queer, subtle nostalgia. This is almost certainly the wrong word. They did not miss the lunatic horrors they had experienced. But they implied that these horrors had, at least, been dished out by a tiger, not by the paltry cats now ruling over them. And they hinted that the mere fact of Russia's survival under a Stalin, as under an Ivan the Terrible, evidenced some apocalyptic magnificence or creative strangeness of destiny. The debate between themselves and terror was an internal, private one. An outsider demeaned the issues by overhearing it and responding to it too readily.

So it is with the great Russian writers. Their cries for liberation, their appeals to the drowsy conscience of the West are strident and genuine. But they are not always meant to be heard or answered in any straightforward guise. Solutions can come only from within, from an inwardness with singular ethnic and visionary dimensions. The Russian poet will hate his censor, he will despise the informers and police hooligans who hound his existence. But he stands toward them in a relationship of anguished necessity, be it that of rage or of compassion. The dangerous conceit that there is a magnetic bond between tormentor and victim is too gross to characterize the Russian spiritual-literary ambience. But it gets nearer than liberal innocence. And it helps explain why the worst fate that can befall a Russian writer is not detention or even death but exile in the Western limbo of mere survival.

It is just this exile, this ostracism from the compact of pain which now obsesses Solzhenitsyn. For this haunted powerful man, there is a real sense in which reincarceration in the Gulag would be preferable to glory and immunity in the West. Solzhenitsyn detests the West, and the oracular nonsense he has uttered about it points as much to indifference as to ignorance. Solzhenitsyn's theocratic-Slavophile reading of history is perfectly clear. The French Revolution of 1789 crystallized man's secular illusions, his shallow rebellion against Christ and a messianic eschatology. Marxism is the inevitable consequence of agnostic liberalism. It is a characteristically Western bacillus that was introduced by rootless intellectuals, largely Jews, into the bloodstream of Holy Russia. The infection took because of the terrible vulnerabilities and confusions of the Russian condition after the first great military disasters of 1914. Communism is a travesty of the true ideals of suffering and brotherhood that made Russia the elect of Christ. But 1914 saw Mother Russia fatally dishevelled and defenseless against the plague of atheist rationalism. Hence the tremendous importance that Solzhenitsyn attaches to the first year of the World War, and his resolve to explore every material and spiritual aspect of 1914 and of the events leading up to March, 1917, in a row of voluminous "fact-fictions."

But in this demonology Lenin poses a problem, of which Solzhenitsyn has long been aware. Marxism may have been a Western and Hebraic disease, but Lenin is an arch-Russian figure and the Bolshevik victory was essentially his doing. Already in Solzhenitsyn's earlier writings there were traces of a certain antagonistic identification of the author with the figure of Lenin. In a sense that is only partly allegorical, Solzhenitsyn seems to have felt that his own uncanny force of will and vision were of a kind with Lenin's and that the struggle for the soul and future of Russia lay between him and the begetter of the Soviet régime. Then, by a turn of fate at once ironic and symbolically inescapable, Solzhenitsyn found himself in Zurich, in the same prim, scrubbed, chocolate-box arcadia of exile in which Lenin raged away his time before the 1917 apocalypse. He had left out a Lenin chapter in "August 1914" and had much Lenin material in hand for later volumes—or "Knots," as he now calls them. But the Zurich coincidence was too rich to be left fallow. From it comes the interim scenario *Lenin in Zurich* (Farrar, Straus & Giroux).

The result is neither a novel nor a political tract but a set of vignettes in depth. Solzhenitsyn aims to establish Lenin's fallibility. News of the Russian Revolution takes the Bolshevik leader totally by surprise. What he has been concentrating his conspiratorial genius on is a wildly involuted and harebrained scheme to involve Switzerland in the war and consequent social unrest. Lenin worries over his breakfast. He dabbles fastidiously in each and any contrivance that may secure funds for his embryonic movement. He aches for the other woman in his austere life, the thrilling Inessa

Armand, and accepts ideological deviations from her that would bring down anathema on any other disciple. Above all, like Solzhenitsyn himself, he finds the antiseptic tolerance of his Swiss hosts maddening:

> All Zurich, probably a quarter of a million people, locals or from other parts of Europe, thronged there below, working, making deals, changing currency, selling, buying, eating in restaurants, attending meetings, walking or riding through the streets, all going their separate ways, every head full of thoughts without discipline or direction. And he stood there on the mountain knowing how well he could direct them all, and unite their wills.
>
> Except that he lacked the necessary power. He could stand here up above Zurich, or lie in that grave, but he could not change Zurich. He had been living here for more than a year, and all his efforts had been in vain, nothing had been done.

And, to make matters worse, the good burghers are about to stage another one of their tomfool carnivals.

Lenin will get back to Russia in the famous "sealed carriage," with the connivance of the German imperial government and general staff (anxious to get Russia out of the war). But this brilliantly ambiguous escapade is not the product of Lenin's cunning or political means. It springs from the teeming brain of Parvus, alias Dr. Helphand, alias Alexander Israel Lazarevich. Despite a full-scale biography by Z.A. Zeman and W.B. Scharlau, "The Merchant of Revolution," much about Parvus remains unclear. He was an amateur revolutionary whose foresight sometimes exceeded Lenin's own. He was a fundraiser of genius for the Bolsheviks, but also a double or triple agent acting as go-between for Turkish, German, and Russian parties. He was a dandy and cosmopolite, at once fascinated and amused by the fanatic asceticism of Lenin's ways. The opulent villa that Parvus built for himself in Berlin, and in which he died, in 1924, was later used by Himmler to plan "the final solution."

The meeting between Parvus and Lenin is the crux of Solzhenitsyn's book. There are fine touches in it, as two kinds of corruption, that of worldly intrigue and that of an agnostic will to power, circle each other. There are also grating undertones. Parvus is the wandering Jew incarnate, the supreme fixer. He invests in chaos as he does on the bourse. Without Parvus, Solzhenitsyn intimates, Lenin might not have succeeded. Lenin, with his own Tatar strength, becomes the carrier of a foreign virus. In the original, these ethnic-symbolic allusions are, one suspects, underlined by the analogies between the Lenin-Parvus dialogue and the great dialogues on the metaphysics of evil in Dostoevsky's *The Brothers Karamazov*. Indeed, if "August 1914" can he said to illustrate, not altogether coherently, Solzhenitsyn's Tolstoyan side, his epic vein, *Lenin in Zurich* is a frankly Dostoevskian work, drawing both on Dostoevski's Slavophile politics and on his dramatic pamphleteering style. It is intriguing but scrappy and, in many respects, very private.

The privacy of Abram Tertz's *A Voice from the Chorus* (Farrar, Straus & Giroux) is of an entirely different order. Tertz is the pen name of Andrei Sinyavsky, who became famous with the publication in the West, from 1959 to 1966, of a series of critical essays and fantastic tales, blending surrealism with acid political and social satire. It was the work and example of Pasternak, at whose burial in May, 1960, he took a prominent part, that seem to have compelled Sinyavsky toward opposition and the dangerous road of publication abroad. He had begun, like so many of his generation, as a Communist idealist or even Utopian. *Doctor Zhivago*, the revelations concerning the true nature of Stalinism in Khrushchev's Twentieth Party Congress speech, and his own sharp-eyed observations of Soviet reality disillusioned Sinyavsky. By means of critical argument and poetic invention, he sought an alternative meaning of Russian existence.

For a time, "Abram Tertz"—the name is that of the hero of an underworld ballad from the Jewish thieves' quarter of Odessa—protected Andrei Sinyavsky. But the secret leaked out, and Sinyavsky, together with his fellow dissident writer Yuli Daniel, was arrested in September, 1965. The trial, in February, 1966, was at once farcical and of extreme importance. The crime of the accused lay in their writings. This fact, added to the ferocity of the sentences imposed, unleashed a storm of international protest. More significantly, it gave impetus to the widespread intellectual dissent and clandestine distribution of forbidden texts (*samizdat*) which are now so vital a part of the Soviet scene.

From 1966 to 1971, Sinyavsky served his term in a succession of forced-labor camps. Twice a month, he was allowed to write a letter to his wife. Oddly, these letters could run to any length (the inmate having to use all the cunning and good will available to him in order to get paper). References to political topics or the literal horrors of camp life would be instantly punished. But within these limits the prisoner could let his mind and pen roam free. "A Voice from the Chorus" is based on Sinyavsky's missives from the house of the dead.

But this is no prison journal. There are few dates or circumstantial details. What Sinyavsky has kept for us is a garland of personal meditations on art, on literature, on the meaning of sex, and, principally, on theology. Sinyavsky's literary range is prodigious: he sets down his reflections on many of the major figures in Russian literature, but also on Defoe, whose *Robinson Crusoe* assumes a direct, evident relevance to his own estate, and on Swift. His inner eye of loving remembrance passes over Rembrandt's "Prodigal Son" and the holy icons, whose magic reflection of suffering becomes clearer and clearer to him. Though the actual details of the play are no longer certain in his mind, Sinyavsky writes a miniature essay on what he now takes to be the core of *Hamlet*—what he calls "the inner music of his image." Over and over, he ponders the creative, fictive genius of human speech, its power to shape worlds.

In the camps, Sinyavsky meets members of various religious sects dogged nearly to annihilation by Soviet repression. They range from strict Orthodoxy to Christian fundamentalism (he records prisoners speaking in tongues) and the Islamic Faith as practiced among the Chechen people of the Crimea. These encounters and his own sensibility impel Sinyavsky toward an ever-deepening religiosity. He studies Church Slavonic and the martyrs' chronicles; he meditates on the unique place Orthodoxy assigns to the Assumption of the Mother of the Lord; he seeks to make out the possible relations between the Russian national character and the special focus of Orthodox theology on the Holy Ghost. Above all else, Sinyavsky bears witness that

> The text of the Gospels explodes with meaning. It radiates significance, and if we fail to see something, this is not because it is obscure, but because there is so much, and because the meaning is too bright—it blinds us. You can turn to it all through your life. Its light never fails. Like the sun's. Its brilliance astounded the Gentiles and they believed.

It was doubtless this ecstatic piety, and its specifically Russian Orthodox flavor of accepted suffering, which enabled Sinyavsky to endure his sentence with something akin to zest. He comes to cherish the slow tempo of camp life: in it "existence opens its blue eyes all the wider." Such is the radiance of spiritual revelation that "when all is said and done, a camp gives the feeling of maximum freedom." Where else do the woods, seen beyond the barbed wire, glow with such pentecostal flame or the stars throw down their spears before His coming?

Punctuating these homilies are the literal "voices from the chorus"—brief interjections, snatches of song, oaths, anecdotes, malapropisms selected from the babble of camp speech. Max Hayward, who with Kyril Fitzlyon has produced what is obviously a brilliant translation, tells us that these fragments are among the most fascinating to come out of modern Russia. He adds that their quality is accessible only to a Russian ear. This is certainly the impression one gets. There are haunting exceptions ("Buy yourself a nice pair of shoes—and you'll feel just like King Lear" or "Till our children's dying day!"), but most of the phrases are poignantly banal.

This is a profoundly moving testimonial by a man of exceptional strength, subtlety, compassion, and faith. Deliberately, perhaps, it leaves a rather dreamlike, muted impression. Sinyavsky read a great deal in the camps. In fact, he wrote a dazzling study of Pushkin while incarcerated. How was this made possible? Did his reading include the prohibited texts of Pasternak, Akhmatova, and Mandelstam to which he makes extended reference? One jotting alludes to what must have been an ideological discussion between a camp commander and the condemned. Was this an exceptional lapse of the usual discipline? One of the voices from the chorus makes a highly significant remark: "There used to be more fun in the camp in the old days. Someone was always being beaten up or hanged. Every day there was a special event." What are the metamorphoses in the politics of hell? There is so much more one would want to learn about from a witness of Sinyavsky's stature. But, again, his message is intended for Russian consumption. We eavesdrop. And Sinyavsky's exile—he now lives in Paris—makes this process the more uncomfortable.

*   *   *

Lydia Chukovskaya's novel *Going Under* (Quadrangle) is far more accessible to the Western reader than either Solzhenitsyn's polemic fragment or Sinyavsky's memoir. The paradox is that Miss Chukovskaya is still "inside," in the twilight zone assigned to writers, artists, and thinkers who have offended the regime and are barred from normal professional life. In the Soviet Union, Chukovskaya's writings circulate, where at all, by clandestine mimeographs. Thus there is a sense in which *Going Under*—pellucidly translated by Peter Weston—is meant for the outside. It is we who are to extract the message from the bottle.

The time is February, 1949, and the *zhdanovshchina*—the purge of intellectuals by Stalin's culture hoodlum, Andrei Zhdanov—is beginning. The action takes place at a rest home for writers in Russian Finland. Nina Sergeyevna, a translator, is one of the fortunate few to whom the Writers' Union has granted a month of pastoral repose away from the stress of Moscow. Ostensibly, she is to rest or get on with her translations. What she is actually attempting to do is to set down an account of her husband's disappearance during the Stalin manhunts of 1938, and thus free herself, at least in part, from a long nightmare. Nothing very much happens at Litvinovka. Nina becomes more or less involved in the lives of Bilibin, a writer who is attempting to come to terms with the demands of his Stalinist masters after a spell at forced labor, and of Veksler, a Jewish poet and war hero. In the drawing room, the literati come and go, spitting venom on Pasternak, their nostrils quivering at the latest rumor of repression in Moscow. The snow glows among the birches, and just beyond the neat confines of the rest home lie the inhuman deprivation and backwardness of rural Russia in the aftermath of total war. Nina's bad dreams draw her back to the infamous queues of the nineteen-thirties, tens of thousands of women waiting in vain in front of police stations for some word of their vanished husbands, sons, brothers. (There are echoes here of Akhmatova's great poem "Requiem.") Bilibin would make love to her, out of the gentleness of his desolation. The N.K.V.D. come for Veksler. War heroes—Jewish war heroes in particular—are no longer wanted. Soon it is March and time to return to Moscow.

Set in a minor key, this short novel echoes and re-echoes in one's mind. Every incident is at once perfectly natural and charged with implication. Walking in the white woods, Nina realizes that the Germans have been there, that the snow masks a literal charnel house. To have fought the Nazis in order to save and consolidate Stalinism—the ironies are insoluble. When the suave hack Klokov denounces the obscurity of Pasternak, Nina's spirit writhes. But in her solitude she is shadowed by the conviction that very great art can belong only to the few, that there is, sometimes in the greatest poetry, an exaction that cuts one off from the common pace and needs of humanity. The narrative is both spare and resonant. Pushkin, Akhmatova, Mandelstam, Pasternak, and Turgenev are obliquely present—especially Turgenev, whose play *A Month in the Country* seems to counterpoint Chukovskaya's scenes. This is a classic.

Under Eastern eyes—Solzhenitsyn makes the point relentlessly—much of our own concerns and literature have a trivial mien. Seen from the Gulag, our urban disarray or racial tensions or economic hiccups look Edenic. The dimensions of cruelty and of endurance in which the Russian imagination works are, to most of us, almost unimaginable. So, even more strikingly, are the mechanisms of hope, of exquisite moral perception, of vital enchantment that produce such books as the memoirs of Nadezhda Mandelstam or the tales of Chukovskaya. We don't really understand the daily breath of terror, and we don't understand the joy. This is because the indissoluble bond between them is for us, at best, a philosophical abstraction. "Driven into a cage," writes Sinyavsky, "the mind is forced to break out into the wider open spaces of the universe through the back door. But for this to happen it must first be hunted down and brought to bay." The "cage" happens to be the name for the barred compartment of Russian railway coaches in which prisoners travel to the camps. Within it, the Solzhenitsyns, the Sinyavskys, the Chukovskayas seem to find their freedom, as did Pushkin, Dostoevsky, and Mandelstam before them. They would not, one suspects, wish to trade with us. Nor is it for us to imagine that we can penetrate, let alone break open, the prison of their days.

October 11, 1976

CAT MAN

THIS REVIEW OUGHT to be about a cat, the most illustrious, compelling cat in the history of literature. Bébert was a Montparnasse tabby, born probably in 1935. He met his second master in occupied Paris in late 1942. "Magic itself, tact by wavelength," as his master described him, Bébert was to be left behind when the master and his wife, Lucette, decamped for Germany in the dread spring of '44. Bébert refused separation. He was carried in the travelling sack. The voyage led through lunar bomb craters, strafed rail lines, and cities burning like mad torches. Under bombardment, Bébert, almost starving, became lost, but rediscovered his master and Madame. The trio crossed and recrossed the collapsing Reich. In a last, despairing lunge, they reached Copenhagen. When the Danish police came to arrest the unwelcome guests, Bébert slipped out across a roof. Caught, the legendary beast was caged in a pound at a veterinary clinic. When his master was released from jail and was recuperating, Bébert had to be operated on for a cancerous tumor. "But the Montmartre tom had been around the block. He withstood the trauma and made a speedy recovery, with the slower and wiser serenity of aging cats, faithful, silent, and enigmatic." Amnestied, Bébert's *patron* headed for home at the end of June, 1951. Four lesser cats—Thomine, Poupine, Mouchette, and Flúte—accompanied them on the voyage. Sphinxlike in years, Bébert, the secret sharer, died in a suburb of Paris at the end of 1952. "After many an adventure, jail, bivouac, ashes, all of Europe ... he died agile and graceful, impeccably, he had jumped out the window that very morning.... We, who are born old, look ridiculous in comparison!" So wrote his grieving master, Louis-Ferdinand Destouches, physician, champion of social hygiene among the destitute, wanderer in Africa and the United States, manic crank.

It is Bébert I want to write about—Bébert the arch-survivor and the incarnation of French cunning. But it is a voluminous biography of his wretched owner that I have before me—of that mad doctor who, under the name Céline (taken from his grandmother), produced some of the greatest fiction and documentary "fact-fiction" not only in this century but in the history of Western literature. Bébert would be a joy to report on. Céline is not.

Frédéric Vitoux's *Céline: A Biography*, translated, heavy-handedly, by Jesse Browner (Paragon), details the Destouches family history and the *misère* of Louis-Ferdinand's parents, living in diverse unsalubrious quarters of Paris before the First World War. It chronicles the bewildering plethora of Louis-Ferdinand's sexual imbroglios, affairs, marriages, and morose peregrinations among the brothels of Paris, London, and colonial Africa. (Dr. Destouches appears to have been a compulsive voyeur, fascinated less by his own sexual experience than by the experiences that his lovers shared with others.) Vitoux is relentlessly informative on his hero's incessant quarrels with publishers, with other writers, with Parisian mundanity. Though it draws heavily on previous chronicles, the coverage of the years of German occupation and of Céline's sardonic, coldly hysterical responses is penetrating. As are the pictures of the hunted fugitive, of the struggle against extradition from Denmark, of the ghostly homecoming. The aura of sanctity that attaches to the deeds of the "slum doctor," of the pathologist struggling against dirt, social injustice, and the ignorance of the destitute, is explored and, to a degree, justified. Frédéric Vitoux argues his brief with tranquil warmth.

Yet the key enigmas remain unresolved. (Shades of the elusive Bébert!) The hallucinatory style with which Céline literally exploded into language and literature when *Journey to the End of Night* appeared, in October, 1932, together with the Jew-hatred first proclaimed in 1937, has always been attributed to a wound Céline suffered on October 27, 1914, when he was on a heroic cavalry mission in Flanders. Céline himself and his apologists cite this wound as the source of the migraines, manic-depressive cycles, and ungoverned rages that subsequently marked Dr. Destouches's private and public pilgrimage as well as the voice and ideology of his writings. The handsome cuirassier, sabre to the wind, had been almost fatally injured, and was thus unhinged into genius and evil. But even Vitoux's careful inventory leaves the facts opaque. It is clear that Sergeant Destouches was wounded in the arm and shoulder, but his captain wrote to Louis's father, "It seems that his wound is not serious." On the other hand, the citation that accompanied the Médaille Militaire awarded him said he was "grievously wounded," and Céline did not return to combat. Was he concussed as he fell from the saddle? Did he endure some psychic shock that thrust him into an abyss of irremediable horror? During convalescence behind the lines, and during the days in London and the Cameroons which ensued, the decorated veteran told of insomnia, of hideous noises in his ears, "whistles . . . drums . . . blasts of steam" that maddened his consciousness. The strategy of apocalyptic pain, of paranoiac suffering and fury, was born. The factual source remains at the unclarified "end of night."

Nor, despite its labored diagnoses, can Vitoux's book throw decisive light on the font and growth of Dr. Destouches's homicidal anti-Semitism. Distaste for Jews ran rife in the French middle and lower middle classes of the late nineteenth and early twentieth centuries. The Dreyfus affair brought latent hatreds into the open.

During Céline's years in obscurity, notably at the Clichy clinic, he had noted with rancor the seeming professional and social success of what he took to be a freemasonry of Jewish physicians and literati. His anarchic pacifism—his conviction that France could not survive another bout of mass slaughter—persuaded him that European Jewry was the principal menace: it, and it alone, could by its internationalism, by its opposition to Hitler, plunge the Continent into a second Armageddon. "Above all, war must be avoided," he wrote. "War, for us as we are, means the end of the show, the final tilt into the Jewish charnel house." Like so many of his generation, Destouches the public-health epidemiologist had imbibed diverse fashionable theories on racial pollution and eugenics. Notoriously, the Jew was the bacillus whose resistant ubiquity infected, with miscegenation, the blood (weakened by war) of nobler breeds. And what of the manifest Jewish role in the birth and dissemination of Bolshevism, the red spectre in the East?

However, even if we mix this potent brew, much remains puzzling in the cry for massacre which rings through *Bagatelles pour un Massacre* and *L'École des Cadavres*. Adjuring Western civilization to eliminate all Jews—men, women, and children—and to eradicate their very shadow from mankind, Louis-Ferdinand Céline in these voluminous tracts exhibited virtuosities of detestation, of incitement for which there are, fortunately, few analogues in literature and political rhetoric. It is, physically and mentally, well-nigh impossible to read those many hundreds of pages. And yet. As one forces oneself to leaf through this or that passage, the flashes of stylistic genius, of verbal incandescence strike one as might a brusque shiver of light across the sheen of a cesspool. (Coleridge noted the transient sparkle of starlight in his brimming chamber pot.) These writings are not the momentary aberration of a crank lamed in brain and body, visited by tormenting headaches and humming in his ears. Their sick and sickening power is that—momentarily, at least—of *Journey to the End of Night* and of the masterpieces to come.

Two conjectures may be worth making. As in Jonathan Swift, so in Céline the wellspring of imagination, of unleashed eloquence, is hatred. Normally, and in respect of aesthetic form, hatred is short of breath; it does not fill major spaces. But in a handful of masters—Juvenal, Swift, Céline—an enraged misanthropy, a nausea in the face of the world, generates full-scale designs. The monotone of loathing becomes symphonic. As Sartre, a close student of Céline, remarked, there is about the urban Jew something that concentrates to a singular pitch the infirm humanity of man. The Jew is not only human but a touch more human than most. In this murky light, hatred of Jews is the natural distillation of a generalized contempt for the human race. Seeking a visible target for his hatred of human ugliness, corruption, greed, vanity, myopia, Destouches swerved onto the Jew. Put *l'homme* where a demented sentence reads *le youpin* ("the kike"), and you have passages of a Biblical greatness—edicts of damnation issued over the Sodom and Gomorrah we have made of our world.

The second point is harder to get in focus. Céline's private manner and literary work are immersed in a black laughter of Rabelaisian proportions. There is in this Cyclopean mirth the notorious merriment of the medical student at his first cadaver. It has a precedent in the riddling, near-hysterical sendup of the tragic plots (which the audience has just experienced) in the Greek satyr plays. Dante lets drop a few mordant jests in Hell. Franz Kafka, having read his "Metamorphosis" to an appalled, speechless group of intimates, doubled over with helpless hilarity. It is at some bizarre level possible to apprehend Céline's anti-Semitic outpourings as parodistic, as some sort of practical joke gone mad. A surrealist clowning, a death's-head Mexican carnival are not far off. *Guignol's Band* is a characteristic Céline title; the "massacre" goes with the "bagatelle" (a word that Céline took to originally signify the tricks and turns of a buffoon or mountebank). A guest at a glittering assemblage of Nazi masters and collaborators, the unkempt Céline did an imitation of Hitler; at the climax, a ranting Führer assured the Jews that he was herding them into camps only so that he might more readily come to a secret agreement with them and share world hegemony. In short, there could be near the rabid heart of Céline's dance for genocide a deranged tomfoolery, the impishness of a child vandal. This is no apologia. It may well make matters worse.

Céline's flight and exile occasioned two further classics. *Castle to Castle* narrates the grotesque twilight of the Vichy régime in Sigmaringen, an operetta town set aside by the retreating Germans for their unwelcome guests. The famous telegraphic and filmic techniques that made the *Journey* a pivot in modern fiction and prose are fiercely compacted here. As only great works of art can, *Castle to Castle* realizes a supreme concision within an extended, open-ended construct. (Observe the economy, the elision, and the breadth in the counter-grammatical French title, *D'un Château l'Autre*.) The depiction of Pétain's miniature court in Sigmaringen Castle between November, 1944, and March, 1945, is incomparable in its hollow laughter. When we follow the scene in which a lone R.A.F. fighter, droning overhead, threatens to scatter the Maréchal's quaking retinue during a ceremonious morning constitutional—Pétain himself, of course, continued to promenade upright, unflinching and cretinously majestic—the sense of a Shakespearean register in Céline becomes insistent.

Here, as in Shakespeare's history plays, the pageant and the proximate ordure, the magnificence of sovereign postures and the underbelly of common need, the monumental and the intimate interact in counterpoint. Here, also, no less than in the masters of the sixteenth century (Montaigne, Rabelais, Shakespeare), a peculiar sensuality of thought is at work: Céline modulates the complex dynamics of political and social debacle into smell, into sound, into the touch of skin and fabric. The despair of the condemned hooligans, the heightened erotic compulsions of fugitives on the rim of the abyss literally leave a taste in Céline's, and the reader's, mouth. And, far more than Shakespeare, Céline uses the electrified sensibility of animals, Bébert first and foremost, to enrich the range of perceptions. (Hence the marvellous encounter between Field Marshal von Rundstedt and Tomcat von Bébert in "Rigodon," the weakest of the three memoirs of exile.) "North" takes up the wild narration of escape, hiding, and Danish incarceration. It excoriates the trial that Céline was subject to in absentia and his official relegation to national disgrace: "Ministers, satraps, Dien-Pen-Hu everywhere! tail-turning and pink underwear!" Vitoux believes that *North* is perhaps Céline's greatest book. Unquestionably, it contains visions of Inferno—of human decomposition on the spectral flatlands of Brandenburg, in blazing Berlin, at the Danish border, and in the papier-mâché aura of Elsinore—that border on Dante. The panoramas of the apocalyptic in Günter Grass, in William Burroughs, in Norman Mailer, and also in the most convincing Vietnam War films and in the journalistic vignettes of black skies over Kuwait all come after Céline.

The preludes to his art are less evident. Rabelais is always invoked. *King Lear* and *Timon of Athens* may have mattered, together with the insight that there are elective affinities between Shakespeare's clowns and his sadists, between Falstaff and Iago, between Malvolio and his merry tormentors. Dostoyevsky remains a possibility. He was much read, dramatized, and imitated in the Paris of the twenties and thirties. Something of the oracular sweep of Victor Hugo's leviathan novels and historical-philosophical epic poems seems to have resonance in the *Journey*. There is the elusive background noise of Rimbaud's lyric execrations. On the whole, however, a pedantic hunt for precedents is futile. *Journey to the End of Night* poured lavalike out of the deeps and crust of language as these had been dislocated by world war. In a Europe in which upward of twenty thousand men had been pounded to mud in a single day of battle, in which a third of a million corpses lay unburied between the lines at Verdun, traditional discourse, the similes of reason, the stabilities of the literate imagination had become a mockery. The shrill in Céline's ear somehow brought with it the new grammars of hysteria, of mass propaganda, of self-deafening. The rock beat, the hammering of heavy metal, of sound as a drug, first detonate inside language in the "Journey." Their suffocating echo has not ceased.

But the bigger question nags. Does aesthetic creativity, even of the first order, ever justify the favorable presentation of, let alone systematic incitement to, inhumanity? Can there be literature worth publication, study, critical esteem which suggests racism, which makes attractive or urges the sexual use of children? (Dostoyevski stands at the edge of this very penumbra.) The liberal case against all censorship is often cant. If serious literature and the arts can educate sensibility, exalt our perceptions, refine our moral discriminations, they can, by exactly the same token, deprave, cheapen, and make bestial our imaginings and mimetic impulses. I have wrestled with this conundrum during some forty years of reading, writing, and teaching. The Céline "case" (as Henry James might have called it, with unquiet fascination) is exemplary either way. By comparison, Ezra Pound's cracker-barrel Fascism, the deeply incised anti-Semitism of T. S. Eliot, and W. H. Auden's call for "the necessary murder" (this time at behest of the left) are thin stuff. It is the sheer weight of Céline's racist vituperations, their material summons to slaughter, the absence of any but fitful or sardonic regrets, inwoven with a structural genius for psychological revelation and dramatic narrative, that press the question. Would that Vitoux had faced these issues.

As luck would have it, the naked savageries come after the *Journey* and do not disfigure, except in an almost farcical, perhaps deliberately loony guise, the best of *Castle to Castle* and of *North*.

It is these inventions which, rightly, secured Céline's inclusion in the Pléiade edition, apex of the French Parnassus, at the time of his death. Nonetheless, there is no escaping the gargantuan trash of the middle years or the unison of hatred, of contempt for woman and Jew, at the backbone of Céline's achievement. In his case, at least, we make out the causal relations, all too taut, between the man and his creations. The dilemma posed by his admirer, contemporary, and fellow-collaborator Lucien Rebatet is even thornier. Both the Germans and Vichy found Céline an embarrassment—they could make nothing of his lacerating drolleries. Rebatet was a true killer, a hunter-down of Jews, Resistance fighters, and Gaullists. Waiting for execution (he was subsequently amnestied), Rebatet completed *Les Deux Étendards* (as yet untranslated into English). This ample novel is among the hidden masterpieces of our time. It is, moreover, a book of unfailing humanity, brimful of music (Rebatet was for a spell France's foremost music critic), of love, of insight into pain. The young woman at the pivot of the tale is no less informed by the radiant pressures of maturing life than is the Natasha of *War and Peace*. What can possibly give us any intelligible grasp of the connections between the abject, twisted Rebatet and the wonders of his fiction? Where are the bridges in the labyrinth of that soul?

I have no answers. My instinct is that *Death on the Installment Plan* and the *Bagatelles* should molder in library stacks. Recent reissues strike me as an unforgivable exploitation for political or market reasons. The great "fact-fictions" stand. Their wild song makes the language live and makes it new. The man Destouches remains inexcusable. But even on this point Bébert might beg to differ.

August 24, 1992

THE FRIEND OF A FRIEND

IT MAY WELL be that scholarship of the very first order is as rare as great art or poetry. Some of the gifts and qualities it exacts are obvious: exceeding concentration, a capacious but minutely precise memory, finesse and a sort of pious skepticism in the handling of evidence and sources, clarity of presentation. Other requisites are scarcer and more difficult to define. The truly great scholar has a truffle hound's nose for the hidden but key document, for the concatenation of apparently disparate circumstances. He glimpses the purloined letter where others stare at wallpaper. Like a dowser, he senses the significant deeps underneath the long-trodden surface. He detects the flaw in the crystal, the false note in the archive, the covert pressure of that which has been falsified or gagged. He adheres obstinately to what Blake called "the holiness of the minute particular" but unfolds from it the application, the generalizing inference, that can alter the whole landscape of our historical, literary, and social perceptions.

But even these talents and their infrequent combination do not determine what is crucial to preeminent scholarship. No less than the master translator or actor or performer of music, the truly great scholar becomes as one with his material, however abstruse, however recondite. He melts the strength of his own personality and technical virtuosity into the historical epoch, the literary or philosophic text, the sociological fabric that he is analyzing and presenting to us. In turn, that fabric, that set of primary sources, will take on something of its interpreter's voice and style. It will become his without ceasing to be itself. There is now an ancient China that is Joseph Needham's, a Hellenistic civilization that speaks in the accents of the late Arnaldo Momigliano, a mapping of grammars which will for a long time to come carry the imprint of Roman Jakobson. Yet in each case the alchemy reinstates the strength of the material.

Gershom Scholem's scholarship was of this rare, life-giving kind. Not only have his studies of the Cabbala altered, albeit controversially, the image of Judaism—the understanding that even an agnostic Jew now has of his psychological and historical provenance—but his explorations, translations, and presentations of Cabbalistic writings exercise a formidable influence on literary theory at large, on the ways in which non-Jewish and wholly agnostic critics and scholars read poetry. Scholem's essays, many composed in a pellucid, classical German prose (bad writing is a symptom of poor scholarship), encompass concerns far beyond the Cabbalistic. There has been no shrewder, more sombrely acute commentator on the drama of German Judaism, on the ambiguities in the condition of modern Israel, on the role of Biblical studies and translations in an increasingly secularized age. Scholem's often strangely ironic, subversive addictions were manifold: like William James (and there are other analogies), he took the play of intellect and the pluralities of human feeling for his province. Every manifestation of religious consciousness, of mythical imagining, of creative illusion fascinated him. But so did mathematics, the anatomy of legal discourse, and anthropology. Much of Scholem's voluminous production is esoteric not only in subject matter—the arcana of medieval and Chassidic mysticism, of Gnostic cosmology, of Renaissance hermeticism and magic—but also in its means of statement. Masterpieces of erudition, of problem-solving remain, unavoidably, enclosed in learned journals and in Hebrew. But Scholem's major works, such as *Origins of the Kabbalah* and the spellbinding study of Sabbatai Sevi, the mystical pseudo-Messiah (both published by Princeton), are aimed at the literate public, as are those masterpieces in (relative) miniature: Scholem's personal recollections, his monograph on mystical visions of creation, and his memoir of Walter Benjamin. And in some cases translations into English contain updated material and editorial help lacking in the Hebrew or German first versions. A great servant of insight has been handsomely served.

Scholem and Benjamin first met in 1915, when Benjamin was twenty-three and Scholem seventeen. Their friendship has become the stuff both of legend and of scholarly investigation. It manifests strong points of affinity. Benjamin and Scholem were German Jews uncannily alert to the marginal yet also creative ambience of their personal and social condition. They were men of the mind—of learning, of citation and commentary in an almost rabbinic vein. Each was, in his own quarter, an addict of ancient books, a systematic bibliophile and collector. They were virtuoso practitioners of German prose in very distinct registers but with a shared purity of expression, whose very mastery told of something not wholly native, not unconsciously inherited. There was in both Scholem and Benjamin a streak of anarchy, a radical distrust of established structures and conventions. (Both succeeded in slipping into Switzerland during the First World War, Scholem having feigned severe neurotic symptoms when summoned by his draft board.) Most important, both Benjamin and Scholem chose to approach central philosophic, historical, and psychological problems from an exotic edge. Scholem revolutionized the study of Judaism by his philological-editorial investigations of extreme esoterica—

of sometimes crazed heresies, of pathologies of speculative reverie. Analysis of children's books and toys; of nineteenth-century photographs; of the "lost" dramaturgy and emblem books of the German baroque; of the emporiums and department stores that sprang up in the Paris of the Second Empire led Benjamin to suggestions, to "illuminations" (his own designation, borrowed from Rimbaud), that are today at the heart of structuralism, of cultural sociology, and of semiotics.

But the differences between the two men were trenchant. Paradoxically, Scholem's immersion in religious mysticism originated in a deeply ironical, skeptical world view. I had the testing privilege of knowing Scholem in his later years, of seeing him in Jerusalem, Zurich, and New York. I cannot even begin to venture an informed guess as to whether this inspired expositor of the Cabbalistic meditation on the self-divisions of the Divine Oneness, on the emanations of light from the Godhead, on the "breaking of the vessels" at the moment of creation believed or did not believe in God. The quizzicalities in Scholem's smile and the hints of a deep-lying Voltairean merriment were legion. Benjamin, on the other hand, was that rare creature: a modern mystic, an initiate of occult realms of foresight, of hermetic symbolism, of white magic. Benjamin, who gave to the sociological-economic context of our consciousness a new precision, who was swiftly responsive to the media revolution in photography, film, and radio, who made a more or less private, heretical Marxism a vital component of his outlook, was the real Cabbalist. (He also experimented with drugs—a foray into unreason from which Scholem recoiled.)

An interest in Zionism was a powerful bond between the two men, though the ways they were to put it into practice were to prove from the outset irreconcilable. With astringent clairvoyance, Scholem sensed the potential for catastrophe in the German-Jewish amalgam. It became blindingly plain to him that a serious commitment to Jewish identity must entail knowledge of the Hebrew language and life in Israel. There is in Scholem's reconquest of the Cabbalistic past for Jewish cognition and for the general history of religious thought a vehement "Zionism," a return to a Holy Land. Benjamin flirted ardently with the notion of emigration to what was then Palestine. Time and again, he eagerly informed Scholem of his intended study of Hebrew. In 1929, and again in the mid-nine-teen-thirties, under the aegis of an impatient Scholem, Benjamin declared himself to be on the verge of departure from a doomed Europe. Nothing came of these urgent, troubled impulses. Scholem went to Jerusalem in 1923. He died, honored, his great work done, in 1982. Benjamin, worn to utter despair, hunted, his writings dispersed or fragmentary, committed suicide in a sordid hole on the French-Spanish frontier in 1940. (Rumor had it that the straggling refugees who had made it across the border would be returned to the French police and thus to Nazi mercies.)

But it could not have been otherwise. Walter Benjamin was among the last and most inspired of Central Europeans, where centrality implies both a geographical notion—that of the spaces defined for emancipated Judaism by Frankfurt-Vienna-Prague-Paris—and the concept of the European historical genius as it is articulated in French and in German. Like Adorno, like Ernst Bloch and other founders of and witnesses to the so-called Frankfurt School of critical theory and of cultural philosophy, Benjamin could not sever his own polyglot identity, his role in the intelligentsia, his very physique—that of the coffeehouse sage par excellence—from the fatality of Europe. And he left for too late the chance of escape to America—a chance that his peers and friends (Adorno, Bloch, Horkheimer, Brecht) seized upon with varying degrees of insightful opportunism.

A key thread in *The Correspondence of Walter Benjamin and Gershom Scholem: 1932–40*, translated by Gary Smith and André Lefevere (Schocken), is the fascinating difference between Scholem's Messiah and Benjamin's. For Scholem, the messianic—whose immensely rich, diverse forms he had diagnosed in monographs, in his magisterial *Major Trends in Jewish Mysticism*, and, above all, in his epic of Sabbatai Sevi—was inseparable from a material, historically grounded homecoming to Israel. It was with arch delight that Scholem insinuated into the Cabbalistic repertoire a parable he himself had invented: that of a coming of the Messiah which would leave all things *very slightly* altered and would therefore be unnoticed—except in Israel, the establishment of which state would itself be the best available evidence of the messianic. Benjamin's vision, which centered on Paul Klee's depiction of the "Angelus Novus"—the angel of history, whom a stormwind always backs away from us—was altogether other. The messianic did not signify Zionism. It implied the recovery of the voices of the humbled and the defeated, plowed under by history and historians. It would restore the lost Adamic tongue that secretly underlay all human languages, and whose generative presence made both possible and impossible the act of translation. For Benjamin, the coming of the Messiah would reveal itself via a transparency to truth, to social justice, to loving rationality extending beyond Judaism and the rebirth of Israel (miraculous as he sensed that to be).

The translation of this correspondence has the virtue of clarity. (There are a hundred and twenty-eight letters in all; some letters prior to 1932 seem to have perished, and there is a touch of wizardry to Scholem's discovery of his own side of the exchange in East Germany in October, 1966.) It does not (it cannot) convincingly echo the differences in the tonality of the two writers—differences that reveal persistent dissonances in their tempers. Beneath even the most affectionate—at moments, teasing—manner of Scholem runs a thread of authority, of exasperation in the face of illusion and of what he takes to be breaches of logic. Benjamin's tonality is one of flickering subtlety, of a seemingly evasive yet finely inward attempt to give expression to intangibles, to necessary ambiguities, to a vibrato of perceptions and intentions which he himself characterized by the word "aura."

In the early spring of 1934, for example, Scholem's harried clearsightedness as to the European situation and Benjamin's incapacity to don the indispensable life belt brought the relationship near to breaking. Benjamin on the third of March:

> My existence is about as precarious as it could be and depends each day anew on the good Lord himself—to say the same thing in a more prudent way. And by that I do not mean just the help I get from time to time, but also my own initiative, which is more or less aimed at a miracle.

Benjamin's waiting for the miraculous had a tenor at once therapeutic—it kept him alive—and disabling, in that it further diminished the utility, the moral and metaphysical status, of mere rational action. Scholem's view of possible divine aid was pragmatic. He strove to find a professional berth for Benjamin in Israel; he labored to get Benjamin's works published or noticed. But his vexation is unmistakable. "How your situation will really develop is becoming increasingly uncertain to me," he wrote, and "Many facts of our correspondence must have escaped your memory, as you no longer remember what seemed to draw you to an explanation of your situation. . . . We are debating with feigned positions, and I do not view this with pleasure."

Moreover, it wasn't only Benjamin's vacillations with regard to refuge in Palestine which provoked Scholem but, from 1924 onward, his exceedingly complicated involvement with Marxism. Scholem knew of Benjamin's personal, erotic relationship with a woman of Communist persuasion. He knew of his friend's trip to Moscow in 1926. Scholem's older brother had played a prominent, tragic role in the German Communist Party. Scholem bitterly resented the growing influence of Brecht's work and person over Benjamin (who spent crucial weeks with Brecht in the latter's Danish exile). Scholem's politics, if any, were those of disenchantment, of fastidious irony, even sarcasm, at the inveterate spectacle of human folly and barbarism.

But Scholem misread Benjamin's heretical, profoundly inventive resort to Marxist theories of history and to the rhetorical instruments of dialectical materialism. Certain friendships from within Communism helped Benjamin to lighten the dark of his almost unnatural solitude. At numerous points in the political awfulness of the nineteen-thirties, Communism, even Stalinism, seemed to offer the only effective resistance to the triumphant tide of Fascism and Nazism. Scholem had no access to Benjamin's posthumously published Moscow diary. In it he would have found clear evidence of Benjamin's skepticism, of his aversion to the actual climate of Soviet society. Yet that aversion did not negate the suggestive strength of Marx's analyses of nineteenth-century capitalism or the instigations to an economic-materialist understanding of the creation and dissemination of intellectual and artistic works which we find in Marxist aesthetics. Benjamin's pioneering studies of the mass reproducibility of art works through photography and color facsimile, his probing insights into the interface between high culture and the market, his preliminary analyses for an intended magnum opus—an anatomy of "Paris, the Capital of the Nineteenth Century"—were underwritten by a personal struggle with Marxist principles. Hence the affinities with the strategically astute, personalized Marxism of Brecht's plays and critical tracts.

Above all, Scholem bridled at what he intuited, uneasily, to be Benjamin's imaging of Marxism as a natural variant of Judaic messianic eschatology—of the central Judaic investment in millenarian hope. Grimly informed, Scholem saw the political oppression, the human misery to which Marxism-Leninism and its fellow-travellers were heading. He did not choose to perceive the tragic dimensions of that degeneration from messianic ideals, from the Utopian but incessant call for social justice as it is already eloquent in the Prophets. Benjamin's partly mystical annunciation of a "recuperation of history"—of the imposition on history of moral criteria—had arisen precisely from a Moscow-Jerusalem dream. Without this doomed hybrid, he could not have produced much of his finest work—in particular, his terse, terminal masterpiece, "Theses on the Philosophy of History." Much later, reflecting on Benjamin's genius and on the series of miracles which had made possible the survival of the "lost" texts, Scholem would concede (I heard him do so) that his friend's intricate dance with and around Marxism had had its uses. At the time, it struck him as a vulgar waste and betrayal of rare gifts.

What kept the dialogue going through thick and thin, what gives it enduring stature, is the successive discussions of Kafka. Subconsciously, perhaps, Benjamin and Scholem reverted to Kafka each time their mutual relations were under stress. The result is a series of readings—of critical delineations—of a penetrative originality. By comparison, the self-serving juggleries of current deconstruction or post-structuralism are embarrassing. Over and over, Scholem and Benjamin bring to bear on Kafka's elusive inexhaustibility an imaginative reach very nearly equal to its object. One would like to quote page after page. I limit myself to two examples. Here is Scholem to Benjamin on September 20, 1934 (in reference to *The Castle*):

> And yet Kafka's women bear the signs of other things to which you pay too little attention. The castle or officialdom with which they have such a horribly undefinable but precise relationship is clearly not just your primal world, if it is that at all. If it were the primal world, then what need would there

have been to make the women's relationship to it into a riddle? Everything would have been clear, whereas in reality everything is not clear and their relationship to officialdom is very exciting, especially since officialdom itself even warns against them (for instance, through the mouth of the chaplain). Rather, the castle or officialdom is something the "primal world" must first be related to.

You ask what I understand by the "nothingness of revelation"? I understand by it a state in which revelation appears to be without meaning, in which it still asserts itself, in which it has *validity* but *no significance*. A state in which the wealth of meaning is lost and what is in the process of appearing (for revelation is such a process) still does not disappear, even though it is reduced to the zero point of its own content.

The discrimination between *"validity"* and *"significance"* is of the utmost pertinence to all of Kafka's works.

Or take Benjamin's great letter—an essay of extreme density—dated June 12, 1938. Even extended quotation would do little justice to its depth:

> Kafka eavesdropped on tradition, and he who listens hard does not see.
>
> The main reason why this eavesdropping demands such effort is that only the most indistinct sounds reach the listener. There is no doctrine that one could learn and no knowledge that one could preserve. The things one wishes to catch as they rush by are not meant for anyone's ears. This implies a state of affairs that negatively characterizes Kafka's works with great precision. ... Kafka's work represents tradition falling ill. ...
>
> This much Kafka was absolutely sure of: First, that someone must be a fool if he is to help; second, that only a fool's help is real help. The only uncertain thing is: Can such help still do

a human being any good? ... Thus, as Kafka puts it, there is an infinite amount of hope, but not for us. This statement really contains Kafka's hope; it is the source of his radiant serenity.

Note—and this is characteristic of Benjamin's allegories of reading—how the analysis itself becomes a parable in Kafka's manner.

An immense sadness shadows even the more informal and momentarily optimistic of these letters. They were sent as Europe went into nightmare. In Palestine, moreover, Scholem not only experienced directly the violence of early clashes between Arabs and Jewish settlers but had unflinching intuitions of the intractable enmities that lay ahead. And yet this is, in its own way, a book of rejoicing. It celebrates the elixir of intellectual passion—the capacity of the human mind and nervous system to plunge into abstract, speculative interests even in, or most particularly in, the face of personal adversity and sorrow. It bears unstinting witness to the strength within outward weakness which has often been the password to survival of humanism and of the hunted. Here, at last, and not on the laconic plaque in a grim cemetery wall, Walter Benjamin has his *in memoriam*. And it is one wholly inseparable from the wonder, perhaps deeper than love, that is friendship.

January 22, 1990

BAD FRIDAY

OUR VEXED CENTURY would be much thinner without the witness of Simone de Beauvoir, without the power of that prodigious woman to make her ardent life a critique of gender, of society, of literature and politics. And Hannah Arendt persists as a pivotal figure in political and social theory, and as one of the compelling voices out of the totalitarian dark. But neither woman was a philosopher in any strict sense. Here extreme precision is needed. Philosophic thought is that which bears on questions rather than answers; where answers arise, they turn out to be new questions. The honor of the craft is that of disinterestedness, of an abstention from practical yield. The philosophic stance—notably in its metaphysical reach and in where it touches (as it must, whether in acquiescence or denial) on the theological—is, in the rigorous sense of the word, unworldly. Characteristically, there lodges in the philosophic sensibility a certain indifference to, or even distaste for, the human body. By these harsh lights, there has been in the Western tradition only one woman philosopher of rank: Simone Weil.

The price that Simone Weil paid for her eminence came near to being wholly unbearable. She consumed her own health to the point of willed early death. She inhabited her body as if it were a condemned hovel. She declared a detestation of her own rudimentary femininity, and stridently suggested that philosophical and mathematical achievements of lasting force were the prerogative of men—that some disorder or weakness in the very grain of womanhood militated against the examined life as demanded by Socrates, by Descartes, or by Kant. (Simone Weil's brother, André, is among the masters of twentieth-century algebraic geometry.) At every possible point and beyond, Simone Weil chose thought against life, logic against the pragmatic, the laser of analysis and enforced deduction against the fitful half-light, the compromise, and the muddle that allow the rest of us to carry on our existence. Like Pascal, like Kierkegaard, and like Nietzsche, but lacking the vanities of eloquence which attach even to these purists, Weil experienced her short life (1909–43) as a trial whose meaning—whose sole dignity—lay in defeat.

The bare facts have been made familiar in biographies like that by her friend Simone Pétrement (1973) and in the closely documented study published in 1981 by Gabriella Fiori. Scholarly publication of Simone Weil's complete writings is currently in progress, and almost every facet of her activities—religious, philosophical, literary, political, social—has been or is being combed through. In ways she would have despised (though ambiguously), the fat men of commentary and adulation are feasting on this most emaciated and self-erasing of lives.

We know of her childhood in the privileged ambience of emancipated French Judaism, of the conspiratorial intimacies and rivalries that knit her to her brother. There have been detailed investigations of the formative impact on Weil of the most charismatic and influential of French lycée teachers, the legendary "thought master" Émile Chartier, who wrote under the name of Alain. Simone Weil immersed herself with equally febrile obsession in diverse Marxist, anarcho-Marxist, and Trotskyite workers' movements and in Greek and Cartesian philosophy. She taught in various provincial secondary schools so far as her chronic headaches allowed. She visited Germany to judge at first hand Hitler's social revolution. Her engagement in the Spanish Civil War ended in macabre farce. (She stepped accidentally into a pan of boiling oil and had to be evacuated in agony.) During the Vichy regime, Weil tilled vineyards, wrote, dabbled in clandestine propaganda and recruitment in and around Marseilles. Having accompanied her parents to safety in New York (only Harlem found grace in her bitter eyes), she tugged at every available string to be allowed to join the Free French in London. There she harried de Gaulle and his staff with heroic schemes. She demanded to be parachuted into Occupied France. She urged an enterprise whereby a bevy of sternly angelic women would enter battle lines in order to tend the wounded and the dying. De Gaulle, who, quite coolly, deemed Weil to be deranged, assigned her the presumably harmless task of social and political planning for postwar France. The voluminous blueprint that resulted remains a classic of urgent impracticality. Self-wasted in mind and body, sick of soul with frustrated ardor, Simone Weil literally passed away in a sanatorium outside London. Her grave, though it is not in consecrated ground, has become a place of pilgrimage.

In *Simone Weil: Portrait of a Self-Exiled Jew* (North Carolina) Thomas Nevin gives only a summary sketch of this *via dolorosa*. Nor does he intend an intellectual biography of Simone Weil in any direct form. His dense study aims to explore and, so far as is possible, validate Weil's obsessions and work by using the fulcrum of Jewish self-hatred—the haunting talent that representative Jewish men and women have exhibited for self-banishment. The acid stain of intellectual and even politically oriented anti-Semitism on Simone Weil's consciousness, on her writings and social reflexes, has long been noted. It has been cogently related to the general theme of self-chastisement, even of masochism, which colors her works and days. But Professor Nevin's is the most thorough, persuasive examination we have so far of this at once repellent and inescapable context. There is not only learning and the poise of doubt in the book; there is courage and a salutary sadness.

Simone Weil's politics were peculiar in the extreme. She sought to conjoin with a partly Platonic ideal of the organic state a sense, both raging and enraged, of the humiliation and suffering visited on industrial labor. By a twist of logic, this young Jew of the French para-Marxist left came to make a series of approbatory comments on Hitler. She lauded his Roman grandeur, his spiritual and administrative seizure of collective hopes and needs: "He commands a country stretched to the maximum, he has a consuming, tireless and pitiless will . . . an imagination that fabricates history in grandiose proportions according to a Wagnerian aesthetic, and well beyond the present; and he is a born gambler." (Dostoyevsky might have written that, or, at certain moments, Trotsky.) To Weil anything was preferable to the unctuous hypocrisies, corruptions, and facile materialism of bourgeois capitalist democracy. Her ferocities on this issue derive from the burning radicalism of Amos and from Jesus' damning of wealth. They come out of Sparta and Lenin. But there lies at the core of her paradoxes and desolation a personal test of rare integrity. Three times, between December, 1934, and late August, 1935, this frail intellectual worked in heavy industry, under pressures and humiliations that almost drove her mad. When she invoked Robespierre, when she fantasized about a centralized revaluation and spiritualization of labor, Weil spoke at first hand. Radical chic was anathema to her.

Like other absolutists of thought, Simone Weil was drawn to violence. Though wrongheaded—she completely misses the festive glitter of archaic heroism—her essay on the *Iliad* does put in high relief the brutalities, the blood lust in the epic. At times, Weil was a pacifist, at other times eager for battle. Her schemes for feminine intervention, for sacrificial enlistment at the point of extreme peril in warfare tell of this same ambivalence. In reference to her Spanish commitment, she wrote: "Criterion: dread and the taste for killing. Avoiding both of these—how? In Spain, this seemed to me a heartbreaking effort, impossible to keep up for long. Make oneself such, then, that one is able to maintain it." The eventuality of torture fixed her mind darkly. She sought to rehearse for it. At moments, a jealousy of suffering possessed her. Her "telescopic sensitivity" (Nevin's apt phrase) isolated and magnified pain and terror both in her and in others. Like Pascal, like certain great painters and narrators of agony (both suffered and inflicted), she imagined materially, she reflected and analyzed with her nerve ends.

The politics in her late essays and in her design for France reborn are a fearful but poignant muddle (and "fearful" is indeed the key). The shadow of Hegel, which Professor Nevin tends to overlook, is pervasive. She believed that Necessity, which is another name for the human condition—for the assembly-line pile drivers of history—bends man to its despotic purpose. To endure, to have some access to that which is divine in destined processes, men and women must have the opportunity to discipline their perceptions, to contemplate with utmost stoic concentration the facts and obligations of their estate. The political-social desideratum is one that insures a space for such acts and, ideally, for such continuities of concentration. (More than once, Weil flirted longingly with fantasies of incarceration.) Famously, she called this posture of contemplative attention *l'enracinement*—"rootedness." It did not escape her notice, as it must not escape ours, that these criteria of rooted meditation—they fascinated T. S. Eliot when he read her—are all too readily reconcilable with certain modes of totalitarian, communitarian political authority, whether of the right or of the left. At her most lucid, Weil strikes one as a bizarre hybrid, an anarchic Platonist who would abdicate to the powers of the state whatever is needed to give privacy to the soul.

This same hybrid construct determines Simone Weil's philosophic essays and fragments. What she strives for obsessively is an amalgam of ancient Greece and Christology—the lessons of Socrates and those of Jesus. There was nothing novel in such a project. From the Gospel of John onward, such a congruence, known as Neoplatonism, has been argued and pursued in Western theology and idealist metaphysics. It is still dreamed of by the Renaissance and by the German philosophers after Kant. It is a part, perhaps subconscious, of the search and wonder of all who pick up a seashell on unbounded ocean shores (Coleridge's image) and hear in its murmuring more than the material echo of their own blood. What was perversely idiosyncratic was Weil's way of proceeding. She inventoried pre-Socratic philosophic fragments, the Platonic dialogues, and the texts of Greek lyric poets and dramatists in order to find passages in which Christ's coming, ministry, and Passion were prefigured. Prefiguration of the Gospels in the Old Testament (in, for instance, the Prophets, in the Psalms of the Suffering Servant, even in the Song of Songs) is, of course, a claim that has been made by Christianity since the time of the Church Fathers. But it is not the Hebrew writings to which Simone Weil adverts in her pilgrim's progress; it is Pythagoras, Pindar, Sophocles, and Plato.

Her dowsing is at once absurd and eerie. Acute Hellenist though she was, Weil was not above distorting and almost falsifying the manifest intent and context of the ancient Greek words. She deliberately confounds the next to nothing we know of Greek mystery cults and Orphic myths of rebirth with the concepts of baptism and of resurrection in Christianity. Her readings of Plato are so selective as to border on travesty. And yet. Her intimations of a common thirst for light on the other side of reason, but rationally urged and somehow communicable, sensible to human thought and discourse, are not always arbitrary. She felt in her bones the often tenuous, subterranean weave of metaphors, of symbolism, of ritual gestures that relate early and later Greek philosophy, and even paganism, to nascent Christianity. When it comes to certain Greek tragic texts, moreover, her commentaries have an aching immediacy. She relives the insolubles of contradictory justice in Orestes' matricide. She identifies, even more carnally and spiritually than Hegel and Kierkegaard did, with the person and fate of Sophocles' Antigone. She, too, knew of the unconditional love of brother and sister. She, too, was resolved on ethical defiance and self-sacrifice in the face of political terror. But, again, it is no accident that her Antigone emerges with more than a hint of Joan of Arc.

Weil's liaison with Roman Catholicism (the erotic tonalities in the word are fully justified) dates back at least to 1935–36. It was then that she began attending Mass, with varying frequency. Her encounter with Gregorian chant appears to have triggered an episode of a mystical and revelatory kind. In this respect, Weil's is not an isolated case. Other Jewish contemporaries of an uprooted and questing nature felt tempted by the aesthetic solemnity of Catholic worship and by the sheer eloquence of the Catholic message within European art and civilization. One recalls Walter Benjamin's immersion in the baroque, the turn toward Christ in Karl Kraus, and—most complex—Proust's resort to the world of the cathedrals and of Christian painting. One remembers the informing role of mystical Catholicism in the symphonies of Mahler. As devastation neared, much in the psyche and the sensibility of the European Jewish élite seemed to cast about for refuge. Characteristically, Simone Weil went a deeper, more jagged way.

She familiarized herself with the liturgy, with the Vulgate Bible of St. Jerome, with sacramental symbolism and doctrine. She met a kindred spirit in St. Augustine (as, on quite another plane, had Hannah Arendt). She sought out the French Thomists—the thinkers and writers who at the time were renewing Catholic awareness of the Church's main philosophical and logical source, Thomas Aquinas. These several impulses gathered all but irresistible force during Weil's exile in the South of France. Best known and best loved of her writings are the letters to the near-blind Dominican priest Joseph-Marie Perrin. It is to him that Weil, in a vein of impassioned, argumentative confessional, offered her inmost. And Perrin seemed destined to receive this tormented soul into the peace of the Church. Weil often knocked at the door, only to step back when it was lovingly opened. The shade of a shadow lay between her fervor, her constant identification of her own physical pains with Christ's suffering, and that act of baptism which now shone as the most natural of resolutions.

She did not take that last step. She reviled Catholic worldliness and the persecution of such inspired heretics as the Cathars. She read Catholicism to be emphatically Roman, which is to say, tainted with the imperialism, the enslavements, the authoritarian pomp of that ancient civilization she so abhorred. In the final reckoning, however, Weil's self-veto had a grimmer origin. She could not espouse a church whose roots lay in the synagogue.

Thomas Nevin is right, of course. Here, too, the crux (insidious image) is that of Simone Weil's self-denial, her repudiation of her own Judaism. Nauseatingly, she protested to the Vichy authorities that she ought not to be barred from employment under the race laws—she was not a Jew! Judaism was unacceptable to her. Only a handful of Jews escaped her sometimes hysterical censure: Amos, the teller of retribution on Israel; Job; Spinoza, who had been ostracized from the community. Relevant documents are sickening. Faced with early but unmistakable evidence of the Holocaust in progress, she took refuge in hostile silence, in "a frozen stare." In her notebooks she pondered the peculiar deracination and pariahdom of the Jew. "The so-called Jewish religion is a national idolatry that has lost all reality since the destruction of the nation," she wrote. "That is why a Jewish atheist is more atheistic than any other. He is so less aggressively, but more profoundly." With a very few, largely poetic exceptions, "the Old Testament is a tissue of horrors," celebrating a blood-hungry tribal deity whose primitive features and attributes come close to being those of a satanic Great Beast. Weil clawed at whatever she could find that had given

Judaism hope: "If the Hebrews, as a people, had carried God within them, they would have preferred to suffer the slavery inflicted by the Egyptians—and provoked by their own previous exactions—rather than to win freedom by massacring all the inhabitants of the territory they had to occupy." This in the midnight of the gas ovens.

Her attendant tastes in literature and in theological tonality were concordant. It was in T. E. Lawrence of Arabia that she envisioned the truest type of modern heroism. And it was in ascetic and mendicant Catholicism, which indicted most brutally the alleged materialism and obdurateness of the Jew, that she felt at home. From Paul of Tarsus to today, the history of Jewish self-hatred is a long and perplexing one. It is quite possible to read both Christianity and Marxism as great Judaic heresies sprung from the opaque pathologies of a suicidal self-rejection. The most ingenious, though in some measure deranged, advocate of Jewish inferiority and racial leprosy in modern polemics, Otto Weininger, was a Jew. Whether Simone Weil's contribution to this garbage was a symptom of some even deeper negation of sexuality and of her own gender, whether it enacted elements of deliberate self-humiliation in the face of what she judged to be a botched life, whether it traced the road to a slow suicide, no psychopathology can adequately explain. Such explanation would, moreover, and by Weil's own imperatives of philosophic integrity, be immaterial.

Why bother then? Simply because Simone Weil has left us a fragmented but substantial corpus of theological, philosophical, and political insights of rare pressure and illumination. Response is so perplexing because an unsparing honesty meshes the inspired with the pathological. Who else save Kierkegaard would at the moment of France's surrender to Hitler have found the sentence "This is a great day for Indo-China," in which a hideous insensibility is perfectly balanced by a political and humane clairvoyance of genius? The fall of metropolitan France was indeed glorious news for the subject peoples it had long lorded over in its far-flung colonies.

For Weil, the "crimes" of colonialism related immediately, in both religious and political symmetry, to the degradation of the homeland. Time and again, a Weil aphorism, a marginalium to a classical or scriptural passage, cuts to the heart of a dilemma too often masked by cant or taboo. She did not flinch from contradiction, from the insoluble. She believed that contradiction "experienced right to the depths of one's being means spiritual laceration, it means the Cross." Without which "cruciality" theological debates and philosophic postulates are academic gossip. To take seriously, existentially, the question of the significance of human life and death on a bestialized, wasted planet, to inquire into the worth or futility of political action and social design is not merely to risk personal health or the solace of common love: it is to endanger reason itself. The two individuals who have in our time not only taught or written or generated conceptually philosophic summonses of the very first rank but *lived* them, in pain, in self-punishment, in rejection of their Judaism, are Ludwig Wittgenstein and Simone Weil. At how very many points they walked in the same lit shadows.

But no analogy suffices. Weil represents what modern physics might call a "singularity." Some of her finest work—on Descartes, on the theory and practice of Marxism—belongs to normal philosophic and intellectual argument. She wrestles with the mystery of God's love as do the saints and doctors of the Church and the visionaries of the Middle Ages and the Baroque. Yet within a hair's breadth, as it were, of her ardent analytic rectitude, of her logical scruples and compassionate questioning, blow those "great winds from under the earth" evoked by Franz Kafka (another cousin in spirit). Some vein of madness is tapped.

The evidence patiently probed in Nevin's unsettling book points toward a twist of feeling at once sharp and deep-buried. In some way, this "chosen outsider" was jealous of God, of His infinite love, which she acknowledged mentally but could not bring to bear on the image she construed of her own identity. Jealous—as, perhaps, were St. Teresa of Avila and St. John of the Cross—of the agonies God had borne in the person of His martyred son. Black waters. To which it may be that the least inadequate response comes from a language at once desolate and sardonic—from the Yiddish, which she ignored or might have despised. Simone Weil was, undoubtedly, the first woman among philosophers. She was also a transcendent *schlemiel*.

March 2, 1992

THE LOST GARDEN

CERTAIN SENTENCES IN the book were right from the outset objects of legend and of parody. There was the opening, astounding in a work of anthropology and Amazonian travel: *"Je haïs les voyages et les explorateurs"* ("I hate travelling and explorers"). There was the coda—a leviathan of a sentence, clause piling on ornate clause, a baroque *sforzando* quavering to rest in the image, at once ludicrous and magical, of "the brief glance, heavy with patience, serenity, and mutual forgiveness, that, through some involuntary understanding, one can sometimes exchange with a cat" (a good stab at translation, yet one that misses both the pathos of *"alourdi de patience"* and the hint of almost theological grace in *"pardon réciproque qu'une entente involontaire permet parfois"*). *Tristes Tropiques* is now almost twenty years old. In the intervening period, Claude Lévi-Strauss has largely accomplished that revolution in anthropology, that renovation in the vocabulary, in the directions of argument proper to "the study of man" which *Tristes Tropiques* called for. He is, so far as the general climate of literacy goes, not only the most celebrated of living anthropologist-ethnographers but a writer whose apparently specialized technical treatises have penetrated sensibility at large. Lévi-Strauss's "structuralism," a term more fashionable than clearly defined, seems somehow pivotal to the current enterprise

in linguistics and psychology, in social studies and aesthetics. But
Lévi-Strauss's fame, the influence he exercises on the tone of our
culture and our high gossip (the suave, nerveless sheen that the
mass media reflect back on the life of the mind), has a paradoxical form. It has grown inversely to his standing with his own professional peers. From the point of view of fellow-anthropologists
and ethnographers, the curve goes something like this: Though
his field work in Brazil in the nineteen-thirties was brief and his
methodology perhaps controversial, Lévi-Strauss later produced a
classic study of kinship relations—*Les Structures Elémentaires de
la Parenté*, published in 1949. Together with a number of technical
papers written during his years in America and shortly thereafter,
this opus constitutes a fundamental development of the understanding of kinship and of primitive society initiated by Marcel
Mauss, Émile Durkheim, and the British school of anthropology. In
the early nineteen-fifties, in collaboration with Roman Jakobson,
Lévi-Strauss began arguing for seminal analogies, for reciprocities
of method and conception, between linguistics and anthropology.
This again was a stimulating move. There is clearly a good deal
to be learned from the possible concordance between the formal
structure of a language and the social structures it organizes and
mirrors (Lévi-Strauss's observation that a society cannot prohibit
that which it cannot name and classify, and that recognitions of allowed or forbidden kinship depend on a corresponding exactness
of linguistic designation, is of obvious depth and value). But such
parallels, where they can be shown to exist, must be handled with
extreme caution. To leap from the monographic scale to a universal model of how the human mind operates, to erect a vast theory
of mind and evolution on so fragile a base, is to abandon the ideals
of science. This, say the anthropologists, is what Lévi-Strauss has
done with, and since, *Tristes Tropiques*. He may be a writer of genius, a shaper of modern myths, a philosopher of sorts, but he is no
longer an anthropologist—responsible to the opaque boredom of

detail, to "that which is the case." A famous precedent lies at hand. To poets and dramatists, to the general public, Sir James Frazer was the prince of anthropologists; to his professional colleagues and immediate successors, he was a word-spinner trapped in a purple haze of his own making. Thus *Mythologiques*, the four-volume "mythology of myths," which has occupied Lévi-Strauss over the past fifteen years, will—when the translation is complete—be our *Golden Bough*.

This is a kind of constellation we recognize: a specialist transcends his own technical discipline and achieves great renown; the colleagues he has left behind close ranks in fastidious dismissal. It is the story of Marx and the academic economists, of Freud and the contemporary psychologists, of Toynbee and the historians. Matters are not sweetened when the new "star" expresses his impatience at the pettiness, at the guild-parochialism, of his sometime peers. (Lévi-Strauss happens to be a virtuoso of disdain.) After a spell—so say intellectual history and hagiography—the work of the great outsider is seen to have altered the whole of the field from which it broke away, and the detractors survive as acid footnotes in the Master's memoirs.

To this the answer must be a troubled yes and no. Whether or not Marx's analyses of social conflict are in any way "scientific," whether or not his predictions have had any verifiable force remain vexed questions. No one would doubt the stature of Freud's achievement, the shaping powers of his philosophic-literary vision on the prevailing climate of Western feeling. But the therapeutic model he sought to universalize, and the neurophysiological foundations he strove to establish for it, are proving increasingly elusive. The "hard-edged" currents in recent studies of the mind and of human behavior are not Freudian. The picture is not one, or not unambiguously one, of individual genius, jealous rejection by lesser colleagues, and subsequent apotheosis. What seems to happen is a development within one sensitive area of a traditional field. This development, which at first observes the conventions and professional idiom of the field, soon becomes too large, too problematic, to be located within established categories. It breaks away, pulling part of the field after it. New orderings emerge: "anthropological linguistics," "semiotics" (which is the systematic investigation of signs and symbols) have emerged from the crisis in classical anthropology, and from Lévi-Strauss's "gravitational pull' toward a combined view of language and biological-social structure. The quarrel between the great man and his pragmatic colleagues is often a symptom of transition and readjustment. There is a sense in which Lévi-Strauss's relation to anthropology was from the beginning as ambivalent, as inherently subversive as, say, was Marx's to classical economic and monetary theory. This "duplicity," this provocation make for the opaqueness and importance of *Tristes Tropiques*.

Its new edition and translation (Atheneum) supersedes the version of 1961. For reasons that have never been entirely clear, several chapters were omitted from the original English-language edition; these are now restored. Alterations made by Lévi-Strauss in the 1968 French edition are incorporated. To translate Lévi-Strauss is not only an arduous task but one performed under the exacting, censorious shadow of the begetter. Though their method is now and again somewhat ponderous and inflationary, precisely because it aims to clarify, to dissect the sinuous rhetoric of the original, John and Doreen Weightman have done an admirable job. One finds oneself reverting from Lévi-Strauss's language to their own when particular difficulties obtrude. And, being the translators of *Mythologiques*, the Weightmans have an unrivalled sharpness in rendering the genesis of Lévi-Strauss's vocabulary, in seeing how and where some of his characteristic attitudes began.

At one level, *Tristes Tropiques* is an intellectual autobiography, ironically perceptive of the distortions, of the self-dramatizations, complacent or condemnatory, that inevitably inflect a self-portrait.

But Lévi-Strauss's recollections of his academic career, at once brilliant and innerly void, lead to a passage that comes as near as any to giving the key to his lifework. Around the age of sixteen, he became acquainted with Freud's theories and the crucial writings of Marx. He saw in both a kind of *geology,* a promise of understanding in depth, a strategy of penetration below the crust of the apparent in man and in social history:

> At a different level of reality, Marxism seemed to me to proceed in the same manner as geology and psychoanalysis (taking the latter in the sense given it by its founder). All three demonstrate that understanding consists in reducing one type of reality to another; that the true reality is never the most obvious; and that the nature of truth is already indicated by the care it takes to remain elusive. For all cases, the same problem arises, the problem of the relationship between feeling and reason, and the aim is the same: to achieve a kind of *super-rationalism,* which will integrate the first with the second, without sacrificing any of its properties.

Difficult as it is, the passage affords an unmistakable clue. Combining Marx and Freud (toward both of whom Lévi-Strauss has a somewhat egalitarian attitude), using the paradigm of geology, with its sense of surface and underlying, formative strata—a paradigm already suggestive of modern linguistics—we must develop a kind of organic, unifying understanding of how "things mean." At this earlier stage in his thinking, Lévi-Strauss called this comprehension of structure a "superrationalism," which is not a helpful term. Today he might call it a *"mythologique,"* a rational logic of the ways ("myths") in which man pictures, articulates, and masters his biological, psychic, social condition. Only such comprehension (a word that entails "completeness"), only such understanding (a word that implies "going deep, going beneath") could justify the proud name "anthropology," *study of man*. To be an anthropologist in this total sense was to fulfill and conjoin the social-economic analyses of Marxism with Freud's reading of consciousness. For this, the young Lévi-Strauss was prepared to abandon philosophy and to head for a minor teaching post in São Paulo.

The conflict between *this* vision and that of the normal field-worker and ethnologist is all too obvious. Lévi-Strauss went on far-reaching, physically taxing expeditions into the interior of Brazil. *Tristes Tropiques* contains a detailed record of his life with several groups of Indians. In one case, this may well have been the first contact with a white man made since chance encounters in the sixteenth century. His notations of native diet, sexual mores, artifacts were copious and disciplined. He ate verminous food, was parched on the great plateaus, and stumbled through untouched forest. But the focus, the framework of diagnosis, was never that of the traditional anthropologist: confronting the elaborate facial designs traced by the Caduveo women, no "scientific" fieldworker would conclude that these women "trace the outlines of the collective dream with their makeup; their patterns are hieroglyphics describing an inaccessible golden age, which they extol in their ornamentation, since they have no code in which to express it, and whose mysteries they disclose as they reveal their nudity." No behavioral psychologist observing the isolated hamlets in the Brazilian interior would confidently affirm that these clusters of inhabitants "developed different forms of madness" in order to cope with rain, malnutrition, and desolation. As Lévi-Strauss traverses the lunar wastes of the interior, moreover, it is not so much the ethnography of the Nambikwara party with whom he is travelling that fascinates him: it is the relation to the Amerindian world of the telegraph line that threads, half abandoned, the barren wastes before them. "Completely virgin landscapes have a monotony which deprives their wildness of any significant value. They withhold themselves from man; instead of challenging him, they disintegrate under his gaze. But in this scrubland, which stretches endlessly into the distance, the incision of the *picada,* the contorted silhouettes of the poles and the arcs of wire linking them one to another seem like incongruous objects floating in space, such as can be seen in Yves Tanguy's paintings."

The symbolism is crucial. Like Joseph Conrad's famous image of a gunboat plopping absurd shells into a shoreline of impenetrable African forest, Lévi-Strauss's evocation of the telegraph line across the Mato Grosso states a fundamental doubt. It speaks of the rapacious illusions of the white man and of technology in their relation to the primitive world. But the rapacity and the illusions extend to, are perhaps most ironically manifest in, the very business of anthropology. Lévi-Strauss's obsessive insight at this point is, as he himself emphasizes, a rediscovery; the dubious nature of the anthropological approach, of the rational study of man as the West has developed it, was already apparent to Rousseau, Lévi-Strauss's true master. Only Western man—beginning as far back as Herodotus—has generated a systematic curiosity about other races and cultures; he alone has gone out to explore the remotest corners of the earth in quest of classification, of a comparative and contrastive definition of his own preëminence. This quest, so often disinterested and sacrificial, has, however, brought conquest and destruction with it. Analytic thought has in it a strange violence. To know analytically is to reduce the object of knowledge, however complex, however vital it may be, to just this: an object. It is to dismember. More than any other "knower," the anthropologist carries destruction with him. No primitive culture survives his visitation intact. Even the gifts he brings—medical, material, intellectual—are fatal to the life forms as he found them. The Western hunt for knowledge is, in a tragic sense, the final exploitation.

It is this fatality that gives to *Tristes Tropiques* its valedictory, even apocalyptic register. "A proliferating and overexcited civilization has broken the silence of the seas once and for all." Wherever the white traveller goes he finds the desolation, the cruel vestiges of the plundering and disease brought by his previous conquests. The Indian tribes, the landscapes the young Lévi-Strauss encountered were not Edenic, not "primitive" in the pure sense. They embodied a long chronicle of infection, ecological waste, and forced dislocation. It was not so much geographical isolation or the difficult terrain that made the forest people inaccessible. It was the brutal fact that complex linguistic-ethnic groups, once at home in a large territory, had now been reduced to a handful. "As far as I know, no one has seen the Mundé again since my visit, apart from a woman missionary who encountered one or two of them just before 1950 along the Upper Guaporé, where three families had taken refuge." Decimation has been the white man's irreparable guilt. But not entirely. Lévi-Strauss is too subtle, too ironic an observer not to suggest that there is in the ruin of primitive cultures a more secret mechanism of limitation, of destined inadequacy. The first explorers to reach Brazil and Central America found civilizations that had "reached the full development and perfection of which their natures were capable." The qualification is obscure but charged with an almost Calvinist edge of fatalism.

This "Calvinism" (Lévi-Strauss himself would prefer to call it "Schopenhauerian pessimism") generates its own punitive allegory. What the ethnographer found in his Amazonian forays was not paradise lost but a parody and a willful destruction of the last groves in the Garden of Eden. It was as if man, having been expelled from the Garden because he grasped the forbidden fruit of the tree of knowledge—a seizure that defines his eminence and solitude in the organic world—had turned back in rage and set out to uproot whatever traces there were in his landscape of the lost Eden. Lévi-Strauss senses in the ecological catastrophe, in our murderous yet also suicidal treatment of the environment, far more than mere greed or stupidity. Man is possessed of some obscure fury against his own remembrance of Eden. Wherever he comes on landscapes or communities that seem to resemble his own image of lost innocence, he lashes out and lays waste.

If *Tristes Tropiques* is, therefore, among the first classics of the current ecological anguish, it is also much more, being, in the final analysis, a moral-metaphysical allegory of human failure. It looks forward with haughty melancholy to the image of the globe—cooling, emptied of man, cleansed of his garbage—that appears in the coda of *Mythologiques*. There is melodrama in this anticipation and a touch of pomp (it is beautifully right that the chair Lévi-Strauss will in a few weeks occupy at the French Academy should be that of Montherlant). But there is also a profound, authentic sorrow. "Anthropology," says Lévi-Strauss in concluding *Tristes Tropiques*, can now be seen as "entropology": the study of man has become the study of disintegration and certain extinction. There is no darker pun in modern literature.

June 3, 1974

SHORT SHRIFT

SHOWN AN EPIGRAM of a line and a half, Nicolas de Chamfort (1741–94), himself a master of mordant brevity, remarked that it would have exhibited greater wit if it had been shorter. The epigram, the aphorism, the maxim are the haiku of thought. They seek to compact the greatest pointedness of insight into the fewest possible words. Almost by definition, and even where it sticks strictly to colloquial prose, the aphorism nears the condition of poetry. Its formal economy aims to startle in a flash of authority; it aims to be singularly memorable, as does a poem. Indeed, celebrated maxims or apothegms often modulate between great poetry or drama and the anonymity of the proverbial. Momentarily, we are at a loss to recall the exact and personal source. Who first taught us that "discretion is the better part of valor" or that "God tempers the wind to the shorn lamb"? In what text do we find the dictum, which helped to initiate an entire revolution in the history of perception and of form, that "nature imitates art"? The terse revelations of Shakespeare, Laurence Sterne, and Oscar Wilde have passed into the glory of common speech.

In French literature, aphorismic and epigrammatic modes play an exceptional role. The composition of *pensées,* of "thoughts" or "reflections" formulated as briefly as possible, is a distinctively

Gallic tradition. In Pascal—and this is a rare accomplishment in any language or literature—the aphorismic strategy extends to the most complex, sublime reaches of theology and metaphysics. In Paul Valéry, it affords a supremely concise elegance to a lifelong meditation on the nature of poetry and the arts. The maxims of La Rochefoucauld, of Vauvenargues, of Chamfort are very likely the most eloquent in the Western tradition. A contemporary poet, René Char, has deliberately effaced the distinction between the *sententia* (the Latin name for a one-sentence dictum or proposition) and the short lyric. At his best, Char, like Valéry, articulates a musical moment in thought.

Why this French predilection for the aphorismic? (In German, the aphoristic manner of Lichtenberg and of Nietzsche is openly indebted to the French precedent.) One answer lies with a proud, explicit Latinity. French literature and thought take pride in their affinity to the Roman source. Roman mores, in the domains both of political power and of discourse, attached eminent value to terseness. Not only was brevity the soul of wit, it was a convention of masculine command and self-command even under extreme pressure of private or civic peril. Much in the French practice of maxims and *pensées* appears to go back directly to the marmoreal authority and lapidary concision of Roman inscriptions. *"Ci gît Gide"* was André Gide's recommendation for his own epitaph. It is from its Latin inheritance that the French language itself draws its ideal of *la litote*. "Understatement" is a lame translation. A *litote,* as we find it persistently in the greatest of all French writers—in Racine—is the tightly, densely concentrated expression of some central immensity, or even enormity, in human recognitions and emotions. It is, at its most characteristic, that rush of silence which pilots report at the center point of a hurricane.

As I have said, the French tradition encompasses within the bounds of the maxim areas as diverse as religion and aesthetics, psychology and politics. But the dominant focus is that of the *mor-*

alistes. Again, translation is awkward. A *moraliste,* particularly as he flourished in the seventeenth and eighteenth centuries, brings to bear universal values and principles on problems of social conduct. He looks sharply at, he "needles," mundane conventions in the implicit light of eternity. The true *moraliste* moralizes only obliquely, by isolating laconically, by giving monumental formulation to some ephemeral but symptomatic gesture, rite, or received verity in the society of his day. The genius of La Rochefoucauld or of Vauvenargues consists in the exact wealth of observed human behavior which underwrites the sparsity, the seeming generality of his notations. Behind La Rochefoucauld's tranquil observation, as radical as any in the annals of insight, that there is something which does not displease us in the misfortunes of a good friend there lies not only a flash of individual scrutiny but a felt knowledge of the ways of the court and of the *beau monde* as comprehensive as that of Saint-Simon or of Proust.

Having emigrated from Bucharest to Paris on the eve of the Second World War, E.M. Cioran has, over the past four decades, established for himself an esoteric but undoubted reputation as an essayist and aphorist of historical-cultural despair. *Drawn and Quartered* (Seaver Books) is the translation of a text published in French, as *Ecartèlement,* in 1971. The maxims and reflections that make up the main part of *Drawn and Quartered* are preceded by an apocalyptic prologue. Gazing upon the immigrants, the hybrids, the rootless flotsam of humanity that now tide through our anonymous cities, Cioran concludes that it is indeed—as Cyril Connolly proclaimed—"closing-time in the gardens of the West." We are Rome in its febrile and macabre decline: "Having governed two hemispheres, the West is now becoming their laughingstock: subtle specters, end of the line in the literal sense, doomed to the status of pariahs, of flabby and faltering slaves, a status which perhaps the Russians will escape, those *last* White Men." But the dynamics of inevitable degradation extend far beyond the particular situation of the capitalist and technological Western sphere. It is history itself that is running down:

> In any case it is manifest that man has given the best of himself, and that even if we were to witness the emergence of other civilizations, they would certainly not be worth the ancient ones, nor even the modern ones, not counting the fact that they could not avoid the contagion of the end, which has become for us a kind of obligation and program. From prehistory to ourselves, and from ourselves to posthistory, such is the road toward a gigantic fiasco, prepared and announced by every period, including apogee epochs. Even utopianists identify the future with a failure, since they invent a regime supposed to escape any kind of *becoming:* their vision is that of *another* time within time … something like an inexhaustible failure, unbroached by temporality and superior to it. But history, of which Ahriman is the master, tramples such divagations.

The human species, intones Cioran, is beginning to put itself out of date. The only interest a *moraliste* and prophet of finality can take in man stems from the fact that "he is tracked and cornered, sinking ever deeper." If he continues on his doomed, sordid path, it is because he lacks the strength needed to capitulate, to commit rational suicide. Only one thing is absolutely certain of man: "He is stricken in his depths … he is rotten to the roots." (The plangent but self-mocking lilt of "rotten to the core, Maude" comes irresistibly to mind.)

What, then, lies ahead? Cioran replies:

> We advance *en masse* toward a confusion without analogy, we shall rise up one against the other like convulsive defectives, like hallucinated puppets, because, everything having become impossible and unbreathable for us all, no one will deign to live

except to liquidate and to liquidate himself. The sole frenzy we
are still capable of is the frenzy of the end.

The sum of history is "a futile odyssey," and it is legitimate—indeed,
compelling—"to wonder if humanity as it is would not be better
off eliminating itself now rather than fading and foundering in
expectation, exposing itself to an era of agony in which it would
risk losing all ambition, even the ambition to vanish." After which
rumination, Cioran bows out with a little pirouette of self-teasing
irony: "Let us then renounce all prophecies, those frantic hypotheses, let us no longer allow ourselves to be deceived by the image of
a remote and improbable future; let us abide by our certitudes, our
indubitable abysses."

The quarrel with this kind of writing and pseudo-thinking is
not one of evidence. The century of Auschwitz and of the ther-
monuclear-arms race, of large-scale starvation and totalitarian
madness may indeed be hastening toward a suicidal close. It is
conceivable that human greed, the enigmatic necessities of mutual
hatred which fuel both internal and external politics, and the sheer
intricacy of economic-political problems may bring on catastrophic
international conflicts, civil wars, and the inward collapse of aging
as well as of immature societies. We all know this. And this knowledge has been the undercurrent of serious political thought, of
philosophic debates on history, since 1914–18 and Spengler's model
of the decline of the West. Nor is it possible to refute an intuitive
sense, a persuasive intimation, of a sort of nervous exhaustion, of
entropy, in the inward resources of Western culture. We seem to
be governed by more or less mendacious dwarfs and mountebanks.
Our responses to crises display a certain somnambular automatism. Our arts and letters are, arguably, those of epigones. Per se,
Cioran's funeral sermon (and it has been uttered by many before
him) may well turn out to be right. As it happens, my own instincts
are only marginally more cheerful.

No, the objections to be urged are twofold. The passages I have quoted bear witness to a massive, brutal oversimplification. The grain of human affairs is, always has been, tragicomic. Hence Shakespeare's centrality and his refusal of absolute darkness. Fortinbras is a lesser being than Hamlet; he will very probably govern better. Birnam Wood will reflower after it has marched on Dunsinane. History and the lives of politics and of societies are far too manifold to be subsumed under any one grandiloquent pattern. The bestialities of our age, its potential for self-ruin are evident; but so is the plain fact that more men and women than ever before in the history of this planet are beginning to be adequately fed, housed, and medically cared for. Our politics are indeed those of mass murder, yet for the first time in recorded social history the notion is being articulated and realized that the human species has positive responsibilities toward the handicapped and the mentally infirm, toward animals and the environment. I have, often enough, written about the venom of current nationalism, about the virus of ethnic and parochial fury which impels men to slaughter their neighbors and reduce their own communities to ash (in the Middle East, in Africa, in Central America, in India). However, subtle but forceful countercurrents are beginning to emerge. Multinational organizations and businesses, the freemasonry of the natural and applied sciences, youth cultures, the revolution in the dissemination of information, and the popular arts are generating wholly novel chances and imperatives of coexistence. They are eroding frontiers. The chances do remain slight; but it may be that they will come in time to inhibit the scenario of Armageddon. It would be fatuous arrogance to rule otherwise. To put it anecdotally, I recall a seminar given by C. S. Lewis. Knowing Lewis's profound nostalgia for what he called "the unbroken image" of the medieval and early-Renaissance cosmos, knowing Lewis's displeasure at the vulgarities and moral confusions of the twentieth-century tone, a graduate student launched on an encomium of times past. Lewis listened for a few moments, his massive head buried in his hands. Then, brusquely, he turned on the speaker. "Do stop mouthing easy rot," he enjoined. "Do close your eyes and concentrate your sensitive soul on exactly what your life would have been like before chloroform!"

The key word here is "easy." There is throughout Cioran's jeremiads an ominous *facility*. It requires no sustained analytic thought, no closeness or clarity of argument to pontificate on the "rottenness," on the "gangrene," of man, and on the terminal cancer of history. The pages on which I have drawn not only are easy to write, they *flatter* the writer with the tenebrous incense of the oracular. One need only turn to the work of Tocqueville, of Henry Adams, or of Schopenhauer to see the drastic difference. These are masters of a clairvoyant sadness no less comprehensive than Cioran's. Their reading of history is no rosier. But the cases they put are scrupulously argued, not declaimed; they are informed, at each node and articulation of proposal, with a just sense of the complex, contradictory nature of historical evidence. The doubts expressed by these thinkers, the qualifications brought to their own persuasions honor the reader. They call not for numbed assent or complaisant echo but for reëxamination and criticism. The question that remains is this: Do Cioran's apocalyptic convictions, his mortal pessimism and disgust occasion original and radical perceptions? Are the *pensées,* the aphorisms and maxims, that constitute his title to fame truly in the lineage of Pascal, of La Rochefoucauld, or of his immediate exemplar Nietzsche?

Drawn and Quartered contains numerous aphorisms on death. This is always a favorite topic for aphorists—for, indeed, is there ever much to be *said* about death? "Death is a state of perfection, the only one within a mortal's grasp" (the point implicit is a feeble, traditional wordplay on the Latin sense of "perfection"). "There is no one whose death I have not longed for, at one moment or another" (echoing La Rochefoucauld). "Death, what a dishonor!

To become suddenly an *object*"—which is followed by the wholly unconvincing assertion that "nothing makes us modest, not even the sight of a corpse." The tone rises to a macabre chic: "Whatever is exempt from the funereal is necessarily vulgar." The climax of portentous silliness is this: "Death is the solidest thing life has invented, so far."

Let us try another theme, that of the acts of writing and of thought. "A book should open old wounds, even inflict new ones. A book should be a *danger*." Quite so—and said, a long time ago, almost verbatim, by Franz Kafka. "One does not write because one has something to say but because one *wants* to say something." Fair enough. "Existing is plagiarism." A witty, suggestive hit. "When we know what words are worth, the amazing thing is that we try to say anything at all, and that we manage to do so. This requires, it is true, a supernatural nerve." True enough; but professed often, and with irrefutable authority, by Kafka, by Karl Kraus, by Wittgenstein and Beckett. "The only *profound* thinkers are the ones who do not suffer from a sense of the ridiculous." Cf. Rousseau and Nietzsche, who arrived at the same finding, but with far greater circumstantial force. (To which caveat, Cioran might reply, "I have invented nothing, I have merely been the secretary of my sensations.") "An author who claims to write for posterity must be a bad one. We should never know *for whom* we write." The admonition may be unexceptionable; a moment's thought of Horace, Ovid, Dante, Shakespeare, or Stendhal reveals its shallowness.

Cioran is the author of an interesting essay on De Maistre, the great thinker of counterrevolution and antidemocratic pessimism. A number of aphorisms—and they are among the more substantial— point to this strain in Cioran's own nocturnal politics: "Never lose sight of the fact that the plebs regretted Nero." "All these people in the street make me think of exhausted gorillas, every one of them tired of imitating man!" "The basis of society, of any society, is a certain *pride in obedience*. When this pride no longer exists, the society collapses." "Whoever speaks the language of Utopia is more alien to me than a reptile from another geological era." "Torquemada was *sincere,* hence inflexible, inhuman. The corrupt popes were charitable, like all who can be bought." I happen to believe that Cioran's stoic élitism, his rejection of meliorism *à l'américaine,* has more truth in it than most of the currently modish brands of ecumenical liberality. But nothing very fresh or arresting is being added here to the plea for darkness in De Maistre, in Nietzsche, or in the visionary politics of Dostoyevsky. The aphorism on Torquemada, for instance, with its modish *frisson,* comes directly out of De Maistre's immensely powerful tractate in favor of the hangman.

The most revealing aphorisms are those in which Cioran testifies to his own bleak, fatigued condition: "All my ideas come down to various discomforts debased into generalities." "I feel effective, competent, likely to do something positive only when I lie down and abandon myself to an interrogation without object or end." There is a lucid pathos in Cioran's confession that he could more easily found an empire than a family, and immediate persuasion in his remark that original sin can be doubted only by those who have not had children. One instinctively trusts and ponders the proposition "I do not struggle against the world, I struggle against a greater force, against my *weariness* of the world." But, as a British idiom has it, a little world-weariness does go a very long way. One hundred and eighty pages, climaxing in the (ludicrous) cry "Man is *unacceptable,*" leave one recalcitrant.

The trouble may well lie with Cioran's dictum that in aphorisms, as in poems, the single word is king. This may be true of certain types of poetry, mainly lyrical. It is not true of the great aphorists, for whom the *sententia* is sovereign, and sovereign precisely insofar as it compels on the reader's mind an internalized but elided wealth of historical, social, philosophic background. The finest aphorismic text of recent decades, T. W. Adorno's *Minima Moralia,* brims with the authority of a true shorthand, of a script whose concision retranslates, compels retranslation, into a full-scale psychology and sociology of observant historical consciousness. Any honest comparison with *Drawn and Quartered* is devastating. No doubt there are better examples of Cioran's work, particularly from before the time when his writings turned into self-repetition. But a collection of this order, all too faithfully rendered by Richard Howard, does raise the question not so much whether the emperor has any clothes as whether there is any emperor.

April 16, 1984

ANCIENT GLITTERING EYES

ON WINSTON CHURCHILL'S eightieth birthday, an English journal of opinion sent felicitations to "the second greatest living Englishman." The panache and impertinence of the compliment lay in the omitted premise. But to logicians and radicals the missing name rang clear: it was that of Bertrand Russell. And the implicit judgment may stick. Indeed, it may reach well beyond English life. It looks as if the presence of Russell will come to inform the history of intelligence and feeling in European civilization between the eighteen-nineties and the nineteen-fifties as does that of no other man. As no single presence has, perhaps, since Voltaire's.

The parallel is both obvious and deep. It springs from the actual wrapper of this handsome book, *The Autobiography of Bertrand Russell* (Little, Brown), with its portrait of Russell made in 1916. His hair is close-folded in the manner of an eighteenth-century wig, the nose is beaked and Voltairean, the lips are sensuous but faintly mocking. Like Voltaire, Russell has lived long and made of this fact a statement of values both festive and stoical. His published work has been immense, an outrage to the sparsities of the modern manner; it comprises some forty-five books. His correspondence has been even larger. Like Voltaire's, it has touched directly on every nerve of its century. Russell has debated philosophy with Wittgenstein and fiction with Conrad and D. H. Lawrence, he has argued economics with Keynes and civil disobedience with Gandhi, his open letters have provoked Stalin to a reply and Lyndon Johnson to exasperation. And, like Voltaire, Russell has sought to make of language—his prose is as supple and lucid as the finest of the classic age—a safeguard against the brutalities and mendacity of mass culture.

It may be that Russell's range is ampler than Voltaire's, although no single work he has produced crystallizes a whole sense of the world as does *Candide*. Only logicians and philosophers of science are qualified to assess the contribution of Russell's *Introduction to Mathematical Philosophy* and of The *Principles of Mathematics*, which he completed in 1903. Together with the *Principia Mathematica*, published in collaboration with Whitehead between 1910 and 1913, these books retain a commanding vitality in the history of modern logical investigation. They anticipate many of the notions that are proving most fruitful in contemporary symbolic logic and information theory. Pure logicians are a rare species. In his capacity for sustained analytic calculation, in his ability to use codes of significant order less encumbered than is ordinary speech by the waste and opacities of customary life, Russell is a peer of Descartes and Kurt Gödel.

Russell's *History of Western Philosophy*, much in the forefront when he received a Nobel Prize in literature in 1950, is *haute vulgarisation* in the best sense. It marches briskly from Anaxagoras to Bergson. It brims with an implicit confidence in the mortality of nonsense. Russell's book on Leibnitz is dated but remains interesting for the comparisons it invites between his own appetite for omniscience and that of the great polymath and rival of Newton. *Our Knowledge of the External World*, based on the Lowell lectures Russell delivered in Boston in 1914, remains perhaps the best introduction to his philosophic style and sinuous empiricism. The problems raised are as old as Plato; this means that attempted solutions are less vulnerable to fashion than in other branches of philosophy. We are an epistemological animal, asking both whence and whither but knowing neither, unable to prove that we do not inhabit a long dream. Russell beautifully charts the strangeness of our condition. He does so again, though less incisively, in *The Analysis of Mind*. Had he produced nothing but these books of philosophic argument and history of ideas, his place would be distinctive.

But the shock of world war and radical changes in his own personality greatly extended and complicated Russell's natural range. Since 1914 there have been few areas of social policy, of international relations, of private ethics that he has not dealt with. His critique of our mores begins in the world of William Morris and Tolstoy; it outlives that of Shaw and Freud; it is active and more irritant than ever in that of Stokely Carmichael. He has sought to plan "The Conquest of Happiness"—whatever the title of the particular discourse or tract. He has spoken as warmly as Montaigne "In Praise of Idleness" and reverted time and again, with the sense of a riddle unsolved, to "Marriage and Morals." He has given the world notice of "Why I Am Not a Christian" but written with a poetic tact alien to Voltaire of the claims of mysticism, of that abrupt logic of the human spirit when it is in a state of rapture. Russell's more immediately political studies and pamphlets would fill a shelf. He inquired early into the "Practice and Theory of Bolshevism" and addressed his uneasy sympathies to "The Problem of China" (another interest shared with Voltaire) long before the present crisis. His study of the "Prospects of Industrial Civilization" relates him to the thought of R. H. Tawney, while his repeated pleas for passive resistance and universal disarmament ally him to that of Danilo Dolci. The dreamer and the engineer have also been present in Russell's genius. He is a Utopian of the short term, a man waking, even at ninety-five, from the simplicities of his dreams and refusing to believe that these cannot bring instant melioration to the morning. The title of one of Russell's tracts, "Has Man a Future?," sums up his quest. The mark of interrogation stands for a persistent skepticism, for a streak of resigned sadness. But the old fox's entire life, marvellous in its diversity and power of creation, has been a striving for a positive answer.

Russell seems to have kept a close record of that life almost from the start—certainly from the moment he went to Cambridge, in October of 1890, and realized that he possessed gifts out of the ordinary. Like Voltaire, Russell has seen his own person move into the light of the historical; time and eminence have in part taken him from himself, and he has watched over the process with ironic precision. *My Philosophical Development* remains an intensely readable record of his passage from Kantian idealism to a kind of transcendental empiricism that I would call Pythagorean ("I have tried to apprehend the Pythagorean power by which number holds sway above the flux"). *The Portraits from Memory*, which resembles and at times completes Keynes's *Essays in Biography*, tells of some of the luminous encounters in Russell's career, and recaptures, so far as any book can, the casual ceremony of intellectual life in the Cambridge of G. M. Trevelyan and Lord Rutherford, of G.E. Moore and E.M. Forster. The formal net of autobiography has grown naturally out of a life so constantly examined. Parts of this volume were assembled and dictated in 1949, other parts probably in the early nineteen-fifties. The material dealt with extends from February of 1876, when the orphaned four-year-old younger son of Lord and Lady Amberley arrived at Pembroke Lodge, the home of his grandparents, until August of 1914, when the forty-two-year-old mathematical logician, Fellow of Trinity College and of the Royal Society, was about to opt for intransigent pacifism and break with much of the world he had adorned. The narrative consists of seven chapters, each followed by a selection of relevant letters. This Victorian device works admirably. Often the letters move subtly against the grain of a much later remembrance, and the dialogue between letter and recollection yields a caustic footnote. Thus, Russell could write to Lucy Martin Donnelly on April 22, 1906, about some of his most abstruse, fiercely taxing endeavors in mathematical logic, "My work goes ahead at a tremendous pace, and I get intense delight from it," whereas Earl Russell, O.M., remarks, forty-five years later, that "It turned out to be all nonsense."

Bertrand Russell was born and brought up an aristocrat. He was the grandson of a Prime Minister and cousin or nephew to a covey of military, diplomatic, and ecclesiastical worthies. Forebears who had visited Napoleon at Elba or defended Gibraltar during the American wars were animate shadows in the nursery. This was the England of espaliers and velvet lawns, of lord and servant. In these opening pages there are dizzying vistas of time. The reader of this review and the writer are, in the allowed sense of the word, contemporaneous with a man who silenced Browning at a dinner party and who, when left in tête-à-tête with William Gladstone, heard cascade upon him the dread pronouncement "This is very good port they have given me, but why have they given it me in a claret glass?" Those now living can seek out a man, still alert, whose servants and early acquaintances clearly remembered news of Waterloo. This is startling enough in itself. But in Russell's case the fact that he came of age in a world almost totally vanished from our grasp, that he belonged to the most confident élite in modern history (the Whig aristocracy of Victorian England), is more than a virtuoso trick of long life. Russell is marked to the very limits of his later radicalism by his origins.

This memoir does nothing to soften his native hauteur. "But what can a charwoman know of the spirits of great men or the records of fallen empires or the haunting visions of art and reason?" he asked Gilbert Murray in 1902, and went on, "Let us not delude ourselves with the hope that the best is within the reach of all, or that emotion uninformed by thought can ever attain the highest level." In February of 1904, Russell ventured "to a remote part of

London" to lecture to the local Branch of the Amalgamated Society of Engineers. His comment at the time was characteristic: "They seemed excellent people, *very* respectable—indeed, I shouldn't have guessed they were working men." Russell grew into one of the genuine mutineers of modern history; his fusillades against capitalism, great-power politics, and the cant of the Establishment have been fierce and prolonged. Pity for the human condition has burned in him till it has all but consumed reason: "Children in famine, victims tortured by oppressors, helpless old people a hated burden to their sons, and the whole world of loneliness, poverty, and pain make a mockery of what human life should be." He has gone to prison, lost academic appointments, and risked ostracism on behalf of his outraged compassion. But Russell's Jacobinism is high Tory; it springs from the certitude that birth and genius impose both the right and the obligation of moral precept. "Echoes of cries of pain reverberate in my heart," says Russell. One wonders whether he is not deceiving himself; the echo chamber lies higher, the pity, like Voltaire's, is cerebral. Fundamentally, Russell's politics of protest seek to realize the hope, so articulate in the small, vibrant coterie of Apostles to which he belonged at Cambridge, that humanity might be elevated to a just plane of social and hygienic well-being so that the elect, the pursuers of beauty and truth, could fulfill their lives without bad conscience. American democracy, argues Russell, is egalitarian and philistine. Thus, it has made room for neither intensity nor loftiness of feeling; "indeed, loftiness of feeling seems to depend essentially upon a brooding consciousness of the past and its terrible power." True politics are the art of securing elbowroom for the best; they will alienate the squalor in the world at large that embarrasses or dissipates the life of the mind. Russell's pity has often been sharp-edged, a weapon against those who would crowd too near his sensibility.

This aristocratic misericord and a betraying preference of the abstract over the disorder of the personal underlie the general tone of the *Autobiography*. They are explicit in what have rapidly become its two most notorious episodes. "I have sought love, first, because it brings ecstasy," writes Russell, "ecstasy so great that I would often have sacrificed all the rest of life for a few hours of this joy. I have sought it, next, because it relieves loneliness—that terrible loneliness in which one shivering consciousness looks over the rim of the world into the cold unfathomable lifeless abyss." But the search not infrequently appears to have brought ruin to others. Russell's first marriage, to Alys, the sister of Logan Pearsall Smith, began in exultation. Russell's recollection of an early visit to his beloved, in January of 1894, when London lay snowbound and "almost as noiseless as a lonely hill top," has the gentle force of Tolstoy's autobiographical narrative of Levin's visit to Kitty near the start of *Anna Karenina*. But the marriage was built on a weird code of sexual reticence that soon produced cruel tensions. In March of 1911, Russell fell in love with Lady Ottoline Morrell, a woman celebrated in the lives and careers of a generation of English poets and politicians. "For one night" with her Russell felt ready to pay the price of scandal and even murder. The end of his marriage to Alys is recounted thus:

> I told Alys that she could have the divorce whenever she liked, but that she must not bring Ottoline's name into it. She nevertheless persisted that she would bring Ottoline's name in. Thereupon I told her quietly but firmly that she would find that impossible, since if she ever took steps to that end, I should commit suicide in order to circumvent her. I meant this, and she saw that I did. Thereupon her rage became unbearable. After she had stormed for some hours, I gave a lesson in Locke's philosophy to her niece, Karin Costelloe, who was about to take her Tripos. I then rode away on my bicycle, and with that my first marriage came to an end. I did not see Alys again till 1950, when we met as friendly acquaintances.

After his term at Harvard, Russell went to Chicago to stay with an eminent gynecologist and his family. He had met one of the daughters briefly at Oxford. "I spent two nights under her parents' roof, and the second I spent with her." It was agreed secretly that the young woman should join Russell in England. By the time she arrived, in August of 1914, world war had broken out. Again, Russell's narrative should be quoted in full:

> I could think of nothing but the war, and as I had determined to come out publicly against it, I did not wish to complicate my position with a private scandal, which would have made anything that I might say of no account. I felt it therefore impossible to carry out what we had planned. She stayed in England and I had relations with her from time to time, but the shock of the war killed my passion for her, and I broke her heart. Ultimately she fell a victim to a rare disease, which first paralysed her, and then made her insane. In her insanity she told her father all that had happened. The last time I saw her was in 1924. . . . If the war had not intervened, the plan which we formed in Chicago might have brought great happiness to us both. I feel still the sorrow of this tragedy.

There is a terrible coldness in both the style and the feelings expressed—a chill, dismissive lucidity in the Augustan manner. In some measure this may result from the detachment of an old man's remembrance. But surely the problem lies deeper. Like Voltaire or perhaps like the Tolstoy of the later years, Bertrand Russell is a man who loves truth or the lucid statement of a possible truth better than he does individual human beings. His ego is of such turbulent richness that egotism makes a world. To it another human person, however intimate, has only provisional access. Russell has recorded at least one definite mystical experience. It took place in 1901 after he had heard Gilbert Murray read part of his translation of Euripides' *The Hippolytus*. He traces to the formidable moment of illumination, of clear trance, that ensued a few hours later his lasting views on war, education, and the unendurability of human loneliness. He emerged convinced "that in human relations one should penetrate to the core of loneliness in each person and speak to that." The conviction was no doubt sincere, but little in this *Autobiography* bears it out. A more pertinent text would seem to be the chapter on "The Ideal" in G. E. Moore's *Principia Ethica*, a work that profoundly influenced Russell's early development; it is "the love of love," which Moore commends "as the must valuable good we know." Set beside the vividness of that realization, love for the actual beloved seems a more pallid joy.

Yet it would be unfair to consider solely what is lofty and bone-chilling in this book. The "ancient glittering eyes are gay." Russell recalls how he read Lytton Strachey's *Eminent Victorians* in jail: "It caused me to laugh so loud that the officer came round to my cell, saying I must remember that prison is a place of punishment." Lunacies and matching asperities out of another age, in an idiom almost extinct, abound: "When the Junior Dean, a clergyman who raped his little daughter and became paralysed with syphilis, had to be got rid of in consequence, the Master went out of his way to state at College Meeting that those of us who did not attend chapel regularly had no idea how excellent this worthy's sermons had been." Russell, like many English dons, is a virtuoso of the undercut. A hilarious vignette of philosophic and personal pomposities in the Cambridge, Massachusetts, of 1914 is capped by the gentle nonce that "There were limitations to Harvard culture. Schofield, the professor of Fine Arts, considered Alfred Noyes a very good poet." A snapshot of Keynes finds him "carrying with him everywhere a feeling of the bishop *in partibus*."

The ironies, moreover, are more than donnish. They deepen to a stream of doubt so erosive that it undermines Russell's own initial values and sweeps before it the science in which he had achieved greatness and the world in which he was most at home. This demolition from within is the high adventure of the first volume (Russell is at work on a second). The labor of abstruse argument that went into the *Principia Mathematica* left Russell exhausted. He reports with absolute candor that his powers of close mathematical reasoning weakened after 1913. It was not mathematical logic alone, however, that weakened its hold. In February of 1913, Russell wrote to Lowes Dickinson a sentence that effectively dooms the criteria of elegant feeling, of academic communion that had dominated his own life until then: "But intellect, except at white heat, is very apt to be trivial." Both the failure of his marriage and the example of Tolstoy lie behind that statement. But so does a precise local circumstance. In the same letter, Russell refers to one greater than himself in philosophy and the analysis of meaning. He reports that Ludwig Wittgenstein, a new arrival from Vienna and Manchester, has been elected to the Apostles "but thought it a waste of time. . . . I think he did quite right, though I tried to dissuade him." The concession is momentous. As the long summer of European civilization drew to a close, Russell outgrew the luxuries of spirit he had prized most. He was to emerge from the war as one set on the road that has led to the Russell International Tribunal in Stockholm.

The myopia, the frivolous malice of many of Lord Russell's recent political pronouncements are revolting. The changes of heart—it was Bertrand Russell who not so very long ago advocated a preventive nuclear strike against the Soviet Union—are risible. Yet even in error and garrulous simplification there is a fierce zest of life, a total gift of self to the claims of ideas and the demands of human conflict. When the whole story comes to be written, it may well appear that few men in history, certainly few in our tawdry age, have done more to dignify the image of life set down by Russell sixty-four years ago:

Often I feel that religion, like the sun, has extinguished the stars of less brilliancy but not less beauty, which shine upon us out of the darkness of a godless universe. The splendour of human life, I feel sure, is greater to those who are not dazzled by the divine radiance; and human comradeship seems to grow more intimate and more tender from the sense that we are all exiles on an inhospitable shore.

August 19, 1967

A TALE OF THREE CITIES

IN THE LAST year, as so often before, the Nobel Prize in Literature has proved a mixed blessing. Elias Canetti's writings are profoundly private and fragmentary. They stem from hidden centers and have unfolded with a cunning patience. Because of the 1981 Prize, much of his that is minor has been rushed into reprint and translation, and the work as a whole, spiralling out of and coming home to one masterpiece, the first and only novel, *Auto-da-Fé*, has shifted out of focus. Canetti himself, moreover, has reacted to the abrupt notoriety bestowed on him in his seventy-seventh year with characteristic irascibility and *hauteur*. He has rounded fiercely, and not altogether fairly, on those who—particularly in England, to which he came as a refugee—failed to keep his books in print or in the light of critical regard during the long years of (relative) obscurity before the Nobel. It is all the more important that the autobiography of this virtuoso of intransigence should now be available outside the incisive, marmoreal German (Canetti is heir to Kleist) in which it was composed. *The Torch in My Ear* is Volume II (translated by Joachim Neugroschel; Farrar, Straus & Giroux). It covers the decade—absolutely decisive for Canetti's development as writer and thinker—from 1921 to 1931. It begins with Elias Canetti as a sixteen-year-old schoolboy in a Frankfurt *Gymnasium,* and closes with Dr. Canetti giving up the chemistry he had studied at the University of Vienna in order to turn to the more potent alchemy of his great fiction. But this is more than the memoir of an exceptionally observant and original witness; it is a vivid image of central European high civilization on the edge of the abyss. It was Canetti's peril and good fortune to come of inward age in a time of twilight.

Readers of Volume I, *The Tongue Set Free*, will recall the writer's formidable widowed mother and the intimacies of tension which bound mother to son. Mme. Canetti's imperceptions could be as coldly strategic as her divinations. In the Frankfurt of the nineteen-twenties, inflation was deepening to lunacy and ruin. All around him, Elias observed insistent symptoms of human wretchedness and despair. When the boy saw a woman fainting with hunger in the street, he demanded some explanation, some reflex of compassion from his mother. "Did *you* remain?" Mme. Canetti asked mordantly, and went on to remind her son that he had best get used to such sights if he was to become a doctor and earn the bourgeois wealth that would guard him from similar misery. Like the crazed child in D. H. Lawrence's story "The Rocking-Horse Winner," young Canetti heard a call for money screaming out of every corner of his mother's expectations. In a riposte that was half ruse, half hysteria, Elias himself, in Vienna a few years later, covered sheets and sheets of paper with the word "money." The alarm that this exercise provoked in a mother always given to taking medical advice was to help bring on her son's liberation and departure from home.

But the final school years had brought other emancipations. The actor Carl Ebert, whom Canetti had admired in classical roles at the Frankfurt Schauspielhaus, gave a Sunday reading from a Babylonian epic older than the Bible: "I discovered *Gilgamesh*, which had a crucial impact on my life and its innermost meaning, on my faith, strength and expectation such as nothing else in the world."

Canetti's summary of this impact can, indeed, serve as epigraph to his œuvre:

> I experienced the effect of a myth: something I have thought about in various ways during the ensuing half century, something I have so often turned over in my mind, but never *once* earnestly doubted. I absorbed as a unity something that has remained in me as a unity. I can't find fault with it. The question whether I *believe* such a tale doesn't affect me; how can I, given my intrinsic substance, decide whether I believe in it. The aim is not to parrot the banality that so far all human beings have died: the point is to decide whether to *accept* death willingly or stand up against it. With my indignation against death, I have acquired a right to glory, wealth, misery ... I have lived in this endless rebellion. And if my grief for the near and dear that I have lost in the course of time was no smaller than that of Gilgamesh for his friend Enkidu, I at least have one thing, one single thing, over the lion man: I care about the life of *every* human being and not just that of my neighbor.

The second major discovery was saltier. Canetti found in Aristophanes a vital clue: "The powerful and consistent way that each of his comedies is dominated by a surprising fundamental idea from which it derives." Such an idea, Canetti concluded, should always be of a public and, in the deeper sense, political order. A radical imagination must seek to o'er-leap the private sphere. And could there be anything more Aristophanic than the spectacle of German life in the grip of fiscal, social, and erotic dissolution?

The supreme analyst of this dissolution was at work in Vienna. With distance, it is becoming more and more obvious that essential traits of sensibility and of expressive style in the West in this century derive from the example of Karl Kraus. The legacy of this apocalyptic satirist is visible all the way from Kafka's vision of language and society to the black, self-lacerating humor in the American urban vein of the nineteen-fifties and sixties. Canetti gives a memorable account of Kraus's celebrated reading-recitals, of one of those mimetic tours de force in which the author-editor of *Die Fackel—The Torch,* which burns also in Canetti's title—educated a generation to the bracing arts of hatred and self-hatred. It was appropriate that it was at a Kraus lecture that Canetti first saw—sitting, as she always did, in the front row—Venetia Toubner-Calderon, the enigmatic and beautiful Veza, whom he was to marry in 1934. More immediately, Kraus's mesmeric effect suggested to Canetti what was to become the pivot of his own questioning: the power of the individual in relation to that of the crowd. Thinking back on Kraus's fantastic vocal register, Canetti notes, "Chairs and people seemed to yield under this quivering; I wouldn't have been surprised if the chairs had bent. The dynamics of such a mobbed auditorium under the impact of that voice—an impact persisting even when the voice grew silent—can no more be depicted than the Wild Hunt." (How many readers, particularly in the Anglo-Saxon world, will identify this penetrating allusion to the myth, probably Celtic in origin, of spectral hounds and hunters crossing the night sky in infernal pursuit? But there are no footnotes in this edition, and the translation is often ingeniously unhelpful.)

No less seminal than Karl Kraus in the education of Elias Canetti were the paintings that he saw and pondered in the great Vienna collections. Two, especially, came to possess him, though with contrary effects. Brueghel's "Triumph of Death" seemed to confirm the message of *Gilgamesh.* The energy of the resistance to death pulsing in the multitudinous figures on the canvas flowed into Canetti's consciousness. Though death triumphs, the struggle is pictured as eminently worthwhile, and it is one that binds all men to each other. The other painting was Rembrandt's colossal "The Blinding of Samson": "I often stood in front of this painting, and from it I learned what hatred is." Moreover, and although he could not yet be aware of it, blinding and blindness were to serve as a leitmotif in Canetti's fiction, travel notes, and philosophic aphorisms. The German title of *Auto-da-Fé* is *Die Blendung*, which signifies both the act of blinding and being dazzled or bewildered to the point of blindness. Canetti's reading of Rembrandt's Delilah seems to echo forward into almost every feminine figure in his subsequent inventions:

> She has taken away Samson's strength; she holds his strength, but still fears him and will hate him as long as she remembers this blinding, and, in order to hate him, will always remember it.

In the summer of 1925, Canetti broke with his *monstre sacré* of a mother. Though still pursuing his studies in science at the University of Vienna, he was now intensely available to the summons of experience—to that which would, if his intimations were accurate, rouse his dormant powers like a fire signal in the night. On July 15, 1927, that signal came, literally. Turning on their own Social Democratic leaders, the more radical workers of Vienna, enraged by a recent miscarriage of justice (workers had been shot down in the Burgenland and their killers acquitted), marched on the Palace of Justice. They set it on fire. That day, Elias Canetti, the lyric metaphysician, the allegorist of violence, came fully into his own: "I became a part of the crowd, I fully dissolved in it." This immersion—the French phrase *bain de foule* exactly renders Canetti's experience—confirmed his resolve to analyze, as Gustave Le Bon had begun to do in the eighteen-nineties, the internal structure, exponential energies, and contagious aura of crowds. It would be 1960 before *Crowds and Power*, a torso of a work, fragmentary in its brilliance, appeared. But the crowd and crowd feelings into which he plunged on that violent summer day were to preoccupy Canetti henceforth. Private obsessions and the public fact, moreover, had fused:

> The fire was what held the situation together. You felt the fire, its presence was overwhelming; even if you did not see it, you nevertheless had it in your mind, its attraction and the attraction exerted by the crowd were one and the same. . . . And you were drawn back into the province of the fire—circuitously, since there was no other possible way.

Both in his meditations on crowds and in his metaphoric appropriations of fire, Canetti found Freud useless. Freud's *Mass Psychology and Ego Analysis* repelled him "from the very first word, and still repels me no less fifty-five years later." Canetti saw in Freud the very embodiment of the secondhand—the edification of dogmatic abstractions on the uncertain bases of other men's deeds and testimony. This rejection has wider resonance. Canetti belongs to the small constellation of first-class minds and sensibilities who have in our time rejected Freud and the psychoanalytic construct as a factitious, antihistorical mythology, whose methodology is, at best, aesthetic and whose evidential material—the dreams, speech acts, gestural styles of fin-de-siècle, primarily female and middle-class Jewish Central Europe—is almost absurdly narrow. This constellation comprises Kraus, Wittgenstein, and Heidegger as well as Canetti himself. It is marked by a tragic sense of life, by an acute alertness to the historical, temporal nature of human discourse, and by grave skepticism as to the ideals or claims of the therapeutic. With the current fading of psychoanalytic presumptions, it may well be these "refusers" of Freud who will prove lasting.

The July uprising had determined Canetti's vocation. Seeking crowds "in history, in the histories of *all* civilizations," he came upon and was fascinated by the history and early philosophy of

China (a fascination that was to animate the novel). Street sounds took on a rich, diverse meaning. The fellow-students with National Socialist sympathies whom Canetti met in the laboratory focussed his attention even more precisely on crowd phenomena and the possibility that the politics of mass manipulation would lead to the collective trance of war. Canetti was now writing "wild and frenzied" poetry. Every new poem was handed to Veza. And she was beginning to know how deeply Canetti loved her. On July 15, 1928, a year to the day after the burning of the Palace of Justice, Canetti left Vienna to spend the rest of the summer in Berlin. After Frankfurt and Vienna, Berlin was to be the third of the cities crucial to his self-discoveries.

Berlin was at that hour the nerve center of modernity. Though the Brown Shirts were increasingly in command of the currents and eddies of street life, the left, both Communist and Socialist, was still present. In the implosive ambience of the city confrontations, practices of psychological and physical aggression, soon to be demonstrated on a global scale, were being rehearsed. Canetti's description is apt:

> The animal quality and the intellectual quality, bared and intensified to the utmost, were mutually entangled, in a kind of alternating current. If you had awakened to your own animality before coming here, you had to increase it in order to hold out against the animality of other people: and if you weren't very strong, you were soon used up. But if you were directed by your intellect and had scarcely given in to your animality, you were bound to surrender to the richness of what was offered your mind. These things smashed away at you, versatile, contradictory, and relentless; you had no time to understand anything, you received nothing but strokes, and you hadn't even gotten over yesterday's strokes before the new ones showered upon you. You walked around Berlin as a tender piece of meat, and

you felt as if you still weren't tender enough and were waiting for new strokes.

The image of "a tender piece of meat" walking around Berlin under a rain of blows is pure Expressionism. It would have amused George Grosz, whom Canetti came to know and admire. Grosz's ferocious drawings threw Canetti into a world of sexual brutality and exploitation. He never queried the truth of Grosz's witness, and it was to influence profoundly the drama of tyrannical eros in *Auto-da-Fé*. Brecht, too, impressed the young visitor, and Canetti glimpsed something of the man's cool but sovereign professionalism. But the great encounter was that with Isaac Babel. Here was a manifest purity such as Canetti was to come upon, later, in the talismanic truth of Kafka. Literature was sacrosanct to Babel. Babel had plumbed the depths of human savagery, but the vision he had of literature made cynicism alien to him. "If he found that something was good, he could never have *used* it like other people, who, in sniffing around, implied that they regarded themselves as the culmination of the entire past. Knowing what literature was, he never felt superior to others." Isaac Babel, Canetti says, kept him from being "devoured" by the voracious city.

Now Canetti's apprenticeship was almost complete. Returning to Vienna in the fall of 1929, he set aside his mother's obstinate dreams of medical or commercial respectability. He would earn his living as a translator his tongues "set free," and begin work on a fiction in several extensive parts, provisionally entitled *The Human Comedy of Madmen*. One more encounter proved pivotal: that with a young philosopher, crippled in body but with an awareness of human beings which at times made him resemble "a Christ on an Eastern icon." Though the dissolution of the individual in a crowd remained for Canetti "the enigma of enigmas," the desolate yet luminous condition of his friend brought the theme of death into the forefront of his concerns. Thinking back on the flames that had enveloped the Palace of Justice, seeing before him a human being possessed, kept alive by abstract thought and the energies of unsparing perception, Canetti found his great theme—that of the quintessential "Book Man," who would, in a final ecstasy of crazed clairvoyance, burn up with all his books. At first, the character was to be named Brand, mirroring the very term "fire" and, perhaps, the fierce absolutist of the spirit in Ibsen's play of that name. Next, he became Kant, touchstone of metaphysicians and archetype of mandarin routine. Finally, the central persona of *Auto-da-Fé* became Kien, a monosyllable that combines the German word for resinous pine-wood with a hint of Chinese tonality. At twenty-four, Elias Canetti was composing one of the most intellectually mature and stylistically controlled novels of our century.

Much that he has published since is of great quality: the ingenious philosophic play *Life-Terms*, the meditative commentary on Kafka's letters to Felice Bauer (*Kafka's Other Trial*, of 1969), the aphorisms and lyric notations in *The Voices of Marrakesh*, and, as I have suggested, certain sections of *Crowds and Power*—the section, for instance, on the role of monetary inflation in the destruction of social identity and ethical discriminations in Weimar Germany. Canetti's autobiography is such as to make one hope for a continuation. Nonetheless, it would be difficult to find anything in Canetti's subsequent writings to match the powers of Opus I. *The Torch in My Ear* provides an absorbing insight into the genesis of a classic.

Inevitably, albeit prematurely, one tries to place Canetti in relation to the entire configuration of Central European and Jewish genius which has so largely determined the climate of modern sensibility. There is not in Canetti the immediacy of mythical creation, the unforced access to specific yet universal symbolic forms, which makes the fictions and parables of Kafka tower over the twentieth-century imagination—Kafka being to his age, as Auden said, what Dante and Shakespeare were to theirs. Nor, one feels, has Canetti the response to physical nature and to the secrecies of the human psyche which gives to the novels—and here the plural matters—of Hermann Broch their patient authority. But it is by these standards that Canetti invites—indeed, compels—judgment. His exacting presence honors literature.

November 22, 1982

LA MORTE D'ARTHUR

ARTHUR KOESTLER'S *DARKNESS AT NOON* is one of the classics of the century. It educated generations to their terrors. *The Spanish Testament* (also known as *Dialogue with Death*) comes close to being of this same stature. *The Sleepwalkers*—particularly the chapters on Kepler—is one of the rare feats of convincing imaginative re-creation of great science, of the poetic logic of discovery. I do not share the certitudes of Koestler's *Reflections on Hanging*, but it endures as one of the great polemic tracts of our time and a pivotal moment in the debate on capital punishment. There are classic chapters in such autobiographical works as *Arrow in the Blue*. But there is a sense in which Arthur Koestler is more than the sum of his writings. There are in epochs and societies men and women who bear essential witness, in whose private sensibility and individual existence the larger meanings of the age are concentrated and made visible. In this black century, the Central European Jew has, more perhaps than any other tribe, borne the enormity of enforced vision and experience. Koestler, who was born in Budapest in 1905, stood on the exact terrain where the nerve ends of twentieth-century history, politics, language, and science touch. Their bitter and bracing currents passed through him. Catalogue the major presences in modernity—the politics of Marxism and of Fascist terror; psychoanalysis and the investigations of the anatomies of the mind; the forward surge of the biological sciences; the conflicts of ideology and the arts—and you will come upon not only Koestler's many books but the man himself. He knew exile and prison, divorce and the bullying solace of alcohol, the ambiguous struggle for privacy in the world of the media. Koestler's cards of identity, genuine and forged, the stamps and visas in his passports, his address books and desk diaries make up the map and itinerary of the hunted in our century.

This is why Arthur and Cynthia Koestler's double suicide, on or immediately before March 3, 1983, reverberates still. This is why it took on so compelling a force of suggestion. Here again, the particular message was writ large. Austerely but poignantly recounted in George Mikes' brief memoir, *Arthur Koestler: The Story of a Friendship* (André Deutsch), the suicide had immediate motives. A progressive, terminal illness would before too long have reduced Koestler to servile pain. But, as always in Koestler's existence, the personal act was prepared for and underwritten by a deliberate and public reflection. Koestler had voiced strong sympathy with the views of a group seeking to clarify the legal and moral issues of freely chosen death. Having faced so much of death in its cruellest and most involuntary forms, having fought so hard against the cold-blooded infliction of judicial death on convicted men and women, Koestler attached enormous value to human freedom, to human dignity in respect of death. A sane man should be allowed the chance to make of his end an act consonant with the crucial worth of liberty of mind and conscience. The legal punishment of failed suicide, as it stands on so many statute books, seemed to Arthur Koestler a barbaric impertinence.

The actual suicide note was written as early as June, 1982. It includes the following passage:

> I wish my friends to know that I am leaving their company in a peaceful frame of mind, with some timid hopes for a depersonalised after-life beyond due confines of space, time and matter and beyond the limits of our comprehension. This "oceanic feeling" has often sustained me at difficult moments, and does so now, while I am writing this.

In fact, and as is well known, Koestler's hopes—or, rather, wishful speculations—were far from "timid." His "oceanic feeling" (the phrase stems from Freud) focussed on the deepening conviction that there were, "out there," psychic presences, ordering energies of a transcendent kind—inaccessible as yet in their occult force, but approachable, or in some ways discernible at the edges of our empirical notice and awareness. Hence Koestler's urgent, often publicly defiant interest in parapsychology, in extrasensory perception, in phenomena extending from spoon-bending to poltergeists. Hence his ardent assembling of "inexplicable" cases of coincidence. Had not Lincoln's secretary, called Kennedy, implored the President not to go to the theatre; had not Kennedy's secretary, called Lincoln, begged the President not to go to Dallas; had Booth not shot Lincoln in a theatre and fled to a warehouse; had Oswald not shot Kennedy from a warehouse and then fled to a theatre? (When Koestler first put this concatenation to me, a wonderfully teasing, ironic, but also obsessed intensity seemed to vibrate in him. And as I hesitated, that smoldering, ironically insistent voice added, "And were they not both succeeded by Presidents named Johnson?") Koestler left a substantial part of his estate for the underwriting of a university chair in parapsychological studies.

Friends, acquaintances who would not follow him along this murky road were more or less gently excluded from intimacy.

Koestler knew full well that his belief in telekinesis and the extra-sensory was making him an outlaw in the world of the exact and natural sciences. He would never be elected a Fellow of the Royal Society. Together with the Nobel Prize, for which he was indeed nominated, that fellowship was his supreme wish. Interestingly, these same two honors also eluded H. G. Wells, who is in some regards Koestler's only true predecessor. Yet both writers had done far more than the great majority of professional scientists to make the stringent beauty and political importance of the sciences available to the literate community.

Another password in Koestler's choice of his intimates was drink. Mikes is affectionately blunt on this matter. It soon became clear to both my wife and me that we could not keep up with the whiskeys before dinner, the wine at dinner, and the numerous brandies thereafter which paced Koestler's evenings. This meant that an acquaintance, an exchange of views, a frequent round of mutual visits extended over the years could not ripen into unguarded closeness. A further obstacle, not alluded to by Mikes, was chess. Koestler played rapidly and sharply. But rather than lose to someone patently his inferior in intelligence, in talent, in knowledge of life, he would break off the game or refuse to play. This also came to be an undeclared cloud on our reciprocal trust, on the simple ease of being together. I ran up against exactly the same inhibition with Jacob Bronowski, that other master from Central Europe, whose death, together with Koestler's, does seem to have reduced palpably the sum of general, of polymathic, intelligence in our affairs. And *he* was a brilliant player.

Koestler's brandies, the spasms of irritation and of exasperated sarcasm which could chill and humiliate those nearest to him had their legitimate source. "A happy man," remarks Mikes, "was a strange curiosity, almost a mystery for him." How could a thinking, a feeling man or woman be happy amid the bestial follies, the waste, the suicidal blindness of contemporary history? To Arthur

Koestler, official rationalism was complacency and an unacceptable pose. Was it really possible to found liberal politics on some
fiction of reason, to pursue science on some unexamined basis of
positivism, when the real world was so manifestly in the grip of
inhuman, inexplicable impulses? If after the early nineteen-fifties
Koestler ceased from intervening publicly in political debates (he
abstained even at the moment of the Soviet invasion of Hungary),
it was out of bleakness. Where they spoke out, the voices of reason
were mocked.

Yet on good days Koestler radiated a rare passion for life, a
deep merriment in the face of the unknown. He seemed to exemplify Nietzsche's insight that there is in men and women a motiva-
tion stronger even than love or hatred or fear. It is that of *being
interested*—in a body of knowledge, in a problem, in a hobby, in
tomorrow's newspaper. Koestler was supremely interested. I imagine that he arranged his appointment with death with that same
watchful, challenging art of attention which he had lavished on
literature and the sciences, on politics and psychology, on the lost
tribes of Israel and French cooking.

George Mikes, himself a Hungarian exile, is too modest about
his own many skills and achievements. He is the author of that
classic tract *How to Be an Alien* and of a whole number of delight-
ful books on the perils of modern times. This is a wise and a witty
portrait of one to whom he meant much. Let me, just for the record, amend a story as Mikes tells it. Koestler had an eagle's aerie
of a house at Alpbach, in the Austrian mountains. During a summer colloquium there, he asked me to bring him into contact with
a minor Hungarian official who was taking part in the proceedings.
The three of us met at nightfall across a café table. Rather abruptly,
Koestler asked if it would be possible for him to revisit Budapest
and stand once more on native ground. After some thought, the
Hungarian said that such a homecoming would be a veritable triumph for Koestler, and that the regime would give him discreet

welcome. But he also said that Koestler's name stood high on a very short list (it also included Silone) of those whom the Soviet authorities so loathed that they might come after them even in Budapest. His safety could not be absolutely guaranteed. The K.G.B. had a way of crossing borders. As Koestler and I walked back to his house, under a tumult of stars and in the clear mountain air, I said to him that to be on that list seemed to me a greater distinction than either a Nobel or a Fellowship of the Royal Society. He stopped short, gave me a characteristic side glance, and said nothing. But he seemed, momentarily, at peace.

June 11, 1984

THE TONGUES OF MEN

TO THE PUBLIC at large, Professor Noam Chomsky, of M.I.T., is one of the most eloquent, indefatigable critics of the Vietnam war and of the role of the military-industrial complex in American life. He has marched on the Pentagon; he has supported the most extreme tactics of pacifist and conscientious dissent; he has labored to extricate his own university and the American academic community from what he judges to be its corrosive entanglements with military technology and imperialist expansion; he has run drastic professional risks on behalf of his beliefs and his intimations of catastrophe. His voice was one of the first to pillory what he sees as the injustice and folly of the Vietnam operation, and it has been one of the most influential in altering the mood of educated Americans and in bringing about the present drive for disengagement.

There is a second Noam Chomsky. To epistemologists, to behavioral psychologists, to theoreticians of child development and education, to linguists, Chomsky is one of the most interesting workers now in their field and a source of heated debate. His contributions to the study of language and mental process are highly technical and of considerable intellectual difficulty. But, like the anthropology of Claude Lévi-Strauss, with which it shows affinities, Chomskian generative and transformational grammar is one of those specialized conjectures which, by sheer intellectual fascination and range of implication, reach out to the world of the layman. Chomsky himself, moreover, is a fluent expositor and willing publicist of his technical work; at his best, he is an "explainer" in the tradition of Mill and T. H. Huxley. Thus a good deal of his professional argument is accessible in part, at least, to the outsider. The effort at understanding is well worth making, for if Chomsky is right, our general sense of man's habitation in reality, of the ways in which mind and world interact, will be modified or, more precisely, will join up with modes of feeling that have not had much influence or scientific weight since the seventeenth and early eighteenth centuries.

The "Chomskian revolution" predates Chomsky. To a greater degree than recent disciples are always ready to acknowledge, the groundwork was laid by Chomsky's teacher, Professor Zelig Harris, of the University of Pennsylvania. Harris is himself a linguist of great distinction, and it is in his *Methods in Structural Linguistics*, which appeared in 1951, that certain key notions of grammatical depth and transformation were first set out. Chomsky's *Syntactic Structures*, which is to many the classic and most persuasive statement of his hypotheses, followed six years later. Then, in 1958, came an important paper, "A Transformational Approach to Syntax," read at the Third Texas Conference on Problems of Linguistic Analysis in English, and "Some Methodological Remarks on Generative Grammar," published in the journal *Word* in 1961. In 1963, Chomsky contributed a severely technical and far-reaching chapter on "Formal Properties of Grammars" to Volume II of the *Handbook of Mathematical Psychology*. *Current Issues in Linguistic Theory*, a year later, marked the commanding prestige and wide influence of the whole Chomskian approach. *Cartesian Linguistics* (1966) is an interesting but in certain respects deliberately antiquarian salute to those French grammarians and philosophers whom Chomsky regards as his true forebears. His *Language and Mind* (Harcourt,

Brace & World) was first delivered as the Beckman Lectures at Berkeley in January of 1967 and published a year later. (It has more recently been published as a paperback by Harcourt.) It represents both a summary of generative linguistics and a program for future work. Around this core of his professional writing lie explanatory or polemic interviews—notably with the English philosopher Stuart Hampshire, reprinted in B.B.C.'s *Listener* of May 30, 1968—and a number of recent lectures given in packed halls in Oxford, London, and Cambridge.

The best place to start is Chomsky's assault on Professor B.F. Skinner, of Harvard. Chomsky tells us that hearing Skinner lecture triggered his own line of thought, and the behavioral sciences, as Skinner represents them, are his constant target. Skinner's *Verbal Behavior* came out in 1957. Chomsky's attack, a lengthy review in *Language,* came two years later, but it had already been circulating in manuscript. What Skinner had sought to do was to extrapolate, from his famous work on stimulus-and-response behavior in animals, to human linguistic behavior. He seemed to argue that human beings acquire and make use of language in a far more sophisticated but not essentially different way from that in which rats could be taught to thread a maze. A precise understanding and predictive theory of human speech would, therefore, involve little more than a refinement of those techniques of stimulus, reinforced stimulus, and conditioned response that enable us to teach a rat to press a certain spring in order to reach its reward of food. Concomitantly, the child would learn language skills (what Chomsky was to call "competence") by some process of stimulus and response within a model fully comparable to that which had proved effective—or at any rate in part—in the "teaching" of lower organisms. The qualification is needed because there is of late some doubt about what Skinner's rats have in fact "learned."

Chomsky found Skinner's proposals scandalous—in the restrictions they seemed to impose on the complexity and freedom of human consciousness, as well as in their methodological naïveté. Skinner's alleged scientific approach, said Chomsky, was a mere regression to discredited mentalistic psychology. It could give no true account of how human beings, *who differ in this cardinal respect from all other known life forms,* can acquire and use the infinitely complex, innovative, and at all levels creative instrument of speech. Chomsky saw—and this has, I believe, been his most penetrating insight—that a valid model of linguistic behavior must account for the extraordinary fact that all of us perpetually and effortlessly use strings and combinations of words which we have never heard before, which we have never been taught specifically, and which quite obviously do not arise in conditioned response to any identifiable stimulus in our environment. Almost from the earliest stages of his linguistic life, a child will be able to construct and to understand a fantastic number of utterances that are quite new to him yet that he somehow knows to be acceptable sentences in his language. Conversely, he will quickly demonstrate his instinctive rejection of (that is, his failure to grasp) word orders and syntactic arrangements that are unacceptable though it may be that none of these have been specifically pointed out to him. At every stage, from earliest childhood on, the human use of language goes far beyond all "taught" or formal precedent, and far beyond the aggregate of individually acquired and stored experience. "These abilities," says Chomsky, "indicate that there must be fundamental processes at work quite independently of 'feedback' from the environment." The dynamics of human communication arise from within.

These processes, remarks Chomsky, are likely to be of enormous intricacy. They may well be located in that intermediary zone between "mental" and "physical," between "psychic" and "neurochemical," that our outmoded vocabulary, with its crude but deeply entrenched mind-body distinctions, is poorly equipped to handle. The child hypothesizes and processes information in a variety of very special and apparently highly complex ways which we cannot yet describe or begin to understand, and which may be largely innate, or may develop through some sort of learning or through maturation of the nervous system. The brain produces "by an 'induction' of apparently fantastic complexity and suddenness" the rules of the relevant grammar. Thus we recognize a new item as a sentence in our language not because it matches some familiar, previously taught item in any simple way "but because it is generated by the grammar that each individual has somehow and in some form internalized." Human language, as Chomsky was to reaffirm in 1967, is a unique phenomenon, "without significant analogue in the animal world." It is senseless, contrary to what numerous biolinguists and ethnologists have felt, to theorize about its possible evolution from more primitive, outwardly-conditioned modes of communication, such as the signals apparently conveyed by bird calls. The spontaneous, innovative use of language somehow defines man. It looks as if people are beings "specially designed" to generate rules of immediate linguistic understanding and construction, as if they possess "data-handling or 'hypothesis-formulating' ability of unknown character and complexity."

The vocabulary of the early Chomsky is worth a close look, particularly because its underlying force will be augmented later. "Special design," "data-handling," his later references to the key "presetting" of the brain all point to the image of a computer. Chomsky would deny this, but the evidence is strong that the notion, perhaps partly unconscious, of a very powerful computer deep inside the fabric of human consciousness is relevant to much of his argument. In the history of philosophy and of the natural sciences, such buried pictures or metaphors play a large role. It is doubtful whether the most recent breakthrough in molecular biology would have taken place when the Morse code was the ruling image of quick communication. The uses of "code," "feedback," "storage," and "information" in current genetics point to the implicit presence of computer technology and of the electronic processing of data. The same is true of Chomskian linguistics, and this may prove important when one tries to determine whether or not it is valid.

Chomsky's interpretation of these abilities of "unknown character and complexity" proceeds on two levels. One, highly technical, consists of an attempt to devise and describe a set of rules that will produce, or "generate," grammatical sentences in English, or any other language, and that will not produce ungrammatical ones. The other level can most fairly be termed philosophic or epistemological. Chomsky's views on transformational grammars lead to certain inferences about the nature of the human mind and about the relations between being and perception. Except for purposes of study, these two planes of argument cannot really be kept apart. Nor ought they to be. The difficulty is that Chomsky sometimes argues as if they could, and then, at other—and often decisive—points, he buttresses his formal hypotheses with inferences that are philosophic and introspective in the old, loose sense. Formal logic tends to overlap with hunches that are occasionally quite nebulous.

Around the turn of the century, both mathematics and logic went through a phase of rigorous self-examination. Both sought to establish formally consistent and self-contained foundations for the processes of reasoning and calculation that had developed with tremendous force in earlier centuries, but on a somewhat ad-hoc basis. Extraordinary holes and bits of patchwork had been left in the foundations of logical and mathematical proof and analysis. The results of this shoring up, with which one associates thinkers such as Russell, Carnap, Tarski, and Gödel, include combinatorial logic, the theory of sets, and symbolic notations of great refinement. These tools were applied to mathematical propositions and to formal structures of logical argument. Noam Chomsky set out to apply them to the far more recalcitrant and varied material of actual human speech. (Whether he has in fact done so is one of the very difficult problems of the entire Chomskian achievement.)

Only the analysis of common speech, he insisted, could lead to a genuine understanding of how language is put together.

Chomsky argued that all possible grammatical sentences in English (or any other tongue) could be derived, or "generated," from a small number of basic, or "kernel," sentences, plus a set of rules of operation and transformation. We may think of these rules as in some way comparable to those surprisingly few conventions of addition, subtraction, substitution, and equivalence from which we can build up the enormously manifold and complex structure of arithmetic and algebra. Given the right manipulative rules, few building blocks are needed. The rules of Chomskian grammar "transform" certain primary configurations, such as noun symbol followed by verb symbol, into related configurations, even as algebraic equations will yield other equations if the proper rules of substitution are observed. Thus "John loves Mary" is pivoted, by a transformational rule that is not only specific but also, presumably, of very comprehensive and generalizing power, into "Mary is loved by John." This particular transformation, from active to passive, allows a human speaker to recognize and manipulate correctly the literally innumerable number of similarly organized and related propositions that he will come up against during a lifetime. The fact that the rules for transformation are "correct" insures that no ungrammatical or randomly ordered sentence is generated. If no such mechanism were operative, each new verbal situation—say, "I cut this loaf," "this loaf is cut by me"—would offer intractable dilemmas and demand a new, specific act of learning. This, urges Chomsky, is plainly not the case.

A sentence generated in this way has two distinct levels, and it is by virtue of this duality that Chomsky considers himself related to certain grammarians and logicians at work in France in the sixteen-sixties and after. "John loves Mary" is the *surface structure* of the sentence. It constitutes the sort of "physical signal," or phonetic articulation, to which we can perfectly well apply the traditional syntax we have learned in school: noun, verb, object, and so on. But this surface structure tells us little and obviously differs for every language. "Far below," as it were, lies the *deep structure,* from which our phonetic expression has been generated and of which the spoken, audible sentence is in some respects a projection or mapping.

What is this purported deep structure like? On this point, crucial as it is to his entire theory of language, Chomsky is elusive and not always consistent. It might have been best, though by no means satisfactory, had he said that we cannot adequately describe in words a psychic system that somehow operates before or very far beneath language. In the Kantian sense, there might be a "final skin" of consciousness and self, which we cannot describe because we cannot step outside it. Instead, Chomsky offers suggestions that are often rather obscure and tangential. The deep structure "may be highly abstract." It may or it may not have a close, "point-by-point correlation to the phonetic realization." That is, the visible contours of the landscape may or may not simulate or parallel the subterranean geological strata and dynamics from which it has been shaped and thrown up. What is worse, the visible terrain may be thoroughly misleading. Surface structures—the sentences we actually speak and hear—are not "like" the kernels from which they are generated by transformational rules. The deep structure from which, according to Chomsky, our understanding and use of all languages stem involves properties of a hitherto incomprehensible generality, abstraction, and formal power. We are not, obviously, to think of these "kernels" or primal linguistic units as verbal or syntactic in any ordinary sense. It is, if I follow Chomsky's hints rightly, *relations* that are involved—formidably simplified yet functional "presettings" that relate subject to object, person to verb. Again, I would suppose, the image of a computer, with its ability to transcribe computer speech into a print-out in English or any other idiom, is involved at some vital though perhaps unacknowledged stage in Chomsky's argument.

In any case, what has been shown is this: the unbounded variety of sentences human beings grasp and make use of upon every occasion in their lives can be derived from a limited set of formal counters and from a body of rules, also presumably limited, for the manipulation and rearrangement of these counters. To have shown this—and I think Chomsky has done so—is of itself a feat of great logical force and elegance. Substantively as well as historically, the exemplary suggestion came from mathematics and mathematical logic. In the binary system of notation, for instance, two symbols, 0 and 1, together with a body of rules about how they are to be put together and "read," suffice to operate with any number or group of numbers in the universe. Logic strives for a comparable economy and rigor at the base. Chomsky's hope that human language can be similarly schematized is understandable and intellectually exciting. But there is more to it than that. Chomsky is not arguing a mathematical model, a *hypothesis*—as Renaissance scientists called any of those formal proposals to which they did not necessarily attach material truth. Chomsky addresses himself to the human fact. He contends that only some such scheme of generation and transformation out of deep structures can account for the way in which *Homo sapiens* actually acquires language and communicates. He summarized this contention in his first Locke Lecture, at Oxford last April:

> A person who knows a language has mastered a set of rules and principles that determine an infinite, discrete set of sentences each of which has a fixed form and a fixed meaning or meaning-potential. Even at the lowest levels of intelligence, the characteristic use of this knowledge is free and creative ... in that one can instantaneously interpret an indefinitely large range of utterances, with no feeling of unfamiliarity or strangeness.

The postulate that language is unique to man (with which I entirely concur) and the correlative notion of *deep structures* have wide philosophic consequences. Of late, Chomsky has been readier than before to examine these and to move outside the confines of formal linguistic analysis. The key question is that of the nature and location of these deep structures and of the process through which human beings have achieved their singular capacity to articulate meaning and express imaginary concepts. In his attack on Skinner, Chomsky stressed the "completely unknown" character of the whole business and admitted that it might result from some form of learning or from a gradual maturation of the nervous system. But as his hypotheses have gained confidence and prestige, Chomsky has come to adopt what he himself calls a Cartesian position but what might more exactly be termed a development of Kant's theories of perception.

It is innate ideas or innate programs for all potential experience and mappings of experience that Chomsky is inferring. The existence of an "innate mental structure" seems to him indispensable to the generation of language. The "schema of universal grammar," whereby all men can operate in their own tongue and reasonably acquire another, must be assigned "to the mind as an innate character." Knowledge of language can be gained only "by an organism that is 'preset.'" Only man is innately equipped or programmed in this immensely specific yet creative fashion. All men being thus organized, there exist between them the bond of universal grammar and the concomitant possibility of translation from any one language into all other languages. It follows as well that no lower organic species will be able to master even rudimentary language forms (which is rather different from saying that certain animals may not be taught to mime human speech sounds). As Chomsky notes, recent studies of animal vision suggest that various species see angle, motion, and other complex properties of the physical world according to the special ways in which their nervous systems are patterned or "hooked up." These patterns are innate, and unalterable except through artificial lesion. Precisely in the same way, man communicates reality to himself and to others in linguistic forms because he has been uniquely imprinted with the capacity and need to do so.

We are now back with Kant and those a-priori mental structures or categories of space, time, and identity through which man interacts with the "outside" world and which govern both the freedom and the conceptual limits of that interaction. We are also back with the doctrines of the great grammarians of Port Royal in the second half of the seventeenth century regarding the universal grammar from which all human tongues ultimately derive their local forms.

How far can we probe into these deep structures and "settings" of consciousness? What kind of evidence are we looking for? Again, Chomsky is elusive and inclines toward modest disclaimers: "In fact, the processes by which the human mind achieved its present stage of complexity and its particular form of innate organization are a total mystery, as much so as the analogous questions about the physical or mental organizations of any other complex organism." Inasmuch as Chomsky has just drawn, and shrewdly so, on the positive results being achieved in the study of animal perception, this rider to the sentence is odd. Elsewhere, moreover, he is less circumspect. Linguistic universals, says Chomsky to Stuart Hampshire, must "be a biological property of the human mind." He adds, in a move strikingly reminiscent of those made by Freud when be was hoping for neurophysiological confirmation of his model of the subconscious (confirmation that never came), that there will "definitely someday be a physiological explanation for the mental processes that we are now discovering."

Does this confident assertion signify that generative linguistics is committed to materialism, to a view of consciousness as being purely and simply neurochemical? Some of its adherents seem to believe so. Chomsky's own formulation is subtler. He rightly points out that the boundaries between "mental" and "physical" are continually shifting. Numerous phenomena once regarded as wholly spiritual and outside the reach of empirical study have now become comprehensible in a physiological and experimental sense. There is beginning to be a chemistry of schizophrenia and a biochemistry of dreams as there has for some time now been a physiology of digestion or procreation. It is by keeping our descriptive categories open and negotiable that we can extend knowledge. "What is at issue," says Chomsky, "is only whether the physiological processes and physical processes that we now understand are already rich enough in principle—and maybe in fact—to cover the mental phenomena which are beginning to emerge" (again, the phrasing might be Freud's). The work done in the past fifteen years on the genetic code and on the neurochemistry of nervous impulse goes a long way toward suggesting how fantastically complicated and creative the energies at work in organic molecular processes are. The development of such work may—Chomsky is saying that it must—lead to some understanding of the "anatomy" of innate deep structures and linguistic generation.

In a simplified, obviously abbreviated form, these are the theories Professor Chomsky has put forward over the last twelve years. No one since the great French-Swiss linguist Saussure, in the early part of the century, and I.A. Richards, in the nineteen-thirties, has had more impact on the study of language or done more to suggest that linguistics is indeed a central discipline in the understanding of mind and behavior. But this does not mean that Chomsky's views have been universally accepted. They have been sharply queried by other linguists, and there are now signs that the Chomskian wave may be receding. That such a recession might occur at a moment when Chomsky's ideas are receiving their widest public and "journalistic" echo would be a coincidence common in the history of science and of ideas.

A good deal of the controversy in the profession is of an extremely technical nature. It involves differences of approach in regard to combinatorial logic, mathematical psychology, and semantics which are scarcely accessible to the layman. Nevertheless, a number of salient doubts can be made out. These are stated with great penetration by Professor Charles F. Hockett, of Cornell, in *The State of the Art* (Mouton, 1968). Hockett rejects the whole Chomskian model of the generation of grammatical sentences from hidden finite sets and rules. Chomsky's picture of language, says Hockett, is absurdly over-abstract; it is a fiction patterned not on real human speech but on the artificial propositions and tautologies of formal logic. Hockett's way of putting this decisive point is arduous but unmistakable: A mathematical linguistics on Chomskian lines is an absurdity because human speech is not a "well-defined subset of the set of all finite strings over a well-defined alphabet." In simpler terms: When we deal with human speech we are not dealing with a rigorously definable, closed system all of whose variants can be derived from a single set or cluster of unchanging elements; we are not looking at the periodic table of chemical elements all of whose structures and atomic weights can be reduced to combinations of certain primal, strictly defined units. Chomsky's transformational grammar fails to account for the vital, fascinating ability of human speakers not only to know how to string words together to form a sentence but to know when and how to stop. This is one of those apparently obvious but deep points on which the cogency of a theory of language may well depend. Let me make it as plain as I can. "One plus one equals two" is a completely acceptable English sentence. "One plus one plus one equals three" is already faintly awkward and almost implies a didactic or special context. "One plus one plus one plus one equals four" is intolerable, and so will be all further sentences built on the same pattern. Yet formally all such sentences are transformations of the first by virtue, presumably, of the "additive rule" somehow established in the passage from deep to surface structure. According to Chomsky's theory, nothing is *grammatically* wrong with a string of "one"s connected by "and"s or "plus"es, or, as Professor Victor Yngve, of the University of Chicago, has pointed out, with other, more complex sentences that are incomprehensible. Yet we know, and know at an early, precise point, that we are no longer speaking acceptable English, that we are at best aping a computer language. What gives us this definite but extraordinarily subtle, perhaps "musical," knowledge?

There is no genuine evidence, argues Hockett, for anything like the deep structures that Chomsky postulates. There is, on the contrary, plenty of evidence that different languages handle the world in very different ways and that all languages have in them "sources of openness" that Chomsky ignores. His fundamental error, urges Hockett, is the belief that a study of semantics can ever be separated from a study of the actual grammar and lexicon of the relevant language or family of languages. By patient comparison of languages as they are in fact spoken, and by careful induction, we may come to discover "cross-language generalizations." Joseph H. Greenberg's *Universals of Language*, published in 1962, and comparative analyses of Southwest American Indian languages, now in progress, are steps in the proper direction. The empirically located and verified common traits or language habits that emerge from this kind of ethnolinguistic study may have nothing to do with universal deep structures. A universal grammar in Chomsky's sense is, according to Hockett, a pipe dream. It is not universal kernel sentences and transformational rules but a manifold context of specific political history and social sensibility that makes a man "stand" for office in English English and "run" for it in American.

Hockett's charge that Chomsky leaves out the spontaneous, altering genius of actual speech touches on a larger philosophic dissent. This is well put by Dr. Yorick Wilks in a recent review of *Language and Mind*. Dr. Wilks, it may be worth noting, is a sometime associate of the Cambridge Language Research Unit, a group whose philosophic approach to linguistics may be more searching than Chomsky's and whose "thesaurus method" attempts to deal with units of speed more complex and realistic than those usually cited in generative grammar. Wilks suggests that despite all its acerbity and conviction Chomsky's quarrel with Skinner is quite spurious. The dispute is not between a mechanistic model and a free or idealistic vision of the production of human speech but "between two alternative mechanistic theories: Skinner's the simple one, and Chomsky's the more complicated." In the terms I have been using, the quarrel would be between a model based on an old-fashioned adding machine and one founded on a super-computer. Wilks then argues, in a subtle and incisive critique, that the kind of mechanistic scheme devised by the behaviorists would, if sufficiently refined, produce the types of basic sentences and transformations posited by Chomskian grammar. That is—and this is a penetrating observation—the language picture postulated by Chomsky does not depend necessarily or uniquely on the theory of generation from deep structures. What were called "finite-state" and "phrase-structure" rules of grammar could also do the job: "If anyone came in and watched the two machines chugging away, he could never tell that they had been programmed with quite different rules."

How can we ever hope to look "inside the machine" (an image as Cartesian as it is Chomskian)? Chomsky's "innate structures," says Dr. Wilks, may well represent a "retreat from the facts," a refusal to submit his formal design to any possibility of experimental investigation. How can we expect to find out *what* is innate in the mind? "We can't look; external behavior is no guide at all, and, of course, it's no help to ask what people think." In view of this impenetrability of "innate presettings," it is a very odd step, suggests Wilks, to pass from categories of grammatical description that may be "natural" and "deep" in Western languages to the assertion that there are universal mental patterns underlying *all* languages. Classical Chinese (and what other evidence have we?) seems to have no need of our noun-and-verb structure. How, then, can we assign to it innate grammatical properties obviously patterned on our own habits of syntax? Chomsky may, almost inadvertently, be tending toward a mechanistic doctrine of his own, all the more disturbing in that it would be culturally as well as formally deterministic. Though Wilks does not make the point, the radical humanism of Chomsky's politics would render such a position deeply ironic.

Dr. Wilks's point about Chinese relates immediately to my own main difficulties in regard to Chomsky's theory of language. Some four thousand languages are in current use on our crowded planet. There are numerous territories in Africa, Asia, and Latin America (not to mention corners of Switzerland) that are splintered by distinct, mutually incomprehensible tongues, though these territories are uniform in climate, way of life, and economic needs. These four thousand languages, moreover, are almost certainly the remnants of an even greater number. So-called rare languages disappear every year from active usage and the recollection of aged or isolated informants. This proliferation of human idiom is an immensely exciting but also scandalous fact. Few linguists since Wilhelm von Humboldt, in the early decades of the nineteenth century, have thought hard enough about its enigmatic implications. Today, the professional divisions between formal, mathematical linguistics (if such really exists), on the one hand, and the comparative and anthropological study of actual languages, on the other, have further blurred the issue. I myself am unable to consider intellectually satisfactory or adequate to the truth any model or formula of human verbal behavior that does not in some way account for this fantastic multiplicity. Why four thousand or more languages? Why, by a factor of a thousand, more languages than, say, there are human races or blood types? No Darwinian analogy of variation through natural selection and adaptation will do. The vast variety of fauna and flora represents a wonder of specific adjustment to local conditions and to the requirements of competitive survival. The contrary is true of the proliferation of neighboring tongues. That proliferation has been one of the most evident and intractable barriers to human collaboration and economic progress. It has left major areas of human habitation internally riven and largely isolated from history. Many cultures that have come to stagnation or ruin may have been linguistic dropouts—which is not to say that we have any solid evidence that one language is better suited than another to the realization of individual or social achievement. We know of no people that does not have in its mythology some variant on the story of the Tower of Babel. This is eloquent proof of men's bewilderment in the face of the multiplicity of tongues that has set between them constant walls of seeming gibberish and silence. Translation is not a victory but a perpetual, often baffling necessity.

To my mind, it is now the main job of linguistics, working with anthropology and ethnography, to get our actual language condition into clear focus. (We do not even have a truly exhaustive language atlas as yet. We must learn to ask the right questions about the deeply puzzling phenomenon of linguistic diversity. There *are* clues. But they do not, I think, point in Chomsky's direction.)

The fundamental matter of language proliferation hardly turns up in the theory of generative and transformational grammar. A cryptic remark occurs toward the close of *Language and Mind*: "The empirical study of linguistic universals has led to the formulation of highly restrictive and, I believe, quite plausible hypotheses concerning the possible variety of human languages." First of all, it is a moot point whether this is so. The preliminary investigation of what certain linguists provisionally assume to be syntactic universals has until now been limited to but a few languages, and the results obtained have been at an almost intangible level of generality (i.e., "in all known languages there are verbs or parts of speech that indicate action"). But let us suppose that the kind of empirical study that Greenberg, Hockett, and others are pursuing does in fact produce verifiable "cross-language generalizations." These would not necessarily support Chomsky's theory of universal grammar and innate deep structures. The point is crucial and must be put carefully.

Chomsky postulates "innate presettings" deeply embedded or imprinted in the human mind. They "must simply be a biological property." Now, such settings *could* lead to the production, through transformational rules, of thousands of human languages. They could, but there is absolutely no obvious reason for them to do so. On the contrary: given a scheme of kernel sentences and functional rules, complex but certainly finite, we would expect the generation of a very restricted, clearly interrelated number of human tongues. What we *should* find, if the Chomskian theory of innate biological universals is true, is the order of diversity shown by human pigmentation and bone structure. The degree of variety here is totally different, both qualitatively and quantitatively, from that which we find in language. Let me go further: The linguistics of Noam Chomsky *could* account, and could account with beautiful economy and depth, for a world in which men would all be speaking *one* language, diversified at most by a moderate range of dialects. The fact that generative and transformational grammar would be beautifully concordant with such a result, that such a result is in some manner both natural and obvious to Chomsky's postulates, seems to me to cast serious doubts on the whole model. Like the great language mystics, who extend from Nicholas of Cusa to Jakob Böhme, Chomsky often seems to conjure up the radiant fiction of that single tongue spoken by Adam and his sons but forever lost and pulverized at Babel. In short, key features of the Chomskian language revolution appear to go against the grain of the linguistic situation in which the human race actually finds itself and in which it has existed as far as history and conjecture can reach back.

The controversies initiated by Chomsky's own polemics

against behaviorism are only in their early phase. It may be that the arguments urged against universal grammar will be met and that the notion of deep structures will acquire better philosophic or physiological support. Recently, claims have been put forward suggesting that children between the ages of eighteen months and two years formulate sentences in a way that exhibits deep structures not yet overlaid by any particular language. Notably, it has been claimed that there are Chomskian analogues in the way in which Russian and Japanese children acquire their respective languages. I wonder. But, obviously, time and investigation will tell. One thing is clear: Chomsky is an exhilarating thinker, possessed, as was Spinoza before him, by a passionate appetite for unity, for complete logic and explanation. There is a strong streak of monism in Chomsky's desire to get to the root of things, be they political or linguistic. But it might be, to advance a cautionary platitude, that neither politics nor language is quite like that. Unreason and the obstinate disorder of particular facts may prove resistant to the claims of either political justice or formal logic. It is part of the stature of Chomsky's work that the issues of disagreement raised by it are basic. To me, man looks a queerer, more diverse beast than Chomsky would have him. And Nimrod's tower lies broken still.

November 15, 1969

A DEATH OF KINGS

THERE ARE THREE intellectual pursuits, and so far as I am aware only three, in which human beings have performed major feats before the age of puberty. They are music, mathematics, and chess. Mozart wrote music of undoubted competence and charm before he was eight. At the age of three, Karl Friedrich Gauss reportedly performed numerical computations of some intricacy; he proved himself a prodigiously rapid but also a fairly deep arithmetician before he was ten. In his twelfth year, Paul Morphy defeated all comers in New Orleans—no small feat in a city that, a hundred years ago, counted several formidable chess players. Are we dealing here with some kind of elaborate imitative reflexes, with achievements conceivably in reach of automata? Or do these wondrous miniature beings actually create? Rossini's Six Sonatas for Two Violins, Cello, and Double Bass, composed by the boy during the summer of 1804, are patently influenced by Haydn and Vivaldi, but the main melodic lines are Rossini's, and beautifully inventive. Aged twelve, Pascal seems in fact to have re-created for and by himself the essential axioms and initial propositions of Euclidean geometry. The earliest recorded games of Capablanca and Alekhine contain significant ideas and show marks of personal style. No theory of Pavlovian reflex or simian mimesis will account for the facts. In these three domains we find creation, not infrequently characteristic and memorable, at a fantastically early age.

Is there an explanation? One looks for some genuine relationship between the three activities; in what way do music, mathematics, and chess resemble one another? This is the sort of question to which there ought to be a trenchant—indeed, a classic—reply. (The notion that there *is* a deep affinity is not novel.) But one finds little except shadowy hints and metaphor. The psychology of musical invention—as distinct from mere virtuosity of performance—is all but nonexistent. Despite fascinating hints by the mathematicians Jules Poincaré and Jacques Hadamard, scarcely anything is known about the intuitive and ratiocinative processes that underlie mathematical discovery. Dr. Fred Reinfeld and Mr. Gerald Abrahams have written interestingly on "the chess mind," but without establishing whether there is such a thing and, if there is, what constitutes its bizarre powers. In each of these areas, "psychology" turns out to be principally a matter of anecdotes, among them the dazzling executive and creative showings of child prodigies.

Reflecting, one is struck by two points. It looks very much as if the formidable mental energies and capacities for purposeful combination exhibited by the child master in music, mathematics, and chess are almost wholly isolated, as if they explode to ripeness apart from, and in no necessary relation to, normally maturing cerebral and physical traits. A musical prodigy, an infant composer or conductor, may in every other respect be a small child, petulant and ignorant as are ordinary children of his age. There is no evidence to suggest that Gauss's behavior when he was a young boy, his fluency or emotional coherence, in any way exceeded that of other little boys; he was an adult, and more than a normal adult, solely in respect of numerical and geometric insights. Anyone who has played at chess with a very young and highly gifted boy will have noticed the glaring, nearly scandalous disparity between the ruses and analytic sophistication of the child's moves on the board and his puerile behavior the moment the pieces are put away. I have seen a six-year-old handle a French Defense with tenacious artistry and collapse a moment after the game was ended into a loud, randomly destructive brat. In short, whatever happens in the brain and nervous synapses of a young Mendelssohn, of a Galois, of Bobby Fischer, the otherwise erratic schoolboy, seems to happen in essential separateness. Now, although the latest neurological theories are again invoking the possibility of specialized location—the idea, familiar to eighteenth-century phrenology, that our brains have different areas for different skills or potentials—we simply don't have the facts. Certain very obvious sensory centers exist, it is true, yet we just don't know how or if the cortex divides its multitudinous tasks. But the image of location is suggestive.

Music, mathematics, and chess are in vital respects dynamic acts of location. Symbolic counters are arranged in significant rows. Solutions, be they of a discord, of an algebraic equation, or of a positional impasse, are achieved by a regrouping, by a sequential reordering of individual units and unit-clusters (notes, integers, rooks or pawns). The child master, like his adult counterpart, is able to visualize in an instantaneous yet preternaturally confident way how the thing should look several moves hence. He sees the logical, the necessary harmonic and melodic argument as it arises out of an initial key relation or the preliminary fragments of a theme. He knows the order, the appropriate dimension, of the sum or geometric figure before he has performed the intervening steps. He announces mate in six because the victorious end position, the maximally efficient configuration of his pieces on the board, lies somehow "out there," in graphic, inexplicably clear sight of his mind. In each instance, the cerebral-nervous mechanism makes a veritable leap forward into a "subsequent space." Very possibly this is a fiercely specialized neurological—one is tempted to say neurochemical—ability all but isolated from other mental and physiological capacities and susceptible of fantastically rapid development.

Some chance instigation—a tune or harmonic progression picked out on a piano in the next room, a row of figures set out for addition on a shop slate, the sight of the opening moves in a café chess game—triggers a chain reaction in one limited zone of the human psyche. The result is a beauteous monomania.

Music and mathematics are among the preëminent wonders of the race. Lévi-Strauss sees in the invention of melody "a key to the supreme mystery" of man—a clue, could we but follow it up, to the singular structure and genius of the species. The power of mathematics to devise actions for reasons as subtle, witty, manifold as any offered by sensory experience and to move forward in an endless unfolding of self-creating life is one of the strange, deep marks man leaves on the world. Chess, on the other hand, is a game in which thirty-two bits of ivory, horn, wood, metal, or (in stalags) sawdust stuck together with shoe polish are pushed around on sixty-four alternately colored squares. To the addict, such a description is blasphemy. The origins of chess are shrouded in mists of controversy, but unquestionably this very ancient, trivial pastime has seemed to many exceptionally intelligent human beings of all races and centuries to constitute a reality, a focus for the emotions, as substantial as, often more substantial than, reality itself. Cards can come to mean the same absolute. But their magnetism is impure. A mania for whist or poker hooks into the obvious, universal magic of money. The financial element in chess, where it exists at all, has always been small or accidental.

To a true chess player, the pushing about of thirty-two counters on 8×8 squares is an end in itself, a whole world next to which that of mere biological or political or social life seems messy, stale, and contingent. Even the *patzer,* the wretched amateur who charges out with his knight pawn when the opponent's bishop decamps to R4, feels this daemonic spell. There are siren moments when quite normal creatures otherwise engaged, men such as Lenin and myself, feel like giving up everything—marriage, mortgages, careers, the Russian Revolution—in order to spend their days and nights moving little carved objects up and down a quadrate board. At the sight of a set, even the tawdriest of plastic pocket sets, one's fingers arch and a coldness as in a light sleep steals over one's spine. Not for gain, not for knowledge or renown, but in some autistic enchantment, pure as one of Bach's inverted canons or Euler's formula for polyhedra. There, surely, lies one of the real connections. For all their wealth of content, for all the sum of history and social institution vested in them, music, mathematics, and chess are resplendently useless (applied mathematics is just higher plumbing, a kind of music for the police band). They are metaphysically trivial, irresponsible. They refuse to relate outward, to take reality for arbiter. This is the source of their witchery. They tell us, as does a kindred but much later process, abstract art, of man's unique capacity to "build against the world," to devise forms that are zany, totally useless, austerely frivolous. Such forms are irresponsible to reality, and therefore inviolate, as is nothing else, to the banal authority of death.

Allegoric associations of death with chess are perennial: in medieval woodcuts, in Renaissance frescoes, in the films of Cocteau and Bergman. Death wins the game, yet in so doing it submits, even if but momentarily, to rules wholly outside its dominion. Lovers play chess to arrest the gnawing pace of time and banish the world. Thus, in Yeats's *Deirdre*:

> They knew that there was nothing that could save them,
> And so played chess as they had any night
> For years, and waited for the stroke of sword.
> I never heard a death so out of reach
> Of common hearts, a high and comely end.

It is this ostracism of common mortality, this immersion of human beings in a closed, crystalline sphere, that the poet or novelist who makes chess his theme must capture. The scandal, the paradox of all-important triviality must be made psychologically credible. Success in the genre is rare. Mr. James Whitfield Ellison's *Master Prim* (Little, Brown) is not a good novel, but there are worthwhile points in it. Francis Rafael, the narrator, is sent by his editor to do a cover story on Julian Prim, the rising star in American chess. At first the middle-aged chronicler, established and suburban to the core, and the nineteen-year-old master don't hit it off. Prim is arrogant and abrasive; he has the manners of a sharp-toothed puppy. But Rafael himself once dreamed of becoming a ranking chess player. In the tautest scene in the novel, a series of "pots" games at ten seconds a move between Julian and diverse "pigeons" at the Gotham Chess Club, the novelist and the young killer meet across the board. Rafael almost manages a draw, and there springs up between the two antagonists "a kind of freemasonry of mutual respect." By the last page, Prim has won the United States Chess Championship and is engaged to Rafael's daughter. Mr. Ellison's Story has all the elements of a *roman à clef.* Julian's idiosyncrasies and career could have been based on those of Bobby Fischer, whose personal and professional antagonism toward Samuel Reshevsky—a conflict unusual for its public vehemence even in the necessarily combative world of chess—appears to be the center of the plot. Eugene Berlin, Mr. Ellison's Reshevsky, is the reigning champion. In a game that provides the all too obvious climax, Julian wrests the crown from his hated senior. The game itself, a Queen's Pawn Opening, though very likely based on actual Master play, is of no deep interest or beauty. Berlin's treatment of the defense is unimaginative, and Julian's breakthrough on the twenty-second move hardly merits the excited response provided by the novelist, let alone the Championship. Minor incidents and personalities are also closely modelled on actuality; no aficionado will fail to be reminded of the Sturdivant brothers or mistake the location of the Gotham Club. What Mr. Ellison does convey is something of the queer, still violence chess engenders. To defeat another human being at chess is to humble him at the very roots of his intelligence; to defeat him easily is to leave him strangely stripped. At a boozy Manhattan soirée, Julian takes on Bryan Pleasant, the English film star, at knight odds and a buck a game. He wins over and over, double or nothing, his "queen appearing and slashing at the enemy like a great enraged beast." In a vindictive display of virtuosity, Julian allows himself less and less time. The naked savagery of his gift suddenly appalls him: "It's like a sickness. . . . It comes over you like a fever and you lose all sense of the way things are. . . . I mean who can you beat in fifteen seconds? Even if you're God. And I'm not God. It's stupid to have to say that, but sometimes I have to say it."

That chess can be to madness close allied is the theme of Stefan Zweig's famous *Schachnovelle* published in 1941 and translated into English as *The Royal Game*. Mirko Czentovic, the World Champion, is aboard a luxurious liner headed for Buenos Aires. For two hundred and fifty dollars a game, he agrees to play against a group of passengers. He beats their combined effort with contemptuous, maddening ease. Suddenly a mysterious helper joins the browbeaten amateurs. Czentovic is fought to a draw. His rival turns out to be a Viennese doctor whom the Gestapo held in solitary confinement. An old book on chess was the prisoner's sole link with the outside world (a cunning symbolic inversion of the usual role of chess). Dr. B. knows all its hundred and fifty games by heart, replaying them mentally a thousand times over. In the process, he has split his own ego into black and white. Knowing each game so ridiculously well, he has achieved a lunatic speed in mental play. He knows black's riposte even before white has made the next move. The World Champion has condescended to a second round. He is beaten in the first game by the marvellous stranger. Czentovic slows down the rate of play. Crazed by what seems to him an unbearable tempo and by a total sense of *déjà vu* Dr. B. feels the approach of schizophrenia and breaks off in the midst of a further brilliant game. This macabre fable, in which Zweig communicates an impression of genuine Master play by suggesting the shape of each game rather than by spelling out the moves, points to the schizoid element in chess. Studying openings and end-games, replaying Master games, the chess player is at once white and black. In actual play, the hand poised on the other side of the board is in some measure his own. He is, as it were, inside his opponent's skull, seeing himself as the enemy of the moment, parrying his own moves and immediately leaping back into his own skin to seek a counter to the counterstroke. In a card game, the adversary's cards are hidden; in chess, his pieces are constantly open before us, inviting us to see things from their side. Thus there is, literally, in every mate a touch of what is called suimate—a kind of chess problem in which the solver is required to maneuver his own pieces into mate. In a serious chess game, between players of comparable strength, we are defeated and at the same time defeat ourselves. Thus the taste of ash in one's mouth.

The title of Nabokov's early novel (recently published here by McGraw-Hill) *King, Queen, Knave* refers to a suit of cards. But the primary devices of the book are based on chess. Mr. Black and Mr. White play chess as the erotic mock melodrama nears its anticlimax. Their game precisely mirrors the situation of the characters: "Black's knight was planning to attack White's king and queen with a forked check." Chess is the underlying metaphor and symbolic referent throughout Nabokov's fiction. Pnin plays chess; a chance look at the Soviet chess magazine *8 × 8* impels the hero of *The Gift* to undertake his mythical biography of Chernyshevski; the title of *The Real Life of Sebastian Knight* is a chess allusion, and the intimation of Master play between two modes of truth runs through the tale; the duel between Humbert Humbert and Quilty in *Lolita* is plotted in terms of a chess match whose stakes are death. These points and the entire role of chess in Nabokov's opus are set out in Mr. Andrew Field's admirably thorough and perceptive *Nabokov,*

His Life in Art (Little, Brown; 1967). But Mr. Field rather neglects the masterpiece of the genre. First written in Russian in 1929, *The Luzhin Defense* first appeared in English in 1964, in these pages. The whole novel is concerned with the insubstantial wonders of the game. We believe in Luzhin's chess genius because Nabokov so beautifully conveys the specialized, freakish quality of his gift. In all other respects and moves of life, Luzhin is a shambling, infantile creature, pathetically in search of normal human contact. When he thinks of the matter at all, human relations seem to him more or less stylized movements in space; survival in society depends on one's grasp of more or less arbitrary rules, less coherent, to be sure, than those which govern a *prise en passant*. Personal affliction is an unsolved problem, as cold and full of traps as are the chess problems composed by the hated Valentinov. Only a poet himself under the spell of chess could have written the account of the Luzhin-Turati encounter. Here Nabokov communicates as no other writer has done the secret affinities of chess, music, mathematics, the sense in which a fine game is a form of melody and animate geometry:

> Then his fingers groped for and found a bewitching, brittle, crystalline combination—which with a gentle tinkle disintegrated at Turati's first reply.... Turati finally decided on this combination—and immediately a kind of musical tempest overwhelmed the board and Luzhin searched stubbornly in it for the tiny, clear note that he needed in order in his turn to swell it out into a thunderous harmony.

Absorbed in the game, Luzhin forgets to apply a lit match to his cigarette. His hand is stung: "The pain immediately passed, but in the fiery gap he had seen something unbearably awesome, the full horror of the abysmal depths of chess. He glanced at the chessboard and his brain wilted from hitherto unprecedented weariness. But the chessmen were pitiless, they held and absorbed him. There was horror in this, but in this also was the sole harmony, for what else exists in the world besides chess? Fog, the unknown, non-being. . . ."

For what else exists in the world besides chess? An idiotic question, but one that every true chess player has at some time asked himself. And to which the answer is—when reality has contracted to sixty-four squares, when the brain narrows to a luminous blade pointed at a single congeries of lines and occult forces—at least uncertain. There are more possible variants in a game at chess than, it is calculated, there are atoms in this sprawling universe of ours. The number of possible legitimate ways of playing the first four moves on each side comes to 318,979,584,000. Playing one game a minute and never repeating it, the entire population of the globe would need two hundred and sixteen billion years to exhaust all conceivable ways of playing the first ten moves of Nabokov's Mr. White and Mr. Black. As Luzhin plummets to his death, his carefully analyzed suimate, the chasm of the night and of the chill flagstones below "was seen to divide into dark and pale squares."

So does the world in one's recurrent dream of glory. I see the whole scene before me in mocking clarity. The row of tables at Rossolimo's chess café in the Village or under the greasy ceiling of a hotel lounge in the town of X (Cincinnati, Innsbruck, Lima). The Grand Master is giving a routine exhibition—thirty-five boards in simultaneous play. The rule on such an occasion is that all his opponents play black and move as soon as he steps to the board. The weaker the play, the more rapid his circuit around the room. The more rapid his wolf's prowl, the more harried and clumsy one's answering moves. I am playing a Sicilian Defense, hanging on, trying to parry that darting hand and the punishing swiftness of its visitations. The Grand Master castles on the fifteenth move and I reply Q-QKt5. Once again his step hastens toward my table, but this time, O miracle, he pauses, bends over the board, and, wonder of celestial wonders, calls for a chair! The hall is unbearably hushed, all eyes are on me. The Master forces an exchange of queens, and there surges up in my memory, with daemonic precision, the vision of the Yates-Lasker game in the seventeenth round of the 1924 World Championship in New York. Black won on that March afternoon. I dare not hope for that; I am not mad. But perhaps once, once in my life, a Master will look up from the board, as Botvinnik looked up at the ten-year-old Boris Spassky during an exhibition game in Leningrad in 1947—look at me not as a nameless *patzer* but as a fellow human being, and say, in a still, small voice, *"Remis."*

September 7, 1968

GIVE THE WORD

DID VICTORIAN PUNDITS need less sleep than we do? Consider the facts. They tramped miles over brake and through briar before breakfast or after high tea. At either or both of which collations they would consume flitches of bacon, grilled kidneys, silver-sides of Scotch beef, a garland of mutton chops, kippers and bloaters in silvery shoals, and half a dozen cavernous cups of India tea. They sired more offspring than Jacob the Patriarch. They breathed Homer and Catullus, Plato and Vergil, Holy Scripture and Bradshaw's Railway Guide through their stentorian nostrils. When they voyaged, it was either through Turkestan with a walking stick and one change of flea powder or to the spas of Europe with a pride of steamer trunks, portable escritoires, tooled-leather vanity cases, and mountainous hampers. The Sunday sermons that they orated or listened to ran anywhere up to two mortal hours. A second service, with an average of eleven hymns, four homilies, and assorted benedictions, followed in the afternoon. After which there would be Mendelssohn's "Songs Without Words" at the piano, a reading out loud of two or three of the shorter epics by Clough or Tennyson, a charade featuring General Gordon's celebrated descent of a staircase at Khartoum in the grinning face of death.

Between which accomplishments our sages, scholars, boffins,

and reformers would learn languages, sciences, literatures, and crafts at a rate and with a mastery to make lesser generations cringe. Victorian memories ingested epics, Biblical family trees, the flora of Lapland, Macedonian irregular verbs, Parliamentary reports, local topography, and the names of third cousins with tireless voracity. Victorian wrists and fingers wrote, without typewriters, without Dictaphones, to the tune of thousands of printable words per diem. Histories of religious opinion in six volumes, lives of Disraeli ditto, twelve tomes of *The Golden Bough*, eighteen of Darwin, thirty-five of Ruskin. Trollope had composed his daily stint of several thousand deftly placed words before the professional working day had even begun. Dickens could produce a quire at a time with the printer's devil puffing at the door. But this was only the half of it; for after the public leviathans came the private immensities—diaries that run to thousands of minutely crowded pages, personal reflections, maxims, and exercises in pious meditation straining the hinges of marbled notebooks folio size, and, above all, letters. Letters of a length and deliberation of which we have no present imagining. Letters in the literal thousands and ten thousands: to Cousin Hallam on the Zambezi, to the Very Reverend Noel Tolpuddle concerning the thorny points raised in his nine addresses on infant perdition, letters of credit and discredit, epistles to every member of the family, to the beloved across the street. Written by hand. Very often with a first draft and a manuscript copy (no carbon, no Xerox). With scratchy pens. In the yellowish, straining aura of gaslight. In rooms getting chillier by the hour.

It is late 1866, and a position is to be filled at the British Museum Library. A twenty-nine-year-old bank clerk applies. He writes by hand, of course, in copperplate, and at some break in a ten-hour day. We need to hear him in full:

> I have to state that Philology, both Comparative and special, has been my favourite pursuit during the whole of my life,

and that I possess a general acquaintance with the languages & literature of the Aryan and Syro-Arabic classes—not indeed to say that I am familiar with all or nearly all of these, but I possess that general lexical & structural knowledge which makes the intimate knowledge only a matter of a little application. With several I have a more intimate acquaintance as with the Romance tongues, Italian, French, Catalan, Spanish, Latin & in a less degree Portuguese, Vaudois, Provençal & various dialects. In the Teutonic branch, I am tolerably familiar with Dutch (having at my place of business correspondence to read in Dutch, German, French & occasionally other languages), Flemish, German, Danish. In Anglo-Saxon and Moeso-Gothic my studies have been much closer, I having prepared some works for publication upon these languages. I know a little of the Celtic, and am at present engaged with the Slavonic, having obtained a useful knowledge of Russian. In the Persian, Achaemenian Cuneiform, & Sanscrit branches, I know for the purposes of Comparative Philology. I have sufficient knowledge of Hebrew & Syriac to read at sight the *O.T.* and *Peshito;* to a less degree I know Aramaic Arabic, Coptic and Phoenician to the point where it was left by Gesenius.

James A.H. Murray, son of a tailor in the small town of Denholm, near Hawick, in Teviotdale, did not get the job. But this did not, for even an instant, diminish his conviction that the intimate knowledge of almost anything a man will turn his soul and spirit to is "only a matter of a little application." From this conviction came the greatest intellectual monument of the Victorian age, and the achievement that, more even than the Authorized Version or Shakespeare, incarnates the genius of the English tongue: the Oxford English Dictionary, under James Murray's editorship. The story of its preparation is one of the sovereign adventures of the life of the mind. It is told, beautifully, by K. M. Elisabeth

Murray, Murray's granddaughter, in *Caught in the Web of Words* (Yale).

From earliest childhood in the one buzzing room of a border-country school, Murray had shown prodigious capacities in both the acquisition and the imparting of exact knowledge. When taking over a one-man academy in Hawick, the young Murray, then all of twenty, could confidently advertise, "In addition to the usual elements of education comprising English Reading, Writing, Grammar, and Composition, Arithmetic, Mathematics, Geography, Drawing, Ancient and Modern Languages, Mr. M. will make it his endeavour, to impart to his Pupils, both Male and Female, the leading principles of Moral Science, Political Economy, History, Natural Science, Human Physiology, and the other Branches of Knowledge which must form an important part of every Enlightened System of Education." Soon the Hawick pedagogue "could read in a sort of way 25 or more languages." More than individual talent and formidable assiduity lies behind this encyclopedic zest. Murray exemplifies dramatically the Victorian capacity for squeezing experience to the pips, for making every sensation yield organized knowledge. The wild flowers Murray saw on his upland walks became exact botany. His eye made a live cartography of the contours of moor and beacon. When he picked up a flint or a medieval potsherd, the context of local and national history was firmly in place. There was no waste motion in heart or brain. We find this omnivorous apprehension, at once sensory and abstract, in Browning's verse, in Carlyle's prose, in the prodigal architecture of Gilbert Scott. A tremendous confidence underwrites it, and a gymnastic of concentration and memory. By contrast, our schooling is planned amnesia, our work a hiatus between phone calls.

Murray was fortunate in that his passion for philology, for phonetics, for the organic development of linguistic forms, for dialects and the singular splendor of the English tongue precisely coincided with the start of modern English studies. In London,

F.J. Furnivall, founder and editor of the Early English Text Society; Walter Skeat, the great Anglo-Saxon scholar; and Alexander Melville Bell, Alexander Graham's father and a pioneer in the scientific study and notation of phonetics, could spot Murray's phenomenal gifts. And though English society was rank-ridden to a degree, the eighteen-fifties and sixties brought an intense liberalization in scholarship and the sciences. In the new freemasonry of intellectual pursuit, Murray's humble origins and status, as a schoolmaster and as a correspondence clerk in the Chartered Bank of India, Australia & China, did not matter. The author of *The Dialect of the Southern Counties of Scotland* had made his mark. In Paris, the *Revue Celtique* took respectful note.

As Elisabeth Murray shows, the process that led to the conception of the Oxford Dictionary was halting and uncertain. Noah Webster had challenged and in many respects surpassed Dr. Johnson. In Germany, Jacob and Wilhelm Grimm, with a battalion of helpers, were at work on the great *Deutsches Wörterbuch*. At sixty-one, Emile Littré, philologist, educator, translator of Dante into medieval French, was about to launch on his thirteen-year task of producing a historical dictionary of the French language (another brilliant example of nineteenth-century work addiction). Only Britain lagged behind. And this at a time when empire glowed at high noon, and when conquest and commerce had flung the English language across the globe on a scale undreamed of by the ecumenical aspirations of Latin or the prestigious mundanity of French. Would Macmillan's undertake the task? Should it be organized and sponsored by the Philological Society, with Dr. Furnivall's busy but often bruising talents at the hub? Ought there to be a public subscription? Negotiations dragged as the cost and intricacy of the enterprise began to emerge. It was Henry Sweet, the original of Professor Higgins in Shaw's *Pygmalion*, who perceived clearly that the best chance for "the English Dictionary" was its adoption by the Oxford University Press, and that if there was one man capable of tackling the titanic project it was James Murray, assistant master at the Mill Hill School.

Murray hesitated. More than anyone else associated with the whole idea, he had some notion of the labors and vexations involved. He met with the delegates of the Oxford University Press in April, 1878. It was March, 1879, before an agreement was concluded. Even for that time, the terms offered to Murray were tight: a publication of seven thousand pages, to be completed at the rate of at least eight hundred pages every year. If this schedule could not be met an extension of up to five years was allowed, but with no increase in the editor's total payment of nine thousand pounds. Out of this sum, Murray, to a very large extent, financed his own staff, the physical plant needed to assemble the millions of word slips, and life for himself and a family that was soon to number eleven children. No one in that early spring of the forty second year of the glorious reign of Queen Victoria could have guessed that the O.E.D. would run to more than sixteen thousand pages, that it would cost three hundred thousand pounds to produce, and that neither James Murray nor his heirs would ever receive a penny's profit.

The trouble, to be sure, lay with the editor's majestic vision and his perfectionism. Murray had in mind a lexicon that would literally encompass the entire formal and substantive history of the English language, from its Anglo-Saxon, Latin, and Anglo-Norman roots to the latest ideological, literary, journalistic, and scientific coinage. Illustrations of usage would be drawn not only, as they had been in Dr. Johnson, from eminent and approved authors but from that almost incommensurable spectrum of printed material—literary-technical, ephemeral, colloquial—which articulates the organic existence and echo chamber of a civilization. Moreover, the etymology and, where applicable, the dialectological genesis of every word were to be traced and set down according to the most rigorous standards of modern scholarship (standards evolved in Indo-European studies since the beginning of the nineteenth century and now tightened by the establishment, in which James Murray had himself been instrumental, of phonological analyses). Even with lavish financing and an army of trained auxiliaries, Murray's project would have been overwhelming. Instead, perfection had to be achieved on a shoestring.

Though reticent in her style, Elisabeth Murray speaks in detail of the "triple nightmare" that came to hang over Murray's labors and that almost brought the O.E.D. to a halt. Some five million word slips provided by volunteer readers had to be sorted and stored, to be used in compiling entries listing a word's earliest known appearance in the language and examples of those subsequent, changing usages through which its history could be shown. Both at Mill Hill and, after 1885, at Oxford, the name Scriptorium (soon famous throughout the literate world) stood for an inadequate, often damp, desperately overcrowded garden shed. At no point did the editor and his team have even the physical facilities that would, today, be regarded as minimal for any comparable enterprise. Soon, time became a harrowing factor. As the unprecedented scope and intended excellence of Murray's design began to emerge, the delegates of the University Press fretted. Would the monster see the light of day within the decade, within the lifetime of anyone associated with its inception? On this issue, Murray himself had been far too sanguine. Part I, or "A-ANT," only appeared in January, 1884; completing "B" took till 1888; "C" entered the world in 1895, three years after the date initially fixed for the publication of the entire dictionary. Naturally, the formidable proliferation of Murray's material and the concomitant delays in publication proved to be a financial hecatomb. Subscribers were mutinous, and as costs mounted, sales withered. By 1897, the deficit stood at more than fifty thousand pounds and was rising at the rate of some five thousand a year. Had anyone known that the O.E.D. would take fifty years to complete, the undertaking might well have been stopped.

As it was, James Murray had to fight a constant battle on two fronts. Though thousands of volunteers in Britain and the United States responded to his call for word slips, far too much of what they sent in proved to be sloppy and haphazard. Some sixty-five actual assistants worked on the dictionary during the half century of its genesis. Of these, no more than a handful showed the necessary philological skill and critical judgment. Time and again, sometimes at the galley stage, the editor had to redo his assistants' work himself. For their part, the almighty delegates turned out to be vexatious taskmasters. It was not until 1896 that relations between editor and publisher eased. It was only then that Murray won his battle for perfection and that the Oxford University Press began to realize what glory lay in its keeping. Again, Miss Murray's scruples are almost Victorian, but what we read between her sober lines is a tale of condescension all too characteristic of the treatment Oxford and Cambridge like to mete out to those who love them too well. No college offered a fellowship to Murray. No research post or lectureship was opened to him in England. Potentates and scholars and writers from divers corners of the earth might come to the Scriptorium in fascinated pilgrimage; to the nabobs of Oxford, Murray was a recalcitrant, perhaps unduly privileged employee. When his knighthood came, in 1908, the university took lofty content.

No wonder that Murray was often on the verge of collapse and resignation. In 1887 and again in 1889 and 1890, his robust health and tireless intellect almost broke. In November, 1892, the delegates communicated to their editor the dolorous insight that "the more they endow the Dictionary the slower proportionately it goes." Surely the number of quotations might be reduced, the range of technical words might be narrowed. (What excuse could there be for including so outlandish a term as "appendicitis"?) Murray was ready to resign. Rumors of a suspension of publication appeared in the press. Some future age, under happier conditions, might resume after "F." Public appeals were bruited, letters flew, subcommittees met. Murray won the day. But at a self-destructive price. As early as 1883, he had been working a seventy-seven-hour week—twenty as a schoolteacher, fifty-seven as a lexicographer and a writer, in longhand, of anywhere up to fifteen letters a day. During the summer of 1895, he was working between eighty and ninety hours a week. Looking back on his Sisyphean labors, he was to speak of "troubles and bitterness, of which the world knows, and need know, nothing."

Their fruit, of course, lies in the actual details of *A New English Dictionary on Historical Principles*. But it is in the sheer statistics that lurk the drama and the vision. In Webster, the etymology of "black" takes five lines; in Murray, twenty-three (themselves a classic of concision). In the O.E.D., "do" occupies sixteen times the space allotted to it by Webster. Work on this ubiquitous monosyllable went on from Christmas, 1896, to June, 1897. The longest entry of all turns out to be "set," and here the treatment by Henry Bradley, who was to succeed Murray as the editor, amounts to little less than a miniature treatise on crucial social, philosophical, and scientific aspects of the Western imagination. "Point," on which Samuel Johnson had had his thoughts, consumes eighteen columns; "put," thirty. Personal touches intrude poignantly: sitting by his wife's bedside just after the birth of Elsie Mayflower, on May 1, 1882, and correcting the proofs of the first section of the dictionary, Murray adds to the first column of page 2, as an instance of "a" following an adjective preceded by "as," the words "as fine a child as you will see." Poets and novelists are a fruitful affliction. What in the world does Lord Tennyson mean by "balm-cricket"? Where has Mr. Thomas Hardy dredged up "terminatory"? Browning "has added greatly to the difficulties of the Dictionary," but has proved helpful over his wife's use of "apparitional." James Russell Lowell gives help with the mysterious "alliterates," which turns out to be a misprint for "illiterates." The Chief Rabbi is informative on "Jubilee." The India Office has a letter of 1620 with the first mention of "punch." From New York, *The Nation* gives help with political terms, so many of which are starting to come eastward across the Atlantic. An early entry for "jute" must be checked with the administrator of the Andaman Islands.

Letters to be written and answered by the thousand; readers' slips by the million to be solicited, filed, and crosschecked. James Murray, rather serenely, worked himself to death. In April, 1915, he was completing "T" and planning how to handle the mad swarm of words in "un-." He worked at the Scriptorium for the last time on July 10th, and died on the 26th. The O.E.D. was completed in 1928. But there can, of course, be no completion of such a job. Two massive volumes of a planned four-volume supplement have been published in the nineteen-seventies. And now there is talk of redoing the whole.

But, whatever the future, James Murray's monument and its derivatives—the Shorter Oxford English Dictionary, the Concise Oxford Dictionary, and the two-volume edition in miniaturized format issued in 1971—stand matchless. They are the living history of the English tongue and the dynamic embodiment of its spread over the earth. The master wordsmiths in modern letters—Joyce, Nabokov, Anthony Burgess, John Updike—are Murray's debtors. Where speech is vital and exact, it springs from the O.E.D. and enriches it in turn. To anyone who knows and loves English, the old quiz question "What single work would you take to read on a desert island?" does not require even an instant's thought. The O.E.D. carries within its dark-blue boards the libraries of fact and of feeling. Dip into it anywhere and life itself crowds at you.

November 21, 1977

AN EXAMINED LIFE

MY INDEBTEDNESS TO Robert Maynard Hutchins is great. In 1947, with a French baccalaureate, I journeyed from New York to New Haven for freshman orientation, and found Yale as suffocating and, socially, as sultry as the end-of-summer days. What to do? (It was already September.) I had, by chance, come across a *Time* account of the wild and woolly life of the mind at the University of Chicago. I wrote to its chancellor, reporting on my disarray at Yale. Customary admissions bureaucracy was waived. Summoned to the Midway, I sat the batteries of examinations that determined what subjects and requirements a student could be exempted from. My education had been classical and ultra-literary, so I found myself sweating through superbly taught courses in physics, chemistry, and biology, with some sort of remedial mathematics mercifully added. I received my B.A., at age nineteen, a year later and could get on to the serious business of graduate school. With Allen Tate teaching one literature and Richard McKeon introducing one to Aristotle and Aquinas, the experience was bracing.

For some ill-chosen reason, I decamped to Harvard. It took me only a few weeks to realize my error. At that time, Harvard graduate schools in the humanities were inert craft guilds, academic in the worst sense of the word. Almost desperately, I wrote to the University of Chicago asking for one of its nominations for a Rhodes Scholarship. (I was fairly recently naturalized but no longer a resident of Illinois.) Quite understandably, the dragon in charge of this precious sponsorship turned me down and observed acerbically that I ought to have thought twice before leaving for sclerotic Harvard. Impertinence being the mother of invention, I turned directly to Hutchins. I wrote pointing out that Chicago had not for some time won a Rhodes. Its lofty disdain for athletics and for the qualities of campus charisma that the Rhodes selectors looked for had prevented its nominees from being chosen. My own disqualifications were all too obvious. But I thought I had an outside chance. Hutchins seems to have been amused by this shameless approach. He gave me the nomination. Some months later, a worn-out Rhodes Scholarship board, having to choose between that year's star-studded captain of the West Point corps and me, and knowing of my total nonathleticism, asked me to show in a diagram the difference between a number of backfield formations in American college football. It so happens that I had during my Chicago years become an ardent watcher, particularly of Michigan and Notre Dame. I was on my way to Oxford.

But these debts to Hutchins are personal trivia. What very probably decided my life and work was the sheer genius of intellectual exhilaration, the passionate electricity of spirit, that had made the University of Chicago under Hutchins the best there was. No one who did not experience that formidable vibrato, who did not at first hand witness the extent to which Hutchins's legendary persona, his dictates, his inebriation with excellence set ablaze every aspect of an undergraduate's day, can capture Hutchins's greatness. Harry S. Ashmore's *Unseasonable Truths* (Little, Brown) lists many of the facts, but the spirit eludes him.

Thinking back on those exigent weeks, on the ferocity of the climate and the work load, on the unembarrassed competitiveness and intellectual ambition that the whole system fuelled, I can still feel a hammering excitement that no other university has ever stirred in me. We sat through whole nights arguing Marx or Dewey, analyzing, word for word, a paragraph out of Joyce's *Dubliners* or Tarski's logic. Enrico Fermi, who had set off the controlled chain reaction that made the atom bomb possible, and had done so in a laboratory underneath the unused university football stadium, was reshaping the teaching of physics. It was during a marathon seminar, with the wind whipsawing at some crazily low temperature, that I was induced to grasp what little I can of the true meaning of a quantum jump. It was some junior math instructor (may he in remembrance forgive my obtuseness) who wrote on the board a row of prime numbers and, below it, a row of even numbers. There are as many, he said, in the one line as in the other. And, like a champagne burst inside me, came the recognition of what might be signified by "infinity." To this distant day, I tingle at the recollection of OII—Observation, Information, and Integration, the crowning course in the college. Here an often inspired teaching staff introduced us to the attempt, from Plato to Carnap, to discover a general principle of human understanding, to find logic and meaning in both the world and the thought in which we incorporate the world. Hutchins's vision was radically historical: a mathematical theorem, a literary form, a philosophical idea, even history itself had a history. Nothing could be truly grasped out of its genetic context. The work was often exhausting, and we undoubtedly fell short. But Hutchins's sovereign ruling that it was the highest of privileges to be in an OII section—to take part, be it as the greenest of undergraduates, in the revaluation of knowledge and society—rang true. Plato's Academy, Galileo's dialogues, Hegel's Berlin lectures reborn—one felt it in one's bones. And the best jazz and Caesar salads just off campus, on 63rd Street. And the steel mills in Gary and White City flashing their lights, making their ovens redder when news came through from Newark that Tony Zale, his hand broken, beat Rocky Graziano (a quite mad occasion and ho-sanna I can't separate from the memory of a wretched paper I did on Mill's social theories).

Ashmore, in his biography, puts great emphasis on the famous Great Books program, the core curriculum of classic texts which Hutchins and Mortimer Adler devised for students and adults alike. Unquestionably, this list and the reading groups associated with it were vital to Hutchins. He said:

> This is more than a set of great books, and more than a liberal education. Great Books of the Western World is an act of piety. Here are the sources of our being. Here is the West. This is its meaning for mankind. Here is the faith of the West, for here before everybody willing to look at it is that dialogue by way of which Western man has believed that he can approach the truth.

In the actual life of the university, that credo was implicit rather than explicit. Courses gravitated to canonic and talismanic works. Scientists had to read the classic documents in the history of their pursuit. But what Hutchins communicated was the necessary miracle of personal dialogue with the master spirits past and present. He made of the university a house of live reading, in which voices sprang at you from the page. Indirectly, Hutchins's critique of Thomas Jefferson makes the point. Jefferson was not, Hutchins said, possessed of "what used to be called the 'intellectual love of God,' what we now call 'the pursuit of truth for its own sake.'" Jefferson's aims were social and pragmatic. But it is the disinterested, joyously obsessive pursuit of truth that is the sole authentic purpose of humane learning and the mark of man's singular, often rebuked dignity. To read, to reread passionately, to read "in dialogue" is to advance that purpose. A great university is one in which the necessary arts of reading are central. Hutchins's Chicago was exactly that. I have not found many like it since.

Ashmore provides a warmly sympathetic and thoroughly researched chronicle of Robert Maynard Hutchins's dizzying ascent to national prominence. He tells of the Presbyterian background, of the school days in which the young Hutchins cultivated his oratory, his appetite for hard work, and his almost nonchalant assumption of authority. (Being strikingly handsome and six feet two and a half inches in height helped.) Hutchins spent a brief but fairly miserable time in Europe during the First World War, which made him something of a combative pacifist. He arrived at Yale in 1919, swept through three undergraduate years at characteristic speed, and began law studies before his senior year. At twenty-six, Hutchins was tutoring law and expounding the conviction that the isolation of legal studies from social psychology, from political theory, and from fundamental philosophical debate was indefensible. Colleagues and seniors bridled, but Yale's President James Rowland Angell had a weakness for Hutchins, and in 1927, aged twenty-eight, Hutchins was appointed dean of the Yale Law School. Already he was in touch with men who were to be vital to his intellectual and administrative career: Adler, William O. Douglas, Henry Luce (whose coverage of Hutchins helped make him a national figure). And already he was spelling out his proud credo:

> After all, the great thing about a university is that it can afford to experiment; and I use the word *afford* not in its financial connotation, but to remind us that a university is free to cultivate and exhibit the independence of thought, the willingness to depart from tradition, the readiness to take a chance, if you will, that may come from the possession of a life that is nearly immortal.

Plato might have spoken thus, or Francis Bacon. This was hardly the language expected of a dean, not yet thirty, addressing a coven of recalcitrant law professors.

But others were pricking up their ears. In 1929, Robert Maynard Hutchins, the "boy wonder" of American higher education, was called to the presidency (later the chancellorship) of the University of Chicago. The twenty-two years he spent there were memorable. Hutchins found a distinguished university and made it one of the very great centers of research, scholarship, and instruction in the West. Medical studies, anthropology, social and political inquiry, Oriental and Biblical scholarship, nuclear physics, astrophysics, and mathematics flourished under Hutchins's passionate goading. But at the absolute center of his manifold enterprise lay the reform of the undergraduate curriculum, the transmutation of American pragmatism, professionalism, and fitful literacy into a model of fundamental perception. Henceforth, on the Midway and in those wind-scarred mock-Gothic quads (the Gothic began to look hauntingly real) the Socratic axiom that no unexamined life was worth living became compelling.

Conservative doubts were strong, and there were attempts at sabotage. Dr. Ashmore vividly reports on the successive showdowns with senior faculties and public opinion which Hutchins had to win in order to achieve his aim. Adler's role was abrasive but, to Hutchins, somehow organic. An odd chemistry bonded the two men. The Aristotelian and Aquinist promise of a total organization, of a systematic and hierarchic summa of human knowledge, underwritten, as it were, by an incessant discipline of definition, redefinition, and discourse, had set both men alight. Mortimer Adler knew how to challenge and offend; Hutchins knew how to turn challenge and offense into administrative and pedagogic practice. Equally, moreover, they shared a passion for jurisprudence, in the full sense. As Plato had taught, law is the sinew of the city of man. If that city is to be enlightened, if it is to be a place in which men and women are the custodians of live tradition and the makers of the new, justice must prevail. Hence the pivotal presence of the Chicago Law School, its informing and philosophical proximity to the climate of the college. Hence the stimulating interplay, for any undergraduate interested enough to sit in on the relevant classes or research sessions (even if he could grasp only a mite of what was going on), of Leo Strauss's political philosophy, Edward Levi on the nature of a legal precedent, and Bruno Bettelheim on the closed world of the violent. Here, Hutchins ordained, there was to be none of that "coddling, nursing and pampering of students" characteristic of American education but "quite unknown anywhere else."

Hutchins lectured endlessly up and down the land. His dicta filled the press. Scholars and thinkers of the first rank joined the staff. The undergraduates were a brilliantly motley corps. In my dormitory bustled the star youth-organizer of the American Communist Party; one of the country's top ten poker players; a transfer from European schooling (as I was) who would soon do major work in mathematical logic; a somewhat crazed short-story writer; a future criminal lawyer with a sensibility perfectly attuned to that of his larcenous and homicidal clients; a clutch of Chinese physicists leapfrogging each other toward the Nobel; and an ex-paratrooper whose ability to jump into an upper bunk from a crouching position has left me with an untarnished image of pure carnal grace and discipline.

But all this at a price. Ashmore deals tactfully with the far too public misery of Hutchins's first marriage. He tells of the successive attempts by red-baiters, both in Chicago and in Washington, to smear and to unseat a man whose commitment to liberty of thought and expression was absolute. We learn of Hutchins' major political error: his participation in the movements that strove to keep America out of Hitler's war. But even on this vexatious point Hutchins's motives were worth attending to. He felt, prophetically, that a second world war would immensely expand the authority, the predatory compass, of American government and bureaucracy and at the same time sweep under the carpet the social inequalities and the racial tension that made that democracy so infirm. But when Pearl Harbor came Hutchins unhesitatingly turned the great resources of the university toward research of national urgency. Hutchins's relations with F.D.R., who it seems at one point had considered him as a possible Vice-President, form a fascinating thread in Harry Ashmore's portrayal.

Now the man was worn out. In December, 1950, Hutchins accepted the codirectorship, with Paul Hoffman, of the Ford Foundation. We are, at this point, on page 303 of a biography of five hundred and forty-one pages. The remainder of Hutchins's career (he died in May, 1977) is, in the main, tedium and failure. So, all too faithfully, is the rest of this book. The later years involved Dr. Ashmore, who joined Hutchins in his think-tank ventures. This explains but does not justify the elaborate treatment he gives them. Names of worthies cascade. Orotund pronouncements on "the Basic Issues" of world government, American destiny, the unification of all knowledge, peace on land and sea spangle these labored pages like fading stars. We enter, irretrievably, the factitious pomp and self-delusions of the world of what Ezra Pound once called American "floundations." Hutchins's spell at Ford proved a fiasco. Then came the Fund for the Republic and the endless blueprints for a Platonic Academy in which sages of liberal persuasions would weigh and expound the American polity, the problems of a world parliament, the role of the sciences in a democracy, the laws of the sea and of space. In the fall of 1959, Hutchins installed himself and his myrmidons on a hill in Santa Barbara.

I visited there briefly during the seventies to read a paper. Two impressions have stayed with me: a cranky, aging British pundit who whispered to me that among the water jugs set around the green baize seminar table there was one containing gin, and an almost palpable aura of unreality. Hutchins the mover of mountains now inhabited a domain in which men and women believe they have achieved something when they have written a project paper, spawned a committee, peopled a conference, filled in requests for funding, and published a glossy brochure at the end of the year. This unreality and the bitchiness, gossip, and palace intrigue that filled the vacant days in the California sun give to Ashmore's twilit record an enervating sadness. There were practical spurts. Hutchins's role was considerable in the conception and preparation of the new Encyclopedia Britannica. He and his colleagues vigorously opposed the right-wing philistinism and the mindless chauvinism of what was rapidly becoming Nixon Land. But there was in the fire that, in 1964, roared through Romero Canyon and destroyed Hutchins's home more than a touch of allegory.

What is Robert Maynard Hutchins's legacy? This is not an easy question to answer. By 1953, the College of the University of Chicago had been "normalized," and a period of rancorous mediocrity ensued. Today, the Hutchins style is at work, if at all, in the visionary despotism of John Silber, at Boston University. But Chicago did recover. It is again one of the great universities, and its president, Hannah Gray, is a woman of incisive authority and of a deep commitment to eminence. Hutchins's demanding pride in the institution, if not his actual design, has prevailed. More generally, it is obvious that the debate currently being conducted on the state of the American mind, on the scandal of American secondary schooling, on the intractable but essential dilemma of the relations between democracy and excellence, between social/ethnic justice and intellectual quality (Hutchins was wholly committed to both) is a debate whose origins and many of whose formulations go back to the heady days when Hutchins ran the Yale Law School. To end on a personal note: because of Hutchins, I have known, intellectually and in my bones, what a university can and should be. That is a formidable bounty. The history of how it felt remains to be written.

October 23, 1989

APPENDIX: ALL GEORGE STEINER'S ESSAYS FOR *THE NEW YORKER*

"Life with Father" (*on Winston Churchill*) November 5, 1966

"Beyond the Power Principle" (*on Aron's* Peace and War) January 14, 1967

"Mondo Freudo" (*on Freud and Woodrow Wilson*) January 21, 1967

"The Great Uncommoner" (*on Disraeli*) April 1, 1967

"Ancient Glittering Eyes" (*on Bertrand Russell*) August 19, 1967

"Games People Play" (*on Raymond Roussel*) October 28, 1967

"The Fire Last Time" (*on Styron's* The Confessions of Nat Turner) November 25, 1967

"Cry Havoc" (*on Céline*) January 20, 1968

"Of Nuance and Scruple" (*on Beckett*) April 27, 1968

"A Death of Kings" (*on chess*) September 7, 1968

"Eastward Ho!" (*on Hesse*) January 18, 1969

"Displaced Person" (*on Herzen*) February 8, 1969

"True to Life" (*on Orwell*) March 29, 1969

"Last Stop for Mrs. Brown" (*on C.P. Snow*) July 12, 1969

"Across the River and Into the Trees" (*on Hemingway*) September 13, 1969

"The Tongues of Men" (*on Chomsky*) November 15, 1969

"Through Seas of Thought, Alone" (*on Vico*) May 9, 1970

"Tigers in the Mirror" (*on Borges*) June 20, 1970

"Life-Lines" (*on Arthur Koestler*) March 6, 1971

"A Pillow-Book" (*on Arthur Waley and Japanese and Chinese literature*) June 12, 1971

"The Corn Is Blue" (*on erotic literature*) August 28, 1971

"Under the Greenwood Tree" (*on E.M. Forster's* Maurice) October 9, 1971

"The Arts of Memory" (*on Lewis Namier and "Namierism"*) January 1, 1972

"Gent" (*on Ford Madox Ford's Tietjens novels*) February 12, 1972

"Fields of Force" (*on Chess*) October 28, 1972

"Gamesman" (*on the game Go in literature*) January 27, 1973

"Uneasy Rider" (*on Pirsig's* Zen and the Art of Motorcycle Maintenance) April 15, 1974

"The Lost Garden" (*on Levi-Strauss*) June 3, 1974

"The Forests of the Night" (*on Solzhenitsyn*) August 5, 1974

"Burnt-Out Case" (*on Graham Greene and Rochester*) October 28, 1974

"Through Seas Forlorn" (*on Paul Zweig's* The Adventurer: The Fate of Adventure in the Western World) January 20, 1975

"The Last Victorian" (*on Aldous Huxley*) February 17, 1975

"Scarlet Letters" (*on Updike's* A Month of Sundays) March 10, 1975

"Bookmen" (*on Samuel Johnson*) April 28, 1975

"The Beholder's Eye" (*On Kenneth Clark*) July 28, 1975

"Witches' Brews" (*on Cohn's* Europe's Inner Demons) September 8, 1975

"More Notes from Underground" (*on Dostoevsky*) October 13, 1975

"Woman's Hour" (*on Redinger's* Femininity and George Eliot: The Emergent Self) January 5, 1976

"Crossed Lines" (*on Gaddis'* JR) January 26, 1976

"A Certain Dr. Malraux" (*On André Malraux*) March 22, 1976

"From the House of the Dead" (*On Albert Speer*) April 19, 1976

"Party Lines" (*on Malcolm Bradbury*) May 3, 1976

"The Good Soldier" (*on Garibaldi*) June 28, 1976

"Petrified Forest" (*on Keneally's* Gossip from the Forest *and histori-cal fiction*) August 23, 1976

"Under Eastern Eyes" (*on Russian writers*) October 11, 1976

"Wild Laughter" (*on Karlinksy's* The Sexual Labyrinth of Nikolai Gogol) February 28, 1977

"The Kingdom of Appearances" (*on E. H. Gombrich and art history*) April 4, 1977

"Sleuths" (*on detective novels*) April 25, 1977

"Down Under" (*on the Australian novelists Patrick White and Thomas Keneally*) May 23, 1977

"Unsentimental Education" (*on Fred Uhlman's* Reunion) August 15, 1977

"Stepmother Russia" (*on Bakunin*) September 12, 1977

"By Jove" (*on Holland Smith's* The Death of Classical Paganism) November 14, 1977

"Give the Word" (*on James Murray and the* OED) November 21, 1977

"God's Spies" (*on Greene's* The Human Factor) May 8, 1978

"De Profundis" (*on Solzhenitsyn's* The Gulag Archipelago Three) September 4, 1978

"God's Acres" (*on* The Letters and Diaries of John Henry Newman) October 30, 1978

"Notes From Underground" (*on Hitler*) March 5, 1979

"An Old Man and the Sea" (*on Joseph Conrad*) April 23, 1979

"Wien, Wien, Nur Du Allein" (*on Anton von Webern*) June 25, 1979

"A Duel" (*on Thomas and Heinrich Mann*) July 9, 1979

"Visions and Revisions" (*On St.-John Perse*) September 10, 1979

"Dead Letters" (*on John Barth*) December 31, 1979

"Closing Time" (*on* Fin-de-Siécle Vienna: Politics and Culture) February 11, 1980

"Marche Funèbre" (*on* The Memoirs of Dmitri Shostakovich) March 24, 1980

"The Gift of Tongues" (*on Canetti's* Auto-da-Fé) May 19, 1980

"Excommunications" (*on Solzhenitsyn's* The Oak and the Calf) August 25, 1980

"The Cleric of Treason" (*on Anthony Blunt*) December 8, 1980

"When Burning Sappho Loved and Sung" (*on* The Victorians and Ancient Greece)February 9, 1981

"Scroll and Keys" (*on Anthony Burgess*) April 13, 1981

"De Mortuis" (on *Phillipe Ariès and* The Hour of Our Death) June 22, 1981

"Ladies' Day" (on *Marguerite Yourcenar*) August 17, 1981

"Rare Bird" (*on Guy Davenport*) November 30, 1981

"Strange Interlude" (*on Pryce-Jones'* Paris in the Third Reich) January 25, 1982

"Maestro" (*on Kimball's* Verdi in the Age of Italian Romanticism) April 19, 1982

"Master and Man" (*on Coetzee's* Waiting for the Barbarians) July 12, 1982

"A Tale of Three Cities (*on Canetti's memoirs*) November 22, 1982

"The Strengths of Discouragement (*on Montale*) May 23, 1983

"Liszt Superstar" (*on Liszt*) June 13, 1983

"Killing Time " (*on Orwell's* 1984) December 12, 1983

"Short Shrift (on Drawn and Quartered *and aphorisms*) April 16, 1984

"Born Again" (*on Dostoevsky*) May 28, 1984

"La Morte d'Arthur" (*on* Arthur Koestler) June 11, 1984

"Sleeper Before Sunrise" (*on Rilke*) October 8, 1984

"Dream City" (*on Broch*) January 28, 1985

"Crossings" (*on Feinstein's* The Border) April 29, 1985

"The Demon Master" (*on Strindberg*) May 27, 1985

"Springs of Sadness" (*on Muschg's* The Blue Man and Other Stories) July 8, 1985

"Birth of a Nation" (*on Mack Smith's* Cavour) August 19, 1985

"Night Call" (*on Bulgakov and Stalin*) December 16, 1985

"Power Play" (*on Foucault and French philosophy*) March 17, 1986

"Portrait of the Artist as a Man" (*on Benvenuto Cellini*) April 7, 1986

"Knight of Old" (*on William Marshal*) May 26, 1986

"Black Danube" (*on Karl Kraus & Thomas Bernhard*) July 21, 1986

"The Heart of Matter" (*on Chardin*) November 17, 1986

"Graven Images" (*on Gombrich's* Aby Warburg) February 2, 1987

"Red Octobers" (*on Leonard Schapiro and Russia*) May 4, 1987

"Little-Read Schoolhouse" (*on E.D. Hirsch and literacy*) June 1, 1987

"Cornucopia" (*on Schama's* An Embarrassment of Riches: An Interpretation of Dutch Culture in the Golden Age) September 14, 1987

"One Thousand Years of Solitude" (*on Salvatore Satta*) October 19, 1987

"The Good Books" (*on Robert Alter and religious texts*) January 11, 1988

"Life Size" (*on John Cowper Powys*) May 2, 1988

"Master Class" (*on Alpers'* Rembrandt) May 30, 1988

"The Master's Voice" (*on Wagner*) October 3, 1988

"Poor Little Lambs" (*on John Boswell's* The Kindness of Strangers *and* orphans) February 6, 1989

"Two Hundred Years Young" (*on Schama's* Citizens and the French Revolution) April 17, 1989

"Wording Our World" (*on Cavell's* In Quest of the Ordinary) June 19, 1989

"On Paul Celan" (*on Celan*) Aug. 28, 1989

"An Examined Life" (*on Robert Hutchins & The University of Chicago*) October 23, 1989

"The Friend of a Friend" (*on Walter Benjamin & Gershom Scholem*) January 22, 1990

"Man of Letter" (*on Kafka*) May 28, 1990

"B.B." (*on Brecht*) September 10, 1990

"Grandmaster" (*on Nabokov*) December 10, 1990

"Mars" (*on Kagan's* A New History of the Peloponnesian War) March 11, 1991

"Long Day's Journey Into Light" (*on Goethe*) September 23, 1991

"Golden Boy" (*on Alexander the Great*) December 9, 1991

"Bad Friday" (*on Simone Weil*) March 2, 1992

"Cat Man" (*on Céline*) August 24, 1992

"White Goddess" (*on Friedrich and Elizabeth Nietzsche*) October 19, 1992

"Glenn Gould's Notes" (*on Glenn Gould*) Nov. 23, 1992

"A Terrible Beauty" (*on William Butler Yeats and Maud Gonne*) February 8, 1993

"Rule Britten" (*on Benjamin Britten*) July 5, 1993

"Pressure Cookers" (*on Gay's* The Cultivation of Hatred) October 25, 1993

"Red Guard" (*on Trotsky and Jean van Heijenoort*) December 20, 1993

"Stranglehold" (*on Althusser's* The Future Lasts Forever) February 21, 1994

"The Magus" (*on Einstein*) June 20, 1994

"Franco's Games" (*on Franco*) October 17, 1994

"The Unfinished" (*on Musil's* The Man Without Qualities) April 17, 1995

"Food of Love" (*on Charles Rosen and Romanticism*) July 24, 1995

"Foursome" (*on Pessoa*) January 8, 1996

"Supreme Fiction" (*on John Updike*) March 11, 1996

"A Red Death" (*on the Aldo Moro kidnapping*) March 18, 1996

"Leastness" (*on Beckett*) September 16, 1996

"Stones of Light" (*on Levey's* Florence: A Portrait) January 13, 1997

"Ex Libris" (*on Manguel's* A History of Reading) March 17, 1997

INDEX